The Confessions Of
Saint Augustine

The Confessions Of Saint Augustine

A New Translation with Introductions

by

E. M. Blaiklock

HODDER AND STOUGHTON
LONDON SYDNEY AUCKLAND TORONTO

British Library Cataloguing in Publication Data

Augustine, Saint, Bishop of Hippo
  The confessions of Saint Augustine.—(Hodder
  Christian paperback)
  1. Augustine. Saint. Bishop of Hippo
  2. Christian saints—Algeria—Biography
  I. Title   II. Blaiklock, E. M.   III. Confessions.
  English
  270.2'092'4   BR1720.A9

  ISBN 0 340 32466 X

Hodder and Stoughton Editorial Office: 47 Bedford Square, London WC1B 3DP.

Contents

Translator's Preface

Aurelius Augustinus was born in Thagaste, a small town in Numidia, a Roman province of North Africa, on November 13, 354. He died while the Vandal war-bands were besieging his episcopal see of Hippo in 430. His father was Patricius, a dull and earthy fellow who held a minor post in Rome's municipal administration. His mother was Monica, a firm Christian, or Monnica, as those say, who insist, with no proof, on her Berber origins.

Augustine was therefore a son of the twilight. The more protected parts of the doomed Empire lay in an unnatural calm. It was like the last days of a lingering Canadian Indian Summer, the sun low and glowing in the sky, the leaves brown on the ground, the storming snow unseen but inexorably advancing. The northern provinces had long felt the cold chill. Hadrian's Wall no longer held. The Nile-Danube frontier buckled and bent.

This is what fascinates the classical historian. Augustine's cameo pictures of Thagaste, Madaura, Carthage, Rome, and later of Hippo are of sombre interest. *Morituri nos salutant.* How little does the present know of the future! No one knew, when Augustus was establishing the frontiers of an imperial world, frontiers which were to hold precariously through four vital centuries of history, that the pivot of the human story had been moved one night from the Palatine to Palestine. No one knew in Thagaste that the frightened schoolboy, who was bad-tempered Patricius' son, was to leave behind him writings six times as voluminous as the whole corpus of Cicero himself, establish theology through a millennium and more of strife and strain, and form one of the bridges between a dying world and that world's rebirth.

Arnold Toynbee, most universal of all historians,

confessed, as he launched the second three volumes of his
Study of History in March 1939, that he had derived
enormous encouragement from Augustine's *City of God*
whose quarter-million words were finished when the
Empire's roof was falling in. The bishop of Hippo had
courage enough to take in both hands the heritage of the
Christian faith and all he had stood for, and to commit it to
the keeping of another world.

The Vandals scattered and slew Augustine's parishioners.
Two centuries later the Moslems came that way with the
desert trailing behind them. Augustine's work did not
perish. It was blowing in the air. It steadied Medieval
Christendom in varied ways, shaping Gregory, Charle-
magne and Aquinas, and gusting more widely to touch
Calvin, Luther, Pascal ...

But these pages are not a commentary on the greatest of
the fathers of the Church. The few pages of introduction
which accompany the ten chosen books of the *Confessions*
are no more than a brief guide to reading, and no more is
said of Augustine's theology, its strengths and its weaknesses than Augustine, sometimes with maddening obscur-
ity, says himself. Much of his theology, in fact, was
formulated in the heat of the controversies which filled the
last forty years of his life. The record of those years is the
heaviest tract of study which the student of ancient church
history has to traverse.

That is why, in the following translation, much of that
which Augustine leaves ambiguously or ill expressed,
appears in the rendering without any attempt to elucidate. A
translator often has to face the problem of responsibility. He
is not an exegete, and risks illegitimate intrusion, when or if
he presumes to make lucid in his translation what is dark or
difficult in the original. I have assumed no right to leach
Augustine's style of some of his exasperating rhetoric. It was
not 'false and affected rhetoric', as a hostile Gibbon put it,
simply rhetoric as the schools taught it, and far from the
'splendid eloquence' sometimes attributed to it. Anyone
deeply familiar with the power and eloquence of Classical
Latin can only deplore Augustine's style, loaded with
redundancies, parentheses, provisos, reservations and

second thoughts. It is full of pronouns, sometimes of obscure reference, and reflects, no doubt, the writer's spoken style. From platform and pulpit perhaps, it sounded well. It is a pity that Augustine did not acquire from Cicero's *Hortensius* something more than a zeal for philosophy. But style reflects the man, and the tortured paragraphs, too often encountered, reflect the tangle of his thoughts.

The *Confessions* are no more nor less than the title claims. They set the story of a remarkable life, before men as well as before God, who, as the writer frequently remarks, does know all about it without a sinner to jog his memory. It is Augustine who speaks in the translation here offered, and not a spokesman for him. The translator, none the less, finds prime interest in a fellow human being, rather than in a great father of the Church. The Augustine of these ten books is not Gibbon's 'grave and learned' churchman whose 'strong, capacious and argumentative mind ... boldly sounded the abyss of grace, predestination and original sin', but rather the harassed seeker for truth, so often weak, perpetually hobbled by his senses, demanding proof – in short, a man 'of like passions as we are.' Gibbon saw the formidable Bishop of Hippo, holding his congregation's courage and morale, as Isaiah held Jerusalem when Sennacherib rolled down. The refugees had poured in from Italy, as Alaric looted Rome, and Augustine's own heart must have at times failed him. It is well that those who stand and fight back because a brave leader does, are not fully aware of what is happening in the leader's own mind and heart.

The *Confessions* were written at the turn of the century, and could themselves be coloured a little by the events of the full decade which lies between the events up to Augustine's dramatic conversion, and the reflections and recollections of Book Ten. For all their wordiness they ring with truth, and touch the reader at lower levels of our common humanity than an account less disciplined by prayer might do.

Book Ten seemed to provide a natural conclusion satisfying a modern reader. Some contemporaries might have opted for Book Nine, with the climax of conversion and the model demise of Monica. Conversion is not, however, an end but a beginning, and it is better to let the narrative run on. The mystical ponderings of the last three books are, for all that, quite detachable, and it is even a little difficult to probe the writer's purpose in placing them thus. They seem laboured in their striving for linkage, and are rather the utterance of the Bishop of Hippo than of the embattled man striving Godwards. We have taken leave to omit them.

E.M. Blaiklock
January 4, 1983

Titirangi
Auckland
New Zealand

BOOK ONE

A North African Childhood

Introduction

The first book of the *Confessions* tells of Augustine's childhood. Picture a brown-limbed, active little boy, sharply intelligent, gregarious, sport-loving and with small zeal for school. For all the shaking frontiers, from Hadrian's Wall to the Euphrates, in the mid-fourth century, North Africa was still a peaceful haven at the Empire's heart. On the Saharan frontier there was no doubt the ancient problem of the raiding nomad, but along with Britain the old territories of Phoenician Carthage were prosperous and Roman. The climate was no doubt cooler than it is today. The Arctic cap was still south of Iceland, and the Imperial exploitation of the province had not finally bared all the ranges and coaxed the waiting desert in. Towns and cities, each a little Rome, ran deep into the continental hinterland, and for all the burdens of a tax-ridden age and a pervasive bureaucracy, life could go on with no great change from generation to generation. It so comes about that the *Confessions* are at times a document descriptive of a way of life soon to end, one of the final utterances of a falling world.

It is with no such consciousness that Augustine writes. He is seeking to tell the truth about himself. Perhaps the finest moral quality of this tormented saint is his ruthless search for truth, and if in truth all sin is to be confessed to God and in the hearing of men, he must go back to his life's beginnings. 'When, where, Lord, was I innocent?' Quite forgetful of a tender saying of the Lord: '... of such is the Kingdom of Heaven', he probes memory, and even the forgotten years, understood only by parents' tales and personal observation of infant delinquency, in an attempt to pinpoint the beginnings of sin. Life begins with a wail, a day-old child clings greedily to a mother's breast, before speech a babe flings body, arms and legs petulantly about to enforce compliance with its will, language, he faintly remembers, found its first impetus and employment to the same selfish and demanding end. Had he not also seen the speechless glare of a suckling child at another infant sharing the same bosom? 'Where, when, Lord . . .'

Education in Roman society down to Augustine's middle-class level, was universal, and his sombre account of the agonies of school might have been appreciated in Cowper's, and even Tom Brown's England. He approaches bitterness against his parents who found the merciless beatings he received amusing. In one paragraph, in which he chides such adult heartlessness, his expression of indignation, for all a translator's limited liberty to infuse clarity into an author's overloaded speech, produces a paragraph almost incoherent in its rage. In spite of such discipline, Augustine, in this or his Madaura school, defeated all efforts to teach him Greek, a most lamentable outcome. Yet, he is constrained after forty years to admit that he deserved it all, a bad little lad, full of original sin, but no worse than those who swung the cane, for his shrewd observation had noted the petty jealousies of his teachers, and the adult zeal for the theatre and sport, which allegedly hindered his juvenile application.

Book One gives the first view of Monica, formal in her faith, stern in its application, who deferred Augustine's baptism when he tearfully cried out for it. He was near death with some form of abdominal colic, perhaps food poisoning or a sick appendix which fortunately halted short of rupture. Monica's superstitious notion was that, if the saving rite could be postponed, it would more advantageously avail for the sins of adolescence. Augustine never quite forgave his mother for the calculated risk she took with his soul's salvation.

In short, Augustine can discover small innocence in what will appear to most modern readers as a normal and not unhappy childhood. His most quoted saying heads Book One, but looking back over the long years, the Bishop of Hippo, apart from the terror of the cane, theme of his first prayers, finds little 'restlessness' in the child Aurelius Augustinus of Thagaste – only a clear indication of human depravity.

I

Prayer of Invocation

Lord you are great, and most worthy of praise; great is your worth and your wisdom beyond reckoning. And man, a fragment of your creation, desires to praise you – man, carrying round with him his own mortality, carrying round with him the witness of his sin and the witness that you 'resist the proud', yet desires to praise you, he, a fragment of your creation. You prompt him to take delight in praising you, because you made us for yourself, and our heart is restless until it find rest in you. Grant to me, Lord, to know and understand whether I should first call upon you or praise you, and to know you before I call on you. But who calls on you without knowing you? Not knowing you, he could call upon something other than you are. Or is it rather that you are called upon in order to be known? But 'how shall they call upon one in whom they have not believed? Or how shall they believe without one to preach?' And they shall praise the Lord who seek him, for if they seek him they find him, and finding him shall praise him. I shall seek you, Lord, by calling upon you, and may I call upon you because I believe on you, for you have been made known to us. My faith calls upon you, Lord, the faith you gave to me, which you breathed into me, through the humanity of your son and the ministry of your preacher.

II

The Mystery of God's Indwelling

And how shall I call upon my God, my Lord, and God,

because assuredly I shall call him into myself when I call on him? And what place is there in me which my God can occupy? By what way can God come in to me, God, the maker of heaven and earth? Is it so, my Lord God? Is there anything in me which can contain you? Indeed, do heaven and earth which you have made and as part of which you made me, contain you? Or because nothing which exists would exist without you, does it come about that whatever exists contains you? And so, because I exist, what am I seeking, when I ask you come into me, I, who would not exist unless you were in me? For I am not yet in hell and yet you are there, for 'though I go down to hell, you are there.' I should not therefore exist, my God, I should not exist at all, unless you were in me. Or rather I should not exist unless I existed in you, from whom are all things, through whom are all things, in whom are all things. Even so, Lord, even so. Why then do I call upon you, when I am in you? Or whence do you come into me? Where can I withdraw, outside heaven and earth whence my God may come into me, he who said: 'I fill heaven and earth'?

III

The Mystery of God's Omnipresence

Do therefore the heaven and the earth contain you, since you fill them? Or do you fill them and leave a surplus since they do not contain you? And into what pours over whatever remains of you when heaven and earth are filled? Or have you no need that anything should contain you, who contain all things, because what you fill you fill by containing it? For the vessels which are full of you do not confine you, because though they should be broken you are not poured out, and when you are poured out upon us you do not lie still, but lift us up, nor are you scattered but draw us together. But all things which you fill, you fill them all with your whole self.

Or because all things cannot contain all of you, do they contain a part of you, and do all things at the same time contain the same part? Or has each its own part, the greater more, the lesser less? Is therefore some part of you greater, another lesser? Or are you wholly everywhere, and nothing contains you wholly?

IV

The Mystery of God's Being

What therefore, is my God? What, I ask, but my Lord God? For who is Lord but the Lord? Or who is God but our God? Most high, best, most powerful, utterly almighty, most merciful and most just, furthest and nearest, most beautiful and most strong, constant and beyond understanding, unchanging yet changing all things, never new, never old, yet making all things new; bringing the proud into old age though they know it not; always acting, and ever still, gathering together but never in need, bearing, filling, protecting, creating and nourishing, seeking though you lack nothing. You love but without disturbance, are jealous but without care. You repent but do not grieve, are angry but tranquil. You change your works but not your purpose. You take what you find but have never lost anything, are never in need but take joy in gain, are never covetous but exact due return. Return is made to you abundantly that you may be the debtor, but who has anything that is not yours? What have we said, my God, my life, my delight, or what does anyone say when he speaks of you? Woe to him that says nothing of you, when those who speak much are dumb.

V

A Plea for God's Assurance

Who shall grant me to find rest in you? Who shall grant that you enter my heart and intoxicate it, that I may forget my evils and embrace you, my one good? What are you to me? Pity me that I may speak. And what am I myself to you that you command my love and are angry with me and threaten mighty woes unless I give it? Is it a small woe itself, if I love you not? Alas for me! Tell me by thy mercies, my Lord God, what you are to me. Say to my soul: 'I am your salvation'. So speak that I may hear. Look, the ears of my heart are before you. Lord, open them and say to my soul: 'I am your salvation'. I will pursue that voice and lay hold of you. Do not hide your face from me; let me die, lest I die, that I may see it.

The house of my soul is narrow for your entry. Let it be enlarged by you. It is in ruins. Rebuild it. There is that in it, I confess and know, which may offend your eyes, but who shall cleanse it? Or to whom but you shall I call? Cleanse me, Lord, from my hidden sins, and spare your servant, Lord, from sins outside himself. I believe, and that is why I speak. You know, Lord. Have I not spoken out against my wrongdoings to you, my God, and you forgave me the wickedness of my heart? I do not contend in judgment with you, who are the truth, and I have no wish to deceive myself, lest my wickedness be a liar. That is why I do not strive in judgment with you, for if you, Lord, Lord, were to take note of iniquities, who shall stand?

VI

The Mystery of Being and Becoming

But allow me, for all that, to speak in the presence of your mercy, though I am but earth and ashes, yet suffer that I speak, for, look, it is your mercy, not man who scorns me, to which I speak. And you, perhaps, scorn me but will turn about and pity me. What is it that I want to say, Lord, save that I do not know whence I came to this place, to this, shall I say rather 'dying life' than 'living death'? I do not know. And the comforts of your mercies received me, so I heard from my parents after the flesh, from whom and in whom once you formed me, for I do not remember. Therefore the comforts of a woman's milk received me. Neither my mother nor my nurses filled their own breasts, but through them you gave to me the nourishment of infancy, as you have ordained, and the wealth which reaches to the very foundation of the world. You also granted me to wish for no more than you gave, and to those who nursed me to be willing to give what you gave to them, for the plenty which they had from you they were willing to give to me, in love ordained. The good I had from them was good for them. It was from them, but rather through them, for all things good are indeed, from you, God, and from God is all my health, as I later learned, when you called to me through those very faculties which, both inwardly and outwardly, you supply. For then I knew to suck and to be content with those things which pleased me, and to cry at what hurt my flesh – no more.

Afterwards I began to laugh, at first when I was asleep and then when awake, for this they told me about myself and I believed it, for so we see other babes do. These things about myself I do not remember. And little by little I began to be conscious of where I was, and wanted to show what I wished to those who could satisfy my wants. I was unable to do so, for my wants were within me and they were without, and they were not able, by any perception of theirs, to enter into my soul. So I would toss my limbs about and utter sounds, such few signs as I could make, to indicate my wishes. They were not very plain. And when I was not obeyed, either because I was not understood or for fear of harming me, I would be angry with my unyielding elders and with children who did not do my will, and avenge myself on them by crying. And this, I have learned, is the way with such infants as I have been able to observe, and they, without knowing it, have shown me that such was I, rather than my nurses who did know it.

And, look, my infancy is long since dead and I am living, but you, Lord, who are always living and in whom nothing dies, because, before the first beginnings of the ages and before everything that can even be called 'before', you are, both God and Lord of all things which you have created, and with you abide the causes of all passing things and the unchanging beginnings of all things changeable, and with you live the eternal reasons for all things unreasoning and temporal, tell me, God, who ask of you, you who are merciful, tell me, who am wretched, tell me did my infancy come after any age of mine which died before? Was it that which I passed in my mother's womb? For of that life not a little has been known to me, and I have seen women with child myself. What was even before that, God, my delight? Was I anywhere or anybody? For I have none to tell me that, neither father nor mother were able, nor the experience of others, nor my own memory. Do you laugh at my enquiring of such matters, and bid me praise you for that which I do know, and acknowledge you? I do acknowledge you, Lord of heaven and earth, praising you for my first beginnings and the infancy of which I have no memory; and you have granted man to conjecture much about himself from others and believe much about himself upon the assurances of mere women. For even then I existed and I lived, and even then, towards the end of my infancy, I sought signs by which to make known what I felt to others. Whence could such a living creature appear but from you, Lord? Could anyone be his own creator? Could there be any source from which being and life could flow into us were you not our maker, Lord? To you, being and living are not two separate things, because, in the highest meaning of both words, they merge into one. For you are pre-eminent and unchangeable. In you today does not come to an end, and yet it does since all things are in you, and they would have no means of moving on unless you contained them. Again, because your years do not pass away, your years are today, and however many our days and our fathers' days have been, they have all been part of your eternal today, and therefrom received their bounds and distinctiveness. And so shall pass the future yet to come. But you yourself are as you have always been and shall be, and you will do today, as you have done today, all you have done in the past, and will do in the future. If anyone cannot understand this, what is it to me? Simply let him rejoice and ask the question: What is this? Let him also rejoice and be glad to find you while not finding an answer, rather than in finding an answer to fail to find you.

VII

The Beginnings of Sinfulness

Hear me, God! Alas for human sin! And yet you pity man confessing thus, because you made him (though not his sin). Who shall inform me now of my infancy's sins? In your sight none are clean from sin, even babes a day old upon the earth. Who reminds me? Why, any tiny tot at all, in whom I see what I do not remember about myself. How then did I sin at that time? In that I gaped crying for the breast? If I were to do so now, not indeed for the breast, but gaping for food proper to my years, I should be ridiculed and most justly taken to task for it. Even then, therefore, I did what was blameworthy, but neither custom nor reason suffered me to be blamed, for blame I could not understand, and as we grow up we root out and throw away such things, and I have never seen a person throwing away the good, as he purges out the bad. Perhaps, at the time, it was innocent enough to cry for what could have only been harmfully given, and to be petulantly angry with those who would not obey me, children, elders, and those from whom I was born, and a host of others who paid no heed to the nod of my will. I would try, as far as I could, to hurt them with blows because demands were not granted, which could only have been granted with harm to myself. That I was innocent lay rather in the frailty of my limbs than in my mind's intent. I myself have watched a very small child manifesting jealousy. It could not speak but glared, pale and hostile, at its companion at the breast.

This is common knowledge. Mothers and nurses declare that they can purge these faults, how is beyond me. But is it innocence, when the fountain of milk is richly and abundantly flowing not to welcome another needy creature who must draw its life from the same nutriment? Such conduct is gently tolerated, not because it is trivial or negligible, but because, with lapse of time it will pass away. And though you may overlook it thus far, the same behaviour in some older person cannot be borne with equanimity. So you, my Lord God, who have given life and body to the babe for, as we have observed, you have furnished it with senses, articulated its limbs, adorned it with shape, and, for its completeness and preservation, have woven into it all the urges of a living being, you bid me praise and confess you, and sing psalms to your name. You are God most high, omnipotent and good, had this been all that you had done. You alone could have done it. From you all proportion flows, most beauteous one, for you fashion the universe and order it according to your law.

This period of my life, Lord, I do not remember. I take the word of others. I guess what it was like from observing other infants, sound enough guesses, no doubt, but I do not like counting it a part of my life on earth. It lies in the darkness of forgetfulness, like the months I lay in my mother's womb. Since, then, 'I was shapen in iniquity and in sin did my mother conceive me', where or when was I, who serve you Lord, innocent? But, see, I pass over that time. What is it to me when I recall no trace of it?

VIII

The Coming of Speech

Journeying on from infancy, I passed into childhood. Or rather did childhood come into me, succeeding infancy? Infancy did not depart. Where could it go? And yet it had gone, for I was no longer an infant who could not speak, but a talking child. I remember this and later realised how I had learned to speak, for my elders did not teach me in some set order of instruction, as they later did the alphabet, but I myself with the mind you gave me, God, by means of grunts, sounds and various gestures would strive to make clear what was in my mind and to get what I wanted, but I proved inadequate to express all I wished, and to be comprehensible to everybody.

It exercised my mind, for I marked and understood that, when people spoke of something, and conformably with what they said, turned towards it, the word they uttered to point it out was what they called it. A wish, shown thus by the body's action, is the natural language of humankind. By the face, the movement of the eyes, and the action of other members, or the sound of the voice, folk generally make known what goes on in the mind, as it seeks, retains, rejects or refuses this or that. So it gradually came to me, with constantly hearing them, that words, properly placed in sentences, were the indicators of certain objects. So I began to express my desires when I had trained my vocal organs in the proper signs. Thus sharing with those about me the indications of what I wanted, I became more deeply involved in the perilous community of human life, still under parental authority and the will of my elders though I was.

IX

The Trials and Agonies of School

My God, what manifold wretchedness and derision I then
encountered, for it was set before me as a child that to live
aright was to obey those who counselled me to blossom in
this world, and to excel in the arts of speech, which minister
to the honour of men and to deceptive riches. Thereupon I
was handed over to school to acquire learning, the use of
which, poor creature, I did not understand. Yet, if I was slow
in such acquisition, I was caned. So tradition laid it down,
and our host of forebears had marked out paths of sorrow
for us – a labour and a grief to Adam's sons. But we did
discover, Lord, men of prayer from whom we learned. As far
as we were able, we sensed that you were someone great,
able, though you eluded our senses, to hear us from afar and
aid. As a child I began to pray to you, my help and hiding-
place, and in such prayer I waxed eloquent. I used to plead,
small though I was, but with no small emotion, that I should
not be caned at school. When you did not answer me
(though this implied no folly in my asking), my canings,
which were then a large and weighty trouble in my life, were
laughed at by my elders, even by my parents who had no
wish that any ill befall me.

Lord, is there anyone, and I am not thinking of a
thoughtless devotion, but of someone who thinks deeply,
and clings to you with intense feeling, and in such holy
nearness loves the most afflicted sufferers, who, none the
less, lightly regards the tortures which, the world over, such
sufferers beg in deepest terror to be spared (racks,
fleshhooks and the like)? Yet in such manner our own
parents ridiculed the torments with which we children were
afflicted by our school-teachers. We were in no way less
terrified of them, nor did we less plead to be spared them.
And yet we sinned, performing less well in writing and in
reading, and paying less attention to our lessons than was
required. We were not lacking, Lord, in such memory or

wits you granted according to our years, but it was fun to play. Punishment, to be sure, fell on us from those who were doing as we did, but the triflings of older folk go by the name of 'business'. Children in such case are punished and no one pities either or both – unless some sound judge does approve of my caning, because I played ball as a child, and was hindered by my sport, learning less, the more odiously to play the fool in later years. Did the very man who caned me do anything else? If he was worsted in some petty argument by another teacher, he was more tormented by bitterness and jealousy than I was when I was beaten in a ball game by a competitor!

X

The Folly of Young and Old

And yet I sinned, Lord my God, ruler and creator of all Nature's realm, though of sins only the ruler. I sinned, Lord my God, in doing contrary to the behests of my parents and those same schoolmasters. I might later have used well the learning they wished me to acquire, whatever purpose they had in mind for me. I disobeyed, not by choosing what was better, but for love of sport. I loved proud victories in sporting contests, and liked my ears to be tickled by lying stories, which only made them itch for more. And it was the same enthusiasm which sparkled in my eyes, at the stage-shows, the sport of my elders. Their producers enjoy such high standing that nearly all the audience covet the same for their small children – children whom they are happy to have thrashed, if by such shows they are hindered in their education, the very education by which they want them to produce the same achievements! Look on these things in mercy, Lord, and deliver us who call upon you now. Deliver even those who do not call upon you yet, so that they may call upon you, and you may deliver them.

XI

Illness, and Baptism Postponed

I had heard, while yet a child, of eternal life promised us through the humility of our Lord who came down to the level of our pride, and I was already marked by the sign of his cross and seasoned by his salt from my mother's womb. She greatly hoped in you. You saw, Lord, how one day, without warning, when still a child, I tossed in abdominal colic on the point of death. You saw, for you were even then my guardian, with what stress of soul, and with what faith, in the name of my mother's piety and that of our common mother, your Church, I besought the baptism of your Christ, my God and Lord. My earthly mother was deeply troubled, for from her pure heart and faith in you, and with love more great than mine, she was in travail for my eternal salvation. She was hurrying to procure for me the holy sacraments of initiation and washing on my confession for the remission of sin to you Lord Jesus, when I suddenly recovered. My cleansing was therefore postponed as though I had to be still more soiled by such continued life. Obviously, there would have been greater guilt and more perilous, too, in sin's defilements after that baptism.

So I was even then a believer, with my mother and the whole household. Only my father was not, but, for all that, he did not prevail in me over my mother's faith, so that I should not believe in Christ as he had not yet believed. She was content, my God, that you, rather than he, should be my father. You helped her in this to outweigh her husband whom she, better person though she was, served, serving thereby you, most certainly who so commanded. I ask you, my God, if it be your will that I should know, why was my baptism thus put off? Was it for my good, as one might say, that sin's reins were slackened? Or were they slackened? Why, even now I hear it said about this one or that, like some refrain in my ears: 'Let him alone, let him do it. He is not yet baptised'. Yet in the case of bodily well-being we do not say:

'Let him go on being hurt. He has not yet been healed.' How much better and swiftly, therefore, should I have been on the way to healing, had it come about that my well-being, by my own and my own folks' watchfulness, had been under the tutelage of you, who gave it – better indeed. How many and how mighty billows of temptation seemed to overhang my childhood! My mother already knew of them, and chose to expose to them rather my primal clay, than the image which was to be shaped from it.

XII

God's Overruling of Folly

In my very childhood, however, which was the subject of less apprehension than my youth, I had no love for learning and hated to be driven to it. Yet I was driven, and it did me good, but I did not do well, for unless compelled, I would not learn. Nobody does well unwillingly, even though what he does is good. Nor did those who drove me do well, but good came to me from you, my God. For they did not understand how I should use what they forced me to learn, save it be to satisfy the insatiable desires of an affluent poverty and a shameful glory. But you, by whom the hairs of our head are numbered, employed for my usefulness the error of those who pressed me to learn, as also you used my own error, who did not wish to learn, for my chastisement, of which, so very small a child, and yet so great a sinner, I was not undeserving. And so by those who did not well for me, you did well for me, and justly punished me, a sinner. You have decreed, and so it stands, that every man's undisciplined spirit is his own punishment.

XIII

The Uselessness of Literary Studies

But why it was that, as a small child, I should so hate the
Greek language in which I was instructed, I cannot yet
understand. I was very fond of Latin, not what my primary
teachers taught, but rather those who are called grammar-
ians. For those first elements, comprising reading, writing
and arithmetic, I thought as burdensome and painful as any
Greek. Whence this, save from sin and the emptiness of life? I
was flesh, a wind which moves on and does not come back.
For those first elements were more valuable, because they
were more clear-cut, and by them was created in me what,
once made, I still possess, the ability to read whatever I find
in writing, and to write myself what I wish, while in the other
classes I was forced to remember the wanderings of some
Aeneas (forgetting my own), and to lament dead Dido
because she killed herself for love, while with dry eyes,
wretch that I was, I endured my own death in your sight, God,
my life.

What is more wretched than a wretch that does not pity
himself, yet weeps for Dido's death, which came about
through loving Aeneas, but does not weep for his own death
which came about through not loving you, God, light of my
heart, bread which feeds my inner being, and power which
unites my mind and the core of my understanding? I did not
love you. I was unfaithful to you, and there sounded all
around my unfaithfulness: 'Well done! Well done!' The love
of this world is unfaithfulness towards God, and such
plaudits make some ashamed, if they are not unfaithful too.
I wept not for this, but for Dido dead, 'seeking the end with
the sword' – and I myself, abandoning you, and seeking the
end you have decreed, 'earth to earth'. If I were forbidden to
read these tales I would be sad (that I might not read what
made me sad!). Such madness is considered higher and richer
learning than that by which I was taught to read and write.

But now in my soul let God cry out, and let your truth tell
me: 'It is not so, it is not so. Far better was the former kind of

learning.' Indeed I am more ready to forget about the wanderings of Aeneas and all such matters, than to forget how to read and write. Curtains hang at the doors of grammar-schools, but what they stand for is a veil for evil rather than a tribute to privacy. Let those whom I no longer fear raise a cry against me, as I confess to you, my God, what my soul desires, and assent to blame for my evil ways, that I may love your good ways. Let those buyers and sellers of literary learning not cry out against me, for if I put to them the question whether it is true, what the poet said, that Aeneas came once to Carthage, the less well-educated will reply that they do not know, the more learned will say it is not true. But if I ask them how Aeneas' name is spelt all who have learned to read will answer correctly with the signs which have been conventionally agreed upon. And if I should likewise ask which of the two one might forget with most inconvenience to life, reading and writing, or those fictions of poetry, who, in possession of his wits, will not see what he must reply? I sinned, therefore, as a child, when I loved rather these empty studies than those more profitable ones, or rather hated the one and loved the other. But then: 'one and one, two; two and two, four' was a hateful chant to me, while a choice show of my vanity was the wooden horse full of armed men, Troy's burning and Creusa's ghost.

XIV

Disliking Greek

Why then did I hate Greek literature, which chants the same songs? Homer was expert in weaving such tales, and most pleasantly trifling, yet to me, as a child, he was distasteful. That, I suppose, is what Virgil is to Greek children, when they are forced to learn him, as I was Homer. In truth, difficulty, the sheer difficulty of learning a foreign language, sprinkled with a sort of gall all the sweet pleasures of Greek myths, for not a word of them did I know and yet, to make me know them, I was strongly driven with fierce threats and punishments. True, time was, in infancy, when I also knew no Latin, but I learned Latin by observation, without fear or torment, amid the encouragements of nurses, and the jests and joys of those who laughed and played with me. Thus I learned without pressure of punishment from those who urged me on, for my own heart also urged me on to bring what I thought to utterance, a feat impossible without learning some words, not from those who taught, but from those who talked with me, and in whose ears I brought to life what I had in mind. By this it is clear that a free curiosity is a greater force in learning than a fear-ridden compulsion. But this compulsion restrains curiosity's waywardness, as your laws, God, decree, your laws, from the canes of our masters to the martyrs' trials, for they are potent to mix together the wholesome and the distasteful, recalling us to you from the pestilential pleasure by which we abandoned you.

XV

Prayer for Pardon

Hear my prayer for pardon, Lord, lest my soul faint under your discipline, and do not let me fail in acknowledging before you your mercies, by which you have snatched me from all my most evil paths, that you might grow sweet to me beyond all the allurements I followed, that I might most powerfully love you and hold fast your hand with all my being, and that to the very end you might tear me from temptation.

For, look, Lord, my king and my God, let whatever that is useful which I learned as a child serve you, let what I say, and write, and read, and calculate serve you. When I was learning trifles you disciplined me, and forgave me the sin of the delight I took in what those trifles held. In them I learned many useful words, but such words can be learned in serious contexts, and that is the safe path in which children should walk.

XVI

The Corruptions of Literature

But woe to you, river of man's ways, who shall stem you, how long before you run dry, how long will you roll the sons of Eve into that vast and fearsome sea which they scarce can cross who have climbed upon the Tree? Have I not read in you of Jupiter, now thundering, now fornicating? Truly no one can do both but this is done so that, with feigned thunder playing procurer, real adultery should have authority and encouragement. Yet which of our gowned schoolmasters would hear with tolerant ears a man shouting from their own classroom floor: 'Homer was making these things up, and ascribing the human to the divine. I should prefer it the other way round'? It is certainly a true word that Homer did make it up, attributing divinity to evil men, so that sin should not be considered sin, and whoever committed such sins should seem to be imitating not abandoned men, but the gods of heaven.

For all that, hellish torrent, the sons of men are flung into you, and fees paid, to learn these things and a big show is made of it all when it is on public display in court, and in full view of the laws (which fix salaries for teachers over and above scholars' fees). You beat your banks and roar: 'Here are words for the learning, here is eloquence won, most essential for successful pleading and setting forth your case.' Presumably we would not know such phrases as 'golden shower', 'lap', 'seduce', had not Terence staged an evil youth putting Jupiter forward as an example for his lewdness, as he looks at a picture on the wall showing Jupiter seducing Danae, as they say, by sending a shower of gold into her lap. Observe how he rouses himself to lust as though by divine decree: 'What a god,' he said, 'who by his thunder shakes the highest courts of heaven! Am I, a mere manikin, not to do as he does? I did, and gladly, too.'

No, absolutely no, these words are not more easily learned by filthiness like this. Rather by these words is filthiness of such sort more brazenly committed. I blame not the words. They are like choice and precious vessels. I blame the wine of error which our drunken teachers give us to drink in them. Refuse to drink it, and we would be beaten, nor was there leave of appeal to a sober judge. And yet, my God, in whose sight my recollection need stir no guilt, I willingly learned these things, took pleasure in so doing, and so was called 'a promising child.'

XVII

A Prize Declamation

Permit me, my God, to speak of my intelligence, your gift, and in what absurdities I wasted it. There was laid upon me a task worrisome enough to my soul, to wit that, for the reward of commendation and fear of shame and caning, I should recite the words of Juno, angry and resentful that she could not keep the Trojans' king from Italy – words I had heard that Juno never uttered, but we were compelled to follow the wavering footsteps of poetic fictions, and to say in prose what the poet had said in verse. His language earned the greater praise, for therein the angry and resentful emotions of the character depicted stood out according to that person's majesty, and in words which fitly clothed the theme. What was it to me, my God, true life? Why was my declamation applauded more than that of my contemporaries and classmates? Mere smoke and wind, was it not? And was there nothing else by which to train my wit and tongue? Your praises, Lord, your praises, through your Scriptures might have propped the young shoot of my heart, and saved it from being torn away by empty trifles, the cheap prey of birds.

XVIII

Rules of Grammar or the Rules of Morality?

What wonder, then, that I should be swept off into vanities, and that I went out from you, my God, when those men were set before me as examples, who were confounded if caught using an inelegant expression or making a grammatical mistake in relating some quite innocent thing they had done, but who, if they told of their lustful acts, in rich and well ordered language, precise and proper in its expression would take pride in the applause. O Lord, longsuffering and most merciful and true, who see this and are silent. Will you be silent for ever? And now will you drag from this horrible pit the soul which seeks you and thirsts for your delights, and whose heart says to you: 'I have sought your face, Lord, your face will I seek, for I am far from your face in darkling desire.'

Men neither come to you, nor go from you on their feet or by distance that can be measured. That younger son you told about did not look for horses, chariots or ships. He did not fly on wings which could be seen, or simply walk away, when he set off to waste what you had given him, sweet father, 'in a far country in riotous living' – and sweeter still you were in that you also gave to him when he came back penniless! No, it is lustful desire ('darkling', I called it) which separates us from your face.

Look with forbearance, Lord, my God, on how meticulously men observe the established rules of writing and pronunciation received from those who used the language before them, and how lightly they hold the eternal rules of everlasting salvation received from you. Thus, one who holds and teaches the ancient decrees of pronunciation, and contrary to the teaching of the schoolmen, says 'uman' without its initial aspirate, displeases 'human' beings, more than if, contrary to your laws, himself a 'human' being, he should hate his 'human' fellows. As if he ought to consider any foe more dangerous to him than the hate which thus fires his hostility! By that very hostility he devastates his own heart more than any persecution can. The record of conscience 'that he is doing to another that which he would not wish to have done to him', is deeper within us than any knowledge of letters.

How inscrutable you are, God only great, dwelling silently in the heavens, and by tireless law, meting out the penalty of blindness on illicit lusts, while some man seeking a reputation for eloquence before a human arbiter, with an audience of men around him and in the act assailing his foe with hate, takes the utmost care not to commit a fault of speech, but no care at all lest, through the rage of his spirit, he should destroy a fellow-man – a fellow 'uman being', so to speak.

XIX

The Child is Father of the Man

Such was the way of life, at whose threshold I, wretched child, lay, this was the arena's wrestling pad, where I feared more to be guilty of an inelegance of speech than I took care, if I did, to envy those who did not. These faults I confess to you, my God. For there I was praised by them, whom to please was to me to live honourably. I saw not the chasm of turpitude into which I was cast from your sight. For in your sight what was more vile than I? Thus I even disgusted myself by the countless lies by which I deceived my tutor, my teachers and my parents, all for love of sport, passion for shows, and longing to ape the stage.

I also stole from my parents' cellar and table, spurred by

gluttony or to have something to give other children for playing with me, though, to be sure, they liked play as much as I did. In such play I often cheated to win, myself beaten by a vain passion to excel. What was I so unwilling to have done to me, and what did I so fiercely condemn if I detected it, as what I did to others? And if I should be caught and condemned, I would rather get angry than admit it.

Is that childish innocence? No, indeed, Lord, my God, I confess to you. These very faults, as riper years follow, just as worse penalties succeed the cane, move on from tutors and teachers, nuts, balls and sparrows, to magistrates and kings, gold, properties and slaves. And so, our king, when you said: 'Of such is the kingdom of heaven', it was only the stature of childhood which you commended, as humility's sign.

XX

'Not Unto us, O Lord . . .'

Yet to you, Lord most high, creator and governor of the universe, thanks would have still been due had it been your will that I should not outlive childhood, for even then I was, I lived, I felt, I had a care for my own well-being, a trace of that mysterious unity from which I came, I guarded in my heart of hearts the totality of my senses, and in these same particulars and in what I thought about them, I took pleasure in the truth. I hated being deceived, I had a good memory, I was well instructed in language, I was soothed by friendship, I avoided pain, dejection and ignorance. In such a living creature what was there not to be admired and praised? But all these are my God's gifts. I did not give them to myself. They are good and their total is myself. God then is he that made me, and he himself is my good. And before him I take joy in every good thing I was as a child. This was my sin, that not in him but in his creatures, in myself and others, I sought pleasures, honours, truths, and so fell into

sorrows, all manner of confusion, and mistakes. Thanks be
to you, my sweetness, my honour, my confidence, my God,
thanks to you for your gifts. Preserve them for me. For thus
will you preserve me, and your gifts to me will be increased
and perfected, and I shall be with you, for even my existence
is a gift of yours.

BOOK TWO

The Pear Tree

Introduction

Book Two is the briefest, scarce four thousand words, and the reason may be Augustine's desire to set in high relief the well-known incident of the stripped pear tree. He was in his sixteenth year, a time of idleness at home, which saw, in his view, a frightening initiation into wilful sin.

Augustine must have been about eleven years old when he was sent from the hated elementary school in Thagaste, to the school of grammar and rhetoric at Madaura, a Roman 'colony' as such bastions of Imperial defence were called, some twenty miles away from home. In the somewhat disjointed account of his education touched upon in the first book, Augustine has anticipated incidents and attitudes remembered from his four or five years of secondary education at Madaura. The *Confessions* have been called, not without some reason, the first autobiography in European literature, but no ordered and firm chronology can be demanded of them.

He remembers with anguish how he wept over the death of Dido, a folk-heroine by now in Phoenician North Africa, and how he found the polished comedies of Terence, also a Carthaginian, seductively pornographic. Homer, in his antipathy to Greek, he resisted, but Latin literature he found corrupting. Monica, in spite of her fundamental Christianity, still lingered, as he has already said, 'in the suburbs of Babylon', and Patricius had only a worldly interest in his school career.

No home influence, therefore, constrained him. He matured early, to the somewhat crude delight of his father, and his mother's vague anxiety was restricted to a timid warning against adultery. Thus, when he came home to spend his sixteenth year in idleness, while Patricius saved the funds needed for his further education, the growing boy was open to all the temptations of a pagan secular society. We hear nothing of a Christian cell in Thagaste, though there must have been one to provide the means of baptism, as the incident of Monica's intransigence showed. The impression deepens that it was only after Patricius died, a late-born Christian about A.D. 370, and with her release from the subservience which she considered a wifely obligation, that Monica became the saintly person she is shown to be in her widowhood. We should be glad to know about Monica's spiritual pilgrimage from the 'suburbs' of the world to the clean and open countryside, apart from the anecdotes of her own and her son's recounting.

The year of idleness did immense damage. Augustine, as a street-boy of Thagaste and member of a local gang, 'trod the mire of Babylon.' He tells with wearisome self-flagellation and introspection, with all the wordiness which the Roman rhetorical education in the days of its decadence produced, the tale of the aimless robbing of a neighbour's pear tree by himself and his mindless friends. The occasion loomed large in Augustine's record of his sins. It was sin for sin's sake, he confesses, a sin sought and savoured, inspired by no appetite or motive, mere naked depravity, a classic case of pure vandalism, half a century before the alien German Vandals swarmed ravaging through the province. It was the result, no doubt, of the boy's gregarious nature, his enormous desire to be popular with his peers.

In Augustine's mind, as he described the incident in this book years later, and from his deep preoccupation with Genesis, that forlorn pear tree became his symbol of the Tree of the Knowledge of Good and Evil.

In short it was a morally disastrous year, undisciplined and idle. Patricius was diligently saving to send his son to Carthage, a sacrifice for which Augustine remained, a trifle tepidly, grateful. He had been dux of the school of words at Madaura, and the equivalent of a university education in the city was the obvious sequence.

I

The Purpose of this Book

I wish now to recall my past impurities, and the carnal corruptions of my soul, not because I love them, but in order that I may love you, my God. I do so for love of your love, surveying, in bitterness of recollection, my most evil ways, so that you may become sweet to me, Sweetness which does not deceive, Sweetness joyous and free from care. I am gathering myself together out of the ruin in which I lay shattered while, turning my back on you alone, I was lost in many ways. For once I burned in youth to take my fill of hell, and rashly to grow wild in many a shady love. My beauty withered, and I stank in your sight, as I sought my own pleasure, and desired to stand well in the eyes of men.

II

The Sins of Youth

And what was it that gave me joy but to love and to be loved, love that was not held by that restraint which lies between mind and mind, where runs the boundary of friendship? From the miry, bubbling fleshly lust of youth, fogs arose which overclouded and darkened my heart, so that the difference between a tranquil affection and the blackness of lust was blurred. They boiled together in confusion, and snatched my weak years down the screes of impure desires to plunge me in a whirlpool of manifold wickedness. Your wrath grew strong above me, but I knew it not. I had grown deaf by the clattering of the chain of my flesh (your punishment for my soul's arrogance) and I wandered further from you – and you permitted it, and I was tossed about, poured out and spread wide, as I boiled over in my deeds of passion while you said nothing, my slow-footed Joy. You said nothing then, as I wandered further and further away from you into more and more fruitless seeding-grounds of sorrows, arrogant in my depression and restless in my weariness.

Would that someone then had calmed my wretchedness and turned to use the fleeting beauties of these new experiences, and set down bounds to what was sweet in them, so that the high-tide of my years could have reached its flood in marriage, and its quietness could have been complete in the begetting of children, as your law lays down, Lord – for thus you form the breed of our mortal flesh, and thus are able to reach out a gentle hand to blunt the thorns excluded from your Paradise. For your almighty power is not far away, even when we are far from you. Surely I should have listened more carefully to the voice from the clouds which hide you: 'Yet such shall suffer in the flesh . . . ', but I spare you. And: 'It is good for a man not to touch a woman', and: 'he who is not married cares for the things of God, and how he may please God, but he who is joined in wedlock, thinks of earthly things and how he may please his wife.' I should, therefore, have listened more carefully to these sayings, and 'a eunuch for the kingdom of heaven's sake', have more happily awaited your embraces.

I boiled over, wretched creature, following the drive of my own tide, and abandoning you passed beyond all that you permit, but I did not escape your scourgings, for what mortal can? You were always there, in severe mercy, be-spattering all my unlawful pleasures with the bitterest disillusionments, just so that I should seek pleasure that brings no disillusionment, and in which I would find nothing but you, Lord – nothing but you who add pain to precept, and smite that you may heal, and kill us that we should not die apart from you. Where was I, and in exile how remote, from the joys of your home, in that sixteenth year of my flesh when, in the mad rage of unbridled lust (the shame of men, unsanctioned by your laws) I accepted its dominion over me, and to it made a full surrender. My family took no thought to stay my wild ways by marriage. Their sole care was that I should make the best possible speech and be a persuasive orator.

III

Sixteenth Year

My studies were interrupted in that year. I came back from neighbouring Madaura, where I had gone for my literary and rhetorical education, for the expenses of a longer journey to Carthage were being saved up for me. It was more out of my father's courage than his resources, for he was only a citizen of Thagaste of quite slender means. To whom am I telling this story? Not to you, my God, in whose presence I tell it, but to my fellow men, or what small number of them may chance to come upon these writings of mine. And for what purpose? To be sure, that I, and whoever reads this, may ponder from what depth we must cry out to you. What is nearer to your ears than the heart which confesses, and the life which springs from faith? For who did not then highly praise the man, my father, when beyond his family's means, he provided whatever was needed for a long journey for my studies' sake? For many citizens of far greater wealth took no such trouble for their children. Yet the same father took no thought of the kind of man I was becoming in your sight, or how chaste I was, provided I was cultivated in speech – though uncultivated in your field, God, you who are the only true, good husbandman of that field which is our heart.

But when in that intermediate idleness of my sixteenth year I lived on holiday with my parents (it was due to some domestic need), the brambles of lust grew over my head, there was no hand to root them out. In the meantime my father saw, when I was bathing, that, with puberty upon me, I was showing the signs of restless youth. As if this stirred desire for grandchildren, he gleefully told my mother when he was a little drunk – that state in which the world forgets you who created it, and instead loves what you have created, bent and twisted as it is towards baser things by the will's unseen intoxication. But you had already founded your shrine in my mother's heart, and commenced to build your holy habitation. He was now, only recently converted, under the instruction of the Church. So it was that she was shocked with a pure anxiety and trembling, and, though I was not yet baptised, she still feared for me the crooked paths in which they walk who turn their back to you and not their face.

Alas! And I am taking on myself to say that you kept silence, my God, when I was wandering further away from you! Did you really say nothing to me then? Whose words were they but yours, which through my faithful mother you chanted in my ears? Nothing went down compellingly to my heart. I remember how, in private and with vast anxiety, she warned me not to fornicate, and most of all not to play the adulterer with any man's wife. Women's words these admonitions seemed to me, which I should blush to obey. But they were yours, and I did not know. I thought you were saying nothing, and that it was she who was speaking, through whom truly you were speaking to me, and in whom you were scorned by me, by me your servant, son of your handmaid. But I did not know, and went headlong with blindness so great, that, among my peers, I was ashamed to be outdone in shamelessness, when I heard them boasting of their evil deeds with bragging equal to their filthiness. I took pleasure not only in the act of lust, but from the praise, too, which follows it.

What is more worthy of censure than vice? Not to be reviled, I made myself more vicious, and where there was no foundation for a deed which, had it been done, would put me level with the damned, I would pretend to have done what I had not done, so as not to appear the more abandoned, as I was in fact more blameless, and not to be thought more dastardly, as I was more chaste. See with what companions I walked the streets of Babylon, and rolled in its mire, as if it was spices and precious ointments. And to make me cling the more tightly to sin's very navel, my unseen foe trampled me down and seduced me, because I was easy to seduce. And my earthly mother, though she had herself fled the inner heart of Babylon, dawdled somewhat in its suburbs. Though she had given me advice on chastity, she listened with respect to what her husband said, and felt it would be unhealthy and potentially perilous to confine what could not be cut back to the quick, within the bounds of married love. She had also on her mind the fear that my expectations might be hampered by the fetter of a wife, not those expectations of another world which my mother did have in you, but the hope of learning which both parents deeply desired I should obtain – my father because he scarcely thought of you but had empty hopes of me, my mother because she thought that the common course of education was not only without harm, but actually a help in laying hold of you. Such I imagine, as I look back, as I can, were the notions of my parents. The reins which held me back from pleasure-seeking were loosened, too, beyond the proper measure of discipline, to the point of indiscipline, in fact, with the varied troubles that brings. Through it all, my God, was a murk which hid from me the tranquillity of your truth. My sin oozed like a secretion out of fat.

IV

The Pear Tree

Assuredly, Lord, your law, like the law written on men's hearts which wickedness itself cannot erase, punishes theft. What thief puts up with another thief, even if one is a rich thief and the other spurred by want. I wanted to be a thief. I committed theft, though I was not driven by any want, unless it was a poverty of righteousness and an aversion to it, together with a surfeit of evil. For I stole that which I had in abundance, and of much better quality. Nor did I want to enjoy that which I had stolen. I rather took joy in the theft and the sin itself.

There was a pear-tree next door to our vineyard loaded with fruit, and enticing neither in size nor taste. To shake and rob this tree, a company of wicked boys, we went late one night, for until then, after our unwholesome fashion, had we spun out our play, and we carried off huge loads, not for our own feasting, but to throw to the pigs. Perhaps we ate some, but it was really for the pleasure of doing what was not allowed. Look on my heart, God, look on my heart, on which you had mercy in the lowest abyss. Let my heart tell you what it sought there – to be bad for no reason, and that I should be evil for no other cause than the evil in me. It was foul evil, and I loved it. I loved to destroy myself. I loved my rebellion, not that for which I was in revolt, but rebellion itself, a base spirit, leaping from your firm foundations to utter death, not seeking something shamefully, but shame itself.

V

The Roots of Wrongdoing

Truly, there is a splendour in beautiful bodies, as in gold and silver and the rest. In the touch of flesh, harmony means most of all. Each of the senses has its proper bodily adjustment. Worldly honour and the power to command and to surpass, have their own attractiveness. Hence the desire for revenge. Yet, in winning all of these, Lord, there must be no departure from you, nor swerving from your law. This life we live has its own charm, because of a certain measure of grace, and its conformity with all these lesser beauties. Human friendship, too, is sweet with its lovesome bond, because it brings about the union of many minds. Because of all these good things and their like, sin is committed, when, through an ungoverned bent towards their remoter worth, the better and the highest are abandoned – you, Lord our God, your truth and your law. These lowest goods have their delights, but not as my God does, who made them all. In him the good man finds delight, and he is the beloved of the upright in heart.

Therefore, when enquiry is made about a crime and its cause, it is commonly thought that a desire and opportunity have emerged of laying hold on one of these lesser goods, as we have called them, or a fear of losing the same. Beautiful they are indeed, and charming, though base and low in comparison with the higher goods, and those which make for happiness. A man has killed another. Why? He was in love with his wife or coveted his property, or he wished to filch a livelihood, or he feared to lose some such thing at his hands, or he had been hurt, and blazed to avenge himself. Would one commit a murder without a cause, or for the sheer joy of murdering itself? Who would believe it? It was said of someone that he was so insanely cruel that he was without any reason bad and cruel. Yet a cause is to be set down even for that: 'I do not want', he says, 'my heart or hand to grow slack through inactivity.' And why again? Why so? Presumably because, having laid hold of a city through the practice of crime, he might pursue after honours, authority and riches, and be free of fear of the law and the burdens which arise from lack of personal resources and the consciousness of crime. And so, not even Catalina loved his crimes, but assuredly something else for the sake of which he committed them.

VI

The Ways of Wickedness

What then did I love in you, my theft, that nocturnal wrongdoing of my life's sixteenth year? You were not beautiful because you were theft. Indeed, are you anything to which I can speak? Those pears were beautiful which we stole, for you created them, you most beautiful of all, creator of all, good God, God, highest good and my true good. Those pears were beautiful, but it was not they for which my miserable soul lusted. I had better ones available, but I gathered those simply in order to steal, for, once gathered, I threw them away, eating from them wickedness alone, which I gladly enjoyed. If any of those pears entered my mouth, the crime was their savour. And now, Lord my God, I ask, what was it in my sin which gave me joy? See, it has no loveliness. I do not mean the loveliness that lies in justice and in wisdom, nor that which is in a man's mind and memory, his senses and abounding life, nor the loveliness which makes the stars resplendent and fair in their orbits, or the earth and sea replete with what they bear, by birth replacing that which passes into death. Much less do I mean that sort of corrupted shadowy splendour which lies in deceiving vices.

Pride makes a show of loftiness, but you alone are God most High, and you are over all. What does ambition seek but honour and glory, when you are alone worthy of honour above all things, and glorious for ever? The savagery of potentates desires to be feared, but who is to be feared but God alone, from whose power nothing can be wrested or taken away – when, where, whither or by whom? The enticements of the sensual are seeking to be loved, but what is gentler than your love? Nothing is loved more wholesomely than your truth, lovely and bright beyond all else. Inquisitiveness pretends to be a zeal for knowledge, when you are supremely omniscient. Yes, and ignorance and folly itself is disguised by the name of simplicity and innocence, when nothing can be found more simple than yourself, and what more innocent, seeing it is nothing but their own deeds which are hostile to the bad. Laziness wishes to be called rest, but what sure rest is there save in the Lord? Luxury wants to be called plenty and affluence, but you are the fulness and unfailing store of uncorrupted sweetness. Prodigality affects a show of liberality, but you are the overflowing bestower of all good. Greed wishes to own much. You possess all. Emulation contends for the top place, but what is higher than you? Wrath seeks vengeance. Who avenges more justly than you? Fear is startled by the unaccustomed and the unexpected, which oppose the things it loves, while it takes precaution for its own safety. What is unaccustomed or unexpected in your sight, or who separates you from what you love, and where is settled safety save by your side? Grief pines over what it has lost and in which desire took joy. It would have nothing taken from it, as nothing can be taken from you.

Thus does the heart play the libertine when it turns from you, and outside of you seeks the unalloyed and untainted, which can be found only when it comes back to you. All, in perverted fashion, imitate you, they who make themselves remote from you and lift themselves up against you. Yet, by imitating you thus, they declare that you are the creator of all nature and that therefore there is no place where they can truly retreat from you. What then did I love in that theft of mine? In what way, albeit viciously and perversely, did I imitate my Lord? Was it my pleasure, though it was but by craft, to go contrary to your law because by strong action I was not able to do so, in order only that, prisoner though I was, I might pretend to a limping liberty, and do what was not permitted without penalty in a dim show of omnipotence? Look, here is your servant running away from his master in pursuit of a shadow. Oh foulness, the monster that life is, the depth of death! Was I able to do freely what was unlawful for no other reason but that it was unlawful?

VII

Thanks for Forgiveness

What shall I render to the Lord because my memory thus recalls, and my soul finds no fear therein? I will love you, Lord, and thank you and confess to your name, because you have forgiven evils so great and my heinous deeds. I ascribe it to your mercy and your grace that you have dissolved my sins like ice. And to thy grace I commit the sins I have not yet done, for what evil is there which I am beyond committing, who loved a deed of wrong for its own sake? I confess that all are forgiven me, both the evils I have wilfully done, and those which, thanks to your guidance, I have not done.

Who is there among men, who, considering his own frailty, dares to set down to his own strength his purity and innocence, and therefore loves you less, as if your mercy, by which you pardon those who have turned to you, is less needed by him?

Let no one who, at your summons, has followed your call and so escaped those sins of which he reads in my memoirs and confessions, scoff at me whose malady was cured by the same physician, by whose therapy he was saved wholly or, at least in part, from the disease. Such a person, in fact, loves you as much or more because he has seen me rescued from the debilities of sins so great, by the very one through whom he observes he has been spared their bondage.

VIII

The Pears Again

What profit had I then, miserable creature, in those things which I blush now simply to remember – especially in that theft in which I loved the theft itself and nothing else? It was nothing itself, but I was the more wretched on account of it. Yet, I would not have done it alone, for so I recall my state of mind – I simply would not have done it alone. Therefore I loved the companionship of those with whom I did it. I did not therefore love nothing but the act of theft. No, indeed, nothing else, because that other circumstance was nothing. What am I really saying? Who can teach me save he who enlightens my heart and reveals its darkness? What has come into my mind to look into, discuss and ponder on? For if I had then loved those stolen pears, and had wanted to enjoy them, I might have alone, had the desire been strong enough, committed the sin by which I satisfied my pleasure, and so needed no stimulus from my accomplices to inflame the itch of my own greed. So because my pleasure did not lie in those pears, it lay in the act of evil itself, which the band of sinners committed.

IX

Yet Again the Pears

What was that state of mind? Surely, it was altogether too foul, and woe to me for entertaining it. What was it? Who understands his sins? We laughed as if our hearts were tickled because we had tricked those who did not think we were doing this, and who strongly resented it. Why then was I pleased that I was not doing it all by myself? Was it because no one easily laughs in private? Commonly, indeed, no one laughs alone, yet laughter does sometimes overcome men by themselves and away from others, if something very funny encounters eyes or ears or fancy. Yet I most certainly should not have done it alone.

See, my God, the living memory of my soul before your face. Alone I should not have perpetrated that theft, in which it was not what I stole which delighted me, but the mere fact that I stole – which theft would certainly have not pleased me to commit by myself, nor would I have done so. Oh friendship too unfriendly, inscrutable seduction of the mind, lust to hurt for fun and games, and greed to harm another without desire for personal gain or retaliation, but simply at the word: 'Let's go and do it', and because of shame not to be shameful.

X

'I have Sinned'

Who can straighten out that bent and twisted knottiness? It is foul. I do not want to think of it. I do not wish to see it. It is you that I desire, oh righteousness and innocence, fair and comely to all honourable eyes, and which I desire with desire never to be satisfied. There is rest indeed with you and life beyond turmoil. He who enters into you enters into 'the joy of his Lord'. He shall have no fear, and know the best in the one who is best of all. I slipped away from you, my God, and wandered, straying far from your steady strength, in the days of my youth. Of myself I made a desert land.

BOOK THREE

Son of Tears

Introduction

'And so to Carthage I came', Augustine tells us. A haunting phrase which promises much and tells little. T.S. Eliot ended a movement of 'The Waste Land' with it. He too might have liked to know more of the Punic town, its life, its education. We only know that the boy, seventeen years old, saw some form of emancipation there. He was 'in love with love', he says cryptically, a most perilous preoccupation in a place where 'a whole frying pan of wicked loves sputtered round him'.

Carthage had been Rome's old enemy six centuries before, when the great Phoenician city, a capital of empire on the sea's waist, almost broke the young Italian republic in two mighty wars. The strait proved too narrow, the island of Sicily too dangerous a bridgehead, and the western Mediterranean too small, for two expanding powers to share. Rome won, though some date the downfall of her imperial power from the devastation the Carthaginian Hannibal wrought up and down Italy. But in 146 B.C. in a ruthless war of revenge Rome razed Carthage.

The site was too attractive to leave unused. Julius Caesar and Augustus set the city on its feet again, and by the second century Carthage became a flourishing metropolis with all the busy commerce and seaport vice which polluted Paul's Corinth. By the third century it was a centre of oratory and legal studies, and Tertullian and Cyprian had made it a focus of Christianity, whose bishop held himself equal to the Bishop of Rome. After the Vandals overran the province, just after Augustine's death, Carthage became the capital of the German kings, Gaiseric and his line, a dreadful pirate power in the Mediterranean until, almost a century later, Belisarius from the surviving eastern Empire, crushed and extirpated all the roving pests.

Augustine tells us little of the life he lived. Without unseemly detail he speaks of his obsession with love and the theatre, which he found an intense emotional and erotic stimulus. He found a girl to live with him, a faithful creature who bore him a son (Adeodatus, 'given by God') and whom he discarded heartlessly after fourteen years, under Monica's unceasing pressure.

He was not happy. The enormous restlessness which was part of a ceaseless quest for truth was on him, warring with the basic Catholicism of his childhood. The city did not absorb him. He was not part of the disorder and indiscipline which marred the life and conduct of the university world, where the 'subverters' ('bother-boys', if you will) made mock of scholarship, culture and academic dignity. He seemed to have earned some distinction in study, and later wrote and taught in Carthage, though clear sequences of dates are difficult again to establish.

His main preoccupation is to concentrate on major events which blazed the path to his conversion. In this book there are recorded two significant adventures of the mind. In his rhetorical studies he discovered Cicero's treatise *Hortensius*, named after Cicero's rival and partner, who shared the oratorical honours of court and forum in the years of Cicero's fame. From this book, a lamentable loss to literature, Augustine became fired with a zeal for philosophy. It fed his hunger for the truth, and if his body strove against his mind in these youthful years, that was the way with him. He may have been in rebellion against Monica's Catholicism, even against Monica herself, but he thirsted for certainty. *Hortensius* had stirred him but (and it is significant) Cicero had no word of Christ. He was, in fact, murdered forty years before Christ was born, on a winter day when Mark Antony's assassins caught up with him in the little wood in Caieta. But had the Manichaeans a coherent faith? Augustine's nine years of trifling with this heretical sect began in Carthage. It was a wavering and diminishing subservience, the memory of which always makes Augustine angry. Sometimes, in his scorn, he cannot bring himself to mention the name, so ashamed was he ever to have been deluded by what he came to look upon as pernicious nonsense.

In fact we should be glad to know more of Mani or Manes, a Parthian born in A.D. 215 or 216. He seems to have tried to establish, as sectaries have attempted in many contexts to do, a synthesis of faiths. In Manes' case it was a fragmented Christianity, orthodox and gnostic, along with Zoroastrianism and Buddhism. Something in the Manichaean notion of a primeval conflict of light and darkness, seems to have answered some of Augustine's difficulties over the problem of evil, and perhaps their view of the physical world offered some semblance of order to his mind, confused a little by the varied volume of his reading. As far as we understand the cult, which had adherents from China to Spain, it could do little for Augustine's inability to grasp the spiritual, a confusion which led to the strangest imagery for God. Of the Manichaean asceticism, vegetarianism, the notion of an elect, apart and enlightened, and the claim that the Comforter was incarnated in the founding father himself, he can have had scant approval, even as a rebel against Catholicism.

He was not, however, a man to give up easily, ready though he was to reject what was proven wrong. He met Faustus, in due course, a leading Manichaean whose confessed ignorance disillusioned him. But that story is told later. Monica, as Book Three ends, is holding fast, pleading with and praying for her wandering boy, encouraged at last by a saintly bishop who had once felt the seduction of the Manichaean cult. He assured her that 'the son of these tears' could not be lost. A curious dream had also assured her.

I

Way of Restlessness

I came to Carthage where a whole frying-pan of wicked loves sputtered all around me. I was not yet in love, but I was in love with love, and with a deep-seated want I hated myself for wanting too little. I was looking for something to love, still in love with love. I hated safety and a path without snares, because I had a hunger within – for that food of the inner man, yourself, my God. Yet that hunger did not make me feel hungry. I was without appetite for incorruptible food, not because I was sated with it, but with less hunger in proportion to my emptiness. And so my soul was sick. Its ulcers showed, wretchedly eager to be scratched by the touch of material things which yet, if they had no life, would not be loved at all. To love and to be loved was sweet to me, the more so if I could enjoy the person of the one I loved.

I polluted, therefore, the stream of friendship with the foulness of lust, and clouded its purity with the dark hell of illicit desire. Though sordid and without honour, in my overweening pride, I longed to be a polished man about town. I plunged, too, into the love with which I sought ensnarement, my merciful God. With what gall did you in your goodness sprinkle that sweetness! I was loved. I went as far as the bondage of enjoyment. Because I so desired I was being tied in the entanglements of sorrow, just to be scourged with redhot iron rods of jealousy, suspicions, fears, bouts of rage and quarrelling.

II

The Lure of Drama

The drama enthralled me, full of representations of my own miseries and fuel for my own fire. Why does a man make himself deliberately sad over grievous and tragic events which he would not wish to suffer himself? Yet he is willing as an onlooker to suffer grief from them, and the grief itself is what he enjoys. What is that but wretched lunacy? He is the more stirred by them in proportion to his sanity. When he suffers personally it is commonly called misery. When he feels for others it is called mercy. But what source of mercy is it in imaginary situations on the stage? The hearer is not stirred to help but invited only to grieve, and he compliments the author of such fictions in proportion to his grief. And if those human catastrophes, out of ancient history or simply made up, are so presented that the spectator does not grieve, he goes off disgusted or critical. If he is moved to grief, he stays on, attentive and enjoying it. Tears and sorrows are therefore loved. To be sure we all like joyfulness. No one wants to be miserable though he likes to be sympathetic, and it is only in such case that grief is loved, because it is really without grief. This is a rill from that stream of friendship.

What is its course and flow? Why does it flow down into that torrent of boiling pitch, with its vast tides of foul lusts, into which of its own nature it is transmuted, of its own will twisted and precipitated from its heavenly clearness? Is compassion therefore to be cast aside? By no means. Let there be times when sorrows are welcomed. Beware of uncleanness, my soul, under my protecting God, the God of our fathers, to be praised and exalted for ever, beware of uncleanness. I am not now past compassion, but in those days, in the theatre, I rejoiced with lovers wickedly enjoying one another, imaginary though the situation was upon the stage. And when they lost one another, I shared their sadness with pity — in both ways enjoying it all. But now I sorrow more for one who enjoys his sin, than for one who has suffered pain over the loss of a harmful pleasure or the deprivation of some wretched fragment of happiness. This is truer compassion, but there is no pleasure in the grief it contains. For though he who shows compassion upon the sufferer be commended for his offering of love, yet, he who is genuinely compassionate would prefer that there should be no occasion for compassion. If there be a goodwill which is illwill (an impossibility) he who is truly and sincerely compassionate could wish that there might be those to pity, in order that he might show pity. There is therefore a sorrow which merits approbation, none which is to be desired. So it is with you, Lord God, who love the souls of men far beyond and more loftily than we can, and have pity beyond all admixture of pollution, for you are harmed by no form of sorrow.

But I in those days, wretch, liked to be made sorrowful, and looked for something to be sorry about when, in someone else's woes, though they were mere dramatic fiction, that actor most pleased me and strongly attracted me who drove me to tears. What wonder then, that, an unhappy sheep straying from your flock, and irked by your shepherding, I should become infected with a foul image? Hence my love of sorrows, not those which would bite too deeply (I had no desire to suffer what I watched) but which, heard and imagined, I might scratch upon the skin, so to speak, and which, hard on the scratcher's nails, there followed a feverish boil, putrefaction and loathsome pus. Was such a life, true life, my God?

III

The University Pests

And your faithful mercy enveloped me afar. In what iniquities I consumed myself! In ungodly curiosity deserting you, I was led down to the very depths of infidelity, the fraudulent service of devils to whom I gave as sacrifice my evil deeds – and in all this you thrashed me. I even dared, within the walls of your Church and during the celebration of your sacred rites, to conceive and execute an act of lust, one worthy of death's fruits. You scourged me with grievous punishments, but not as I deserved, my God, my exceeding mercy, my refuge from the fearful perils amid which I walked with right confident neck, to retreat far from you, loving my own ways, not yours, loving a runaway's liberty.

Those studies which were called honourable were directed towards the courts of litigation, where a man is praised in proportion to his craftiness. Such is the blindness of men, who brag about their very blindness. I was already a senior in the school of rhetoric, right proud of myself and swelling with arrogance – although, as you know, Lord, by far a quieter person, indeed quite removed from the subversive doings of the 'Overturners' (this cruel and devilish name was a sort of badge of culture with them). I kept company with them in a sort of brazen bashfulness, because I was not one of them. I consorted with them, and took pleasure in friendship with them at times. But I shrank from what they did, their 'overturnings', I mean, by which they impudently persecuted the modesty of strangers, which they assailed without cause jeering and indulging their own malevolent pleasure. Nothing could be more like the doings of devils than that. There was no more appropriate name for them than 'Overturners'. They were themselves, to begin with, 'overturned' and perverted, for seducing and deceiving spirits were, unseen, making a joke of them, in the very way in which they themselves took pleasure in making fun of others and tricking them.

IV

Encounter with Cicero

Among those people, in my years of weakness, I learned the

books of eloquence, in which I aimed to excel from a damnable and conceited ambition, and in human vain-glory. And in the common course of learning, I came across a book of one Cicero, whose speech almost everyone admires, though not his heart. This book of his, called 'Hortensius', contains an exhortation to philosophy. This book quite changed my outlook, and, Lord, changed my prayers to you and altered my purposes and desires. All my empty hope became suddenly base to me, and with an incredible surge of emotion I began to long for wisdom and its immortality. I began to rouse myself to return to you. It was not to sharpen my tongue, the skill I was buying with the money my mother was providing, (I was in my nineteenth year, my father dead these two years) that I conned that book. It was not its language but its theme, which laid hold of my mind.

How I burned, my God, how, indeed, to fly back from earthly things to you, but I did not know what you would do with me. For with you is wisdom. Love of wisdom is in Greek 'philosophy', with which that book fired me. There are those who lead others astray by philosophy, colouring and painting over their own perverted ways by a great, charming and honourable name. And almost all who, in those and earlier times have been of this kind, are in that book censured and shown up, and in it is made plain the healthy advice of your Spirit through your good and trusty servant. 'Beware lest anyone deceive you by a hollow and deceptive philosophy, which follows the fashion of man, and the basic principles of this world, rather than Christ, in whom there lives bodily all the fullness of God.' And you know, light of my heart, that these apostolic scriptures were not yet known to me. This alone delighted me in that exhortation, that it did not bind me to one sect or another. It merely bade me love, seek, follow after, hold and firmly embrace wisdom, whatever wisdom might be. I was stirred by that word and set fiercely on fire. Only this chilled such hot ardour that Christ's name was not in it. For this name, by your mercy Lord, my saviour's name, your son's, my tender heart had long since devoutly drunken with my mother's milk and kept deeply hidden, and anything which lacked this name, however polished and true as literature it might be, did not wholly carry me away.

V

Disappointment with the Bible

I therefore turned my thoughts to the study of the holy Scriptures, and to see what they were like. And look, I saw something not disclosed to the proud, not made plain to children, something humble in its approach, lofty in its progression, and veiled in mysteries. I was not then fitted to penetrate it, nor bow my head to follow it. For when I turned to the Scriptures, I did not feel as I now speak, but they seemed to me unworthy to compare with the sublimity of Cicero, for my swollen pride shunned their manner, and my keen wit could not penetrate their depths. Yet Scriptures were something which could grow up with children. For my part I scorned to be a child. Blown up with pride, I saw myself a great man.

VI

Encounter with Heresy

So it came about that I fell in with some proud idiots, carnal folk and wordy, with the snares of Satan in their mouths, a birdlime compounded of syllables of your name, Christ's, and that of the Holy Spirit our comforter. These words never left their mouths, as far as sound went and the tongue's clatter. For the rest of their heart was void of truth. There they were saying: 'Truth, Truth'. I was hearing it from them all the time, but it was nowhere in them. They were prattling lies, not of you only, who are Truth itself, but even of the basic stuff of thy created world, and on that theme, for love of you, I have considered it my duty to bypass philosophers who did speak truth, my Father supreme in goodness, and sum of all things beautiful. Truth, Truth, how deeply even then did the very marrow of my mind aspire to you, though those people were always and in many ways sounding your name to me, with the spoken word alone, or in many vast tomes. These were the dishes in which the sun and the moon were served to me, when I was hungry only for you. The sun and the moon are your lovely workmanship, no more, not you yourself nor even your first creatures. Your spiritual works came before these material works, bright and heavenly though they are.

I hungered and thirsted not for those former works, but only for you, the Truth 'in whom there is no variableness nor shadow of turning.' Still there was set before me in those dishes, glittering phantasies, and it would have been better to adore the sun itself than them, for the sun is at least visible to our eyes. Those deceits trick our mind through the eyes. Yet, because I mistook them for you, I fed upon them, not indeed greedily, for you were not as now, a savour in my mouth, nor were you those empty phantoms. Nor was I nourished by them but rather starved. The food we eat in dreams is very like the food of our waking hours, but sleepers are not fed by it simply because they are asleep. But those phantasies were in no wise like you, as you have now told to me, for the reason that they were phantoms of the body, false, less true than those corporeal realities which we discern with our natural sight in the sky or on the earth. This faculty we share with beasts and birds and what we see is more real than our imaginings. Further, our imagining even about such realities is more reliable than it is about greater or infinite objects which do not exist at all. With such vain provender was I fed – and starved.

But you, my Love, for whom I pine that I may be strong, are not yourself those bodies which we see, in the sky though they are, nor yet those things beyond our vision there, for you are their creator and count them among the highest of your creation. How far then are you from those phantasies of mine, phantasies of bodies which do not exist at all, than which the phantasies of bodies which do exist, have more reality! Yet you are not they. Nor are you the soul, these bodies' life. That is why the life of those bodies is better and more sure than the bodies themselves. But you are the life of souls, the life of lives, living life itself. You do not change, life of my soul.

Where were you then and how far from me? I was wandering far from you, shut out even from the husks of those swine I was feeding with husks. How much better are the tales of teachers and poets than those snares, for their verse and poetry, and 'Medea flying' are certainly more useful than 'the five elements' variously concocted to match the 'five dens of darkness', which do not exist but kill the believer. Verse and poetry I can change to real nourishment. Although I would sing 'Medea flying', I did not affirm the truth of the song, and did not believe it, often though I heard it sung. But I did believe those other matters, alas and alas, and such were the steps by which I was led down to the bottom of hell, toiling though I was and seething for want of truth. I confess to you my God, who pitied me though I acknowledged you not, I was looking for you, not by the understanding of the mind by which you set me above the animals, but by the sensations of the flesh. But you were deeper within me than my innermost being, higher than my highest. I met that bold woman bereft of foresight, Solomon's riddle, sitting on the doorstep of her house and saying: 'Enjoy eating the hidden bread and drink the sweet stolen water.' She led me astray because she found my soul out of doors and dwelling in the eye of the flesh and chewing such food as it gave me to devour.

VII

Absurdity of the Heresy

I knew not real truth which is quite different from this, and under the urge of some subtlety of mind threw in my lot with foolish charlatans questioning thus: 'Whence comes evil?' 'Is God bounded by a bodily shape?' 'Has God hair and nails?' 'Are polygamists to be accounted righteous men?' 'Are murderers, or those who make animal sacrifices?' I was distressed that I did not know the answers, and, though I was receding from the truth, I imagined I was moving into it. I did not know that evil was only the deprivation of good, until something ceases altogether to exist. How could I see this whose bodily sight was limited by the visible, and whose spiritual sight was bounded by imagination? I did not know that God was spirit, whose person has neither length nor breadth nor mass, for every mass is lesser in its parts than in its totality. And if it is to be infinite, it is less in some part limited by a fixed space, than in its infinity, and so cannot be wholly everywhere as a spirit is, and therefore God is. And I was totally ignorant of what there is in us by virtue of which we are, as scripture says, 'in the image of God'.

Nor did I know that true justice of the heart which judges not according to custom, but out of the utterly righteous law of God Omnipotent. It was by this law that the moral codes of different times and places took shape as befitted them. Itself remained the same at all times and everywhere, not varying with place and occasion. It was by this law that Abraham, Isaac, Moses, David and all others whom God commended, were righteous. And this was in spite of the fact that they were judged unrighteous by ignorant men measuring by the judgment of their time, and by the norm of their own code, the general habits of mankind – just as if one who knew nothing about armour, and what fitted each part of the body, should try to cover his head with greaves and his legs with a helmet, and complain that they did not fit. Or as if, on a day when the courts are closed in the afternoon, someone should complain that he is not able to keep his shop open, because it is allowed in the morning; or if in a house someone should see a servant busy with something not permitted the butler, or something done behind the stables which is prohibited in the dining room; or who gets angry because, when there is one house and household all do not everywhere share all rights and privileges. Such are those who are angry when they hear that something was allowed the righteous in such and such an age, which is not for righteous men today, and because God ordered one thing for those and for these another, as history dictated. Yet both ages were under the same rules of righteousness, and in one man, on one day, and in the same house, they see one thing fit for one man, another for another, one thing lawful now and not permitted an hour later, one act permitted or commanded in one corner which is forbidden and punished in the next room. Does justice, then, vary and change? No, times, rather, which justice rules, are not the same. That is why they are called 'times'. But men, whose life on earth is brief, because they are not able by their understanding to weave into one the real issues of other ages and peoples outside their experience, but in one body, day or house can see that which fits one member, occasion, part or person, accept this, and are put out by that.

I did not then know or observe such matters. Though the facts were everywhere before my eyes, I did not see them. I sang songs in which I was not allowed to place the metrical feet in any order, but one metre here, another there, nor even put the same foot in any part of the same verse. And the art itself, under which I made my poetry, did not vary its rules from place to place but was consistent. Nor then did I observe that the justice which good and holy men served, in fashion far more excellent and sublime, contained together all its precepts, not variant within itself, though at different times she would distribute and emphasise those proper to the occasion. Thus blinded I would reproach those holy patriarchs, not only for using what was to their hand as God ordered and prompted, but also for prophesying things to come, as God made them clear.

VIII

Sin and its Judgment

Can it be an unrighteous thing, at any time or place, for a man to love God with all his heart, with all his soul and with all his mind, and his neighbour as himself? Therefore those crimes which are against nature are to be everywhere and at all times, both detested and punished, such crimes as those of Sodom were. If all nations were to commit those same sins, by God's law they should all stand impeached under the same charge. For God's law has so made men that they should not use each other. Indeed despite is done to the same fellowship which should exist between man and God, when the same nature of which he is the creator, is soiled by lust's perversity. Those offences which run counter to the customs of men are to be avoided according to the diversity of those customs. A matter agreed upon by the custom of state or people and established by law, is not to be violated at the whim of citizen or alien. Every part which does not agree with its own whole is corrupt.

But when God commands anything against the custom or ordinance of any people, though it be without precedent, it must be done. If it has fallen into disuse, it must be restored. If it has never been written into law before, it must be written now. If it is lawful for a king in a state over which he rules to order that which no one of his predecessors, nor he himself has previously ordered, and obedience is not against the common good of the state (as disobedience would be), and it is a part of man's common social contract to obey its rulers – then how much the more is obedience certainly to be given to God, ruler of all Creation, in all he commands us. For just as among the powers set up by the society of man the greater power is set in authority over the lesser, so is God set over all.

Likewise in crimes involving a vicious desire to do harm, either by insult or injury, both for revenge between enemies, or to lay hold on some commodity not one's own, as between thief and traveller, or to avoid an ill out of fear, or for envy on the part of the less fortunate against the more prosperous, or in his case, who fears another will equal or outstrip him, or even for joy at another's misfortune, like those who watch gladiators, or who deride or play tricks on others. These are the high points of iniquity which sprout abundantly from the lust for power, the lust of the eye and the lust of the flesh, one or another or all three together. Thus we live in sin against three and seven, that psaltery of ten strings, your decalogue, Lord most high and sweet. But what evil deeds can be in you who are incorruptible, or against you who cannot be harmed? Your vengeance falls on what men perpetrate against themselves, because even when they sin against you, they act evilly against their own souls, and iniquity deceives itself, corrupting and perverting its own nature, which you made and set in order. Perhaps it is in undisciplined use of what is permitted them, or in burning to experience what is not permitted and against nature. Or they are held guilty for raving against you with thought or word, 'kicking against the goad'. Or breaking down the proper bonds of human fellowship, they arrogantly exult in cliques and factions, as their likes go or their dislikes.

This is what happens when you are abandoned, fountain of life, the one creator and governor of the universe, and when in personal arrogance one falsehood is even partially desired. By humble devotion a return is made to you. You cleanse us from our evil mode of life. You are graciously forgiving towards the sins of those who confess. You hear the groans of those who are bound and loose us from our self-inflicted bonds, if so be we do not lift up against you the strength of a liberty which is not real, greedy for more and risking losing all, and loving more our own than you, the universal good.

IX

Sin and Justice in God's eyes and Man's

But among vices and crimes and such multitude of evil deeds

are numbered the sins of those who are making progress, who, by those who rightly judge them by the rule of perfection, are censured, but praised by those who hope for fruit as from the cornfield's green blade. Some have the appearance of vice or crime, but are not to be accounted sins because they do not offend you, Lord my God, nor the community at large – when, for example, preparation is made proper to the processes of life and the occasion, and it cannot be said whether it is part of a desire to possess, or when, under constituted authority, there is punishment inflicted in a zeal for correction, and it is not clear whether it is not rather a desire to inflict pain. There is much done which seems to be generally disapproved yet approved by what you say, and much of that is praised by men, but on your testimony, under condemnation. Often the appearance of the deed and the mind of the doer are at variance and also the unknown point of time. You, indeed, give sudden and unforeseen commands, though time was when you forbade the very deed, although you for a while conceal the reason for your command, and although it be contrary to the ordinance of some human community, who doubts but that it must be obeyed, when that community is just and serves you. Blessed are those who know that the command came from you. But all things are done by those who serve you either to procure a present need or to give notice of a future one.

X

Nonsense of the Manichaeans

For my part, ignorant of such matters, I derided your holy servants and prophets. And what was I doing when I derided them but courting your derision, for perceptibly and gradually I was drawn off to believing that a fig wept when it was picked and the mother tree shed milky tears? Yet, if some holy person ate the same fig, provided it was picked by the sin of someone else and not his own, and should digest it in his stomach, he would breathe out from it angels, veritable fragments of God, as he grunts and belches at his prayers. And those fragments of God most high and true, would have been bound up in that fruit, unless they were freed by the teeth and stomach of the holy elect. I believed, poor wretch, that more mercy should be shown to the fruits of the earth than to the human beings for whom they were brought into being. And if anyone who was not a Manichaean, should, in hunger, beg a little, that mouthful, if it were given him, would be condemned to capital punishment.

XI

Monica's Dream

You stretched your hand from above, and drew my soul from this deep darkness, while my mother, your faithful one, wept for me more than mothers weep for their dead children. For by the faith and spirit which you gave to her she saw that I was dead. You heard her prayer, Lord. You heard her and did not despise her tears when they flowed from her eyes and watered the earth beneath her eyes in every place where she prayed. Yes, you heard her. Whence otherwise that dream with which you comforted her and by which she allowed me to live with her and share the same table. At first she had been unwilling, rejecting and detesting the blasphemy of my heresy. For she saw herself standing on a sort of wooden rule and a young man coming towards her, handsome, with cheerful countenance and smiling at her, though she was grieved and overwhelmed with sorrow. He inquired of her the causes of her grief and daily tears (to teach, as the custom is, rather than to learn) and she replied that she mourned my perdition. He ordered her to cast off her care, and told her to look carefully and see that where she was, there too was I.

When she did look carefully, she saw me beside her standing
on the same wooden rule. How could this come about unless
your ears, good omnipotent One, were attuned to her heart,
for you so care for every single one of us, as if we were the
only one, and regard us all as if we were one alone?

And whence came this about that, when she had described
this vision, and I was trying to bend it into the meaning that
she should rather not lose hope and that she would in future
be as I was, straightway she replied, unhesitatingly: 'No, for
that was not told me, where he is there you, too, shall be, but
where you are there he too shall be.' I confess to you, Lord,
as far as I hold it in my memory, and I have often described
it, I was more deeply moved by this, your answer through my
mother, and that she was not put out by my so plausible but
false interpretation, but saw instantly what was to be seen
(which I had certainly not seen before she spoke), that I was
more strongly moved by that than by the dream itself, by
which the joy of a good woman so far in the future, was
predicted so far before, to assuage her present anxiety. For
almost nine years followed in which I wallowed in the mire of
that abyss and falsehood's murk, the more heavily sliding
back as often as I strove to rise. Yet all that time that chaste,
godly and sober widow (such women you love), now cheered
by hope, but no less urgent in tears and sighing, for never an
hour ceased from her prayers to lament about me to you.
And her prayers found entry to your sight though you
permitted me to be tumbled and tumbled again in that black
darkness.

XII

Monica and the Bishop

Meanwhile you gave her another answer, as I recollect. I
pass over many details for I press on to those matters I would
most urgently confess to you. Many I do not remember. You

gave a second answer through a priest of yours, a bishop nourished in the Church and knowledgeable in its books. When my mother asked him to be good enough to speak with me, to show the falsehood of my heresies, disabuse me of evil and teach me what is good (he practised this ministry when he chanced on ready listeners) he refused, wisely as I later found. He replied that I was still unready for instruction, that I was blown up with the novelty of this sect, and had, as she had told him, upset many simple people with a multitude of petty questions. 'Leave him for a time', he said. 'Simply pray to the Lord for him. As he reads he will find for himself what that error is, and how great its impiety.'

He went on to tell how he himself as a small boy had been handed over to the Manichaeans by his mother, who was one of their dupes. He had not only read, but written out almost all their books. It had become obvious to him, without anyone to argue and convince him, how that sect had to be shunned. And that he had done, he said. When he had spoken thus, she would not be satisfied. She pressed the more on him with such entreaty and such tears, that he should see me and talk with me that he said, a little annoyed: 'Leave me, and God go with you. It is not possible that the son of such tears should perish.' She often recalled in conversation with me afterwards, that she had accepted this word as if an oracle had sounded from heaven.

BOOK FOUR

Years of the Locust

Introduction

Book Four covers Augustine's years from nineteen to twenty-eight. He could have told us much about the teaching of rhetoric in Thagaste and Carthage, but Augustine was not eager to say more than he needed of this wasted decade. The memory shamed him. His profession, 'the sale of loquacity' as he called it, would have reminded him, had he read Greek, of Aristophanes' assault on the sophists of eight centuries before, who taught how 'to make the worse appear the better reason' by their manipulation of words and tricks of argument. In the search for truth, though he may have been by nature somewhat gullible, Augustine was scrupulously honest. Rhetoric, he was beginning to feel, was too ready to confuse logic with truth.

Astrology for a while fascinated his active mind, in spite of his friend Nebridius, who here enters the story, and a wise old physician. Meanwhile he was an active and proselytizing Manichaean. The death-bed repentance of one of his converts who sternly forbade him to make light of baptism, shook him badly. With his deep capacity for friendship, Augustine mourned for this friend long and passionately, and found no alleviation in the fables of his cult. Monica, meanwhile, discovering his heresy, for a while forbade him her house.

While in Carthage, he wrote a book, 'On the Beautiful and the Fitting', presumptuously dedicating it to a prominent orator. If it contained much of his contemporary speculation and convoluted thinking, its loss is not significant to literature or philosophy. He also read widely, how wisely we do not know, in liberal arts, including Aristotle. He is not a little proud of his capacity to absorb and understand a broad range of subjects. Gibbon remarks, a trifle loftily, that the superficial knowledge of Augustine was confined to the 'Latin language', and we have no means of knowing how well or how extensively Greek learning was translated into Latin. There is no doubt that Augustine's continued refusal to learn Greek must have restricted his reading damagingly – a lack of which he seems unaware.

Such wider roving was, none the less shaking what was left of his confidence in the world-view and pseudo-scientific teachings of Mani, as the bishop had predicted to the tearful Monica. Perhaps this slow development was the only fruit surviving the locusts of these years. If he covers them with greater haste than he does much else, it is because he sees little dramatic to report. Significant events of the spirit need not, of course, be dramatic.

I

Nine Wasted Years

Over the next nine years, from my nineteenth year to my twenty-eighth, I was led astray myself and I led others astray, deceived and deceiving in all manner of lusts, openly by so-called liberal teaching, privately under the false name of religion, now in pride, then in superstition, and in all things fruitless. On the one hand, I would be seeking empty popularity, cheers in the theatre, poetic competitions, strife for straw crowns, trifles of stage shows, and undisciplined desires. On the other hand, I would be trying to cleanse myself of such pollutions, carrying food to those dubbed 'elect' and 'holy', out of which, in the workshop of their stomachs, they could manufacture for us the angelic and divine beings through whom we were to find release. Such were my preoccupations, along with my friends, in mutual deception. Let the proud deride me, those who have not yet been savingly cast down and crushed by you, my God. Yet I confess my manifold shame to you and praise you. Permit me, I beg, and grant me in present memory to traverse the past tracks of my wandering, and to offer you a sacrifice of jubilation. What am I apart from you, but a guide to downfall? Or what am I, when it is well with me, but a suckling babe enjoying a food incorruptible? What is any man at all, when that is all he is? Let the strong and mighty laugh at us, but let us, the weak and needy, make our confession to you.

II

Words, the Wizard, and the Winds

I taught the art of rhetoric over those years. In zeal for a livelihood, I sold a triumphant wordiness. Yet, Lord, as you know, it was my preference to teach those accounted good. Without guile, I taught them guile, not to use against the life of the innocent, though at times to save the life of the guilty. And from afar, God, you saw me slip in slippery places, and my faith sparking amid much smoke. I did show it, even in that task of teaching those who loved vanity and sought mendacity, for I was one of them. In those days I had a woman, not known as mine in what is called lawful wedlock, simply one tracked down by my vagrant lust when I was devoid of foresight. To her, none the less, I was faithful in our union, and in that union I learned, by personal experience, the wide difference between a marriage contract entered into for begetting children, and the pact of a lustful love. Offspring too follows unsought, and, once born, commands our love.

I recollect an occasion, when I had in mind to enter a theatrical competition, and some sort of soothsayer asked me what fee I would pay him to win. I, however, detesting and abominating such foul rites, replied that though the garland should be of indestructible gold, I would not permit a fly to be killed for my victory. In his sacrifices he was intending to kill living creatures, by such rites, it seemed, purposing to call in demonic support. But this evil I cast aside, not from holiness towards you, God of my heart, for I did not know how to love you. I could only meditate on 'inner illumination'. Sighing for such fictions, does not the soul commit uncleanness against you, put trust in falsehood and feed the winds? To be sure, I did not want him to sacrifice to devils for my sake. Yet, by that very superstition, was I not sacrificing myself to them? For what else is 'feeding the winds' but precisely that – by our straying to become the objects of their pleasure and derision?

III

Encounter with a Wise Physician

And so I went on consulting those charlatans they call astrologers, because they used no sacrifice nor directed any prayers to a spiritual being for divination's sake. None the less true Christian piety consistently rejects and condemns their doings. It is a good thing to confess and say to you, Lord: 'Have mercy on me, heal my soul, for I have sinned against you.' This is not to abuse your lovingkindness and to be more free to sin, but to bear in mind the Lord's word: 'Look, you have been made whole. Sin no more lest something worse happen to you'. All that health they strive to slay with assertion: 'It is from heaven that the cause of sin comes inescapably upon you', and 'Venus did this, or Saturn, or Mars' – presumably that man, flesh and blood and proud corruption, should be without guilt, while the creator of heaven and the stars should be blamed. And who is this but our God, sweetness and well-spring of righteousness, who shall render to each according to his works. 'A broken and a contrite heart you will not despise.'

There was at that time a most clever and honoured physician, a wise man, too, who, in his capacity as proconsul, had once placed the crown of contest on my head, a sick head at that. Nor was he acting as a doctor, for you are the restorer for this disease, you who 'resist the proud and give grace to the humble'. Yet you did not fail me by that old man, or cease the healing of my soul. I grew quite closely acquainted with him, and hung eagerly and attentively on his words. His conversation was entertaining and serious, by the lively nature of his thought rather than by elegance of his words. When he gathered from what I said that I was addicted to books of astrology, in a kind and fatherly way he urged me to throw them away, and not to bestow vainly the care and attention which useful studies demanded on such a triviality. He added that, in young manhood he had himself studied that practice, as a possible mode of livelihood. He

argued that, if he had understood Hippocrates, he might well
understand those writings also, but he had given it up and
followed medicine for no other reason than that he had
found the other utterly deceitful. Being an upright man, he
had no wish to earn his living by deceiving people. 'And you',
he said, 'earn your living by the profession of rhetoric, and
are following this delusion under no bond of common
necessity, but by free choice of study. That is why you should
the more heed what I say about it, who worked so hard to
master it because it was intended to be my only source of
income.' When I asked him why so many true prophesies
were made by it, he replied, as well he might, that it was the
operation of chance which brought this about, and chance,
in the nature of things, penetrated all life. For if someone, he
said, should happen to look into the pages of some poet, who
had in mind to write about quite another matter, his verses
often strangely corresponded to a situation in hand. It was
not a matter for wonder, he said, if out of the mind of man,
not knowing its own working, but by some higher instinct,
by chance and not manipulation, some word should emerge
corresponding to the affairs and actions of the inquirer.

Either from him or through him, you established for me,
and marked upon my memory, the course of investigation I
should from then on pursue. But at the moment, neither he
nor my dearest friend Nebridius, a truly good and righteous
young man, who ridiculed this whole sort of divination, were
able to persuade me to abandon it because the authority of
the leaders of the cult more powerfully swayed me. And I
had not yet found the sort of irrefragable demonstration I
was seeking, which might make it plain to me beyond all
doubt, whether the true predictions of those experts were the
result of speculation, chance, or the art of the astrologers.

IV

Death of a Friend

In those years when I first began to teach in my native town, I had found a close friend in a fellow-student. He was of my age, and blossoming into young manhood along with me. He had grown up with me as a child. We had gone to school and played together. Yet he was not my friend in the manner that true friendship should be measured. That comes only when those who are drawn together are bound by that love shed in our hearts by the Holy Spirit which is given us. Yet it was a sweet friendship, warmed by our zeal for the studies we shared. I had led him astray from the true faith, in which he, as a young man, was not genuinely and deeply grounded, into those superstitious and destructive myths on account of which my mother mourned for me. That man was my fellow-wanderer in the spirit, and my soul could not be without him. But look, you, pressing ever on the back of those who run away from you, at once the God of all vengeance and the fountain of mercies, who turn us to yourself by the strangest means, took this person out of my life after less than a year of friendship, a friendship sweet to me beyond all the sweetnesses of life.

Which man can number the praises you have merited in his one single person? What did you then do, my God, and how beyond plumbing is the abyss of your judgments? For when he was tossing in a fever and lay senseless in the sweat of death, when hope for him was abandoned, without his knowledge, he was baptised. I thought little of it, taking it for granted that his soul would retain what he had learned from me, not what happened to an unconscious body. It turned out far otherwise. He was restored and made well. And just as soon as I could speak with him – and that was as soon as he could speak with me, for I never left him, and we quite depended on each other – I tried to scoff, expecting him naturally to scoff with me, at that baptism which he had received when he could not think or feel anything at all. He had learned that he had received it. But he shrank from me as if I were an enemy, and with amazing and sudden frankness, told me, if I wished to be a friend, to cease such speech. I was dumbfounded and upset, and I postponed my inclinations until his convalescence, and until he was fit and well, when I could talk as I would with him. But he was torn violently from my madness, that in your presence he should be withdrawn for my blessing. A few days later, when I was not there, he relapsed into his fever and died.

With what sorrow my heart was darkened. Everything in view looked like death. My native place seemed torture, my father's house sheer unhappiness. Whatever I had talked about with him, now that he was gone, seemed awful torment. My eyes looked everywhere for him, and did not find him. I hated every place, for he was not there, and no place could say to me: 'Here he comes,' as they could when he was merely absent. I became a puzzle to myself, and asked my soul why it was so sad, and so tormented me. It had no reply to give. And if I said: 'Trust in God', my soul would quite properly not obey me, because the one most dear that I had lost was a truer and better man, than the phantasm it was bidden trust in. Tears alone were sweet to me, for they had taken my friend's place in my soul's affections.

V

The Meaning of Tears

And now, Lord, these things have passed away and by time my wound is eased. May I hear from you who are Truth, and move my heart's ear to your lips so that you can tell me why weeping is so sweet to those in sorrow. Have you, although you are everywhere, cast afar our sorrow from you? Or do you remain constant in yourself, while we are tossed about by trials? Yet, unless we direct our lamentations to your ears, what hope is left to us? How then is sweet fruit gathered from the bitterness of life, from groaning, weeping, sighing and complaining? Does the sweetness lie in this, that we hope that you hear us? This is a true element in prayer, the hope we have of breaking through. Was that so with that sorrow and grief over what I had lost and by which at that time I was overwhelmed? I did not hope that he would come to life again, nor, for all my tears, did I pray for this. I only grieved and wept for him. I was unhappy and had lost my joy. Or is weeping a bitter thing, but because of our aversion to the things which once gave that joy, can some pleasure come in our very shrinking from them?

VI

The Lost Friendship

But why do I speak of those things? It is not the time to enquire about them, but to confess to you. Unhappy I was, and unhappy is every soul bound by mortal friendships, and who is torn to shreds at their loss, and becomes aware of a misery which was, in fact, present prior to the loss. So, then, was I. I wept most bitterly, but in bitterness found relief. Thus was I unhappy, but I held my unhappy life more dear than my friend himself. Though I should have been glad to change it, I was more unwilling to lose it than I had been to lose him. And I do not know whether I would have lost it for him. The tale or fable about Orestes and Pylades has it that they were willing to die together for each other, because it was worse than death not to live together. But an odd kind of emotion arose in me quite contrary to theirs. Equally, I had the deepest disgust with living, and the fear of dying. I suppose that, the more I loved him, so much the more did I loathe and dread death as a most fearsome enemy. I thought of death as being on the way to make a sudden end of all mankind, as it had been able to do with him. Thus I was, as I remember it. See my heart, my God. Look within, because I remember, my hope, you who clean me from the impurity of such affections, turning my eyes to you, and plucking my feet from the snares. I wondered that other mortals could go on living, because he whom I had loved, as if he was never going to die, was dead indeed. And I wondered the more that I, who was like his second self, should be alive when he was dead. Someone described well his friend: 'half of my soul'. For I felt his soul and my soul were one soul in two bodies. That is why life was a horror to me, because I did not wish to be only half alive. Perhaps for that reason I was afraid to die, in case he, whom I loved much, should thus be wholly dead.

VII

Retreat to Carthage

O madness which does not know how to love men in the way man should love his fellow! Foolish man, who so impatiently endures man's common suffering! I was then that foolish man. So I stormed, sobbed, wept in turmoil, beyond rest or counsel. I bore along with me my lacerated and bloodied soul, itself impatient with my bearing it. But I could find no place to put it down – not in pleasant woods, nor amid dance and song, in sweet-scented gardens, elaborate banquets, in the pleasure of brothel or bed, nor even in books and poetry did it become quiet. Everything irked me, even the light of day, and whatever was not he was vile and wearisome to me, except groans and tears, in which alone I found a crumb of rest. As soon as I took my soul away from these, an enormous pack of wretchedness bore me down, which I knew, Lord, could be lifted and lightened by you alone. Yet I was both unwilling and inadequate for that, because I did not then think of you as solid and substantial. At that time it was not you, but empty phantasy and my own error which was my God. And if I should try to rest my burdened soul on that, to give it some relief, it slid through emptiness, and again fell heavily upon me. I remained for myself an unhappy place, where I could not live, nor from which I could retreat. For whither could my heart escape my heart? Whither could I escape myself? Whither should I not have pursued myself? And yet I fled my native land, for my eyes looked less for him in a place where they had not been accustomed to seeing him. From the town of Thagaste I came to Carthage.

VIII

Remedies for Sorrow

Time takes no holiday, nor rolls round our senses with nothing to do, but causes strange notions in our minds. It daily comes and goes, and by its coming and going it planted in me other hopes and other memories, and little by little recharged me with the delights I knew before. To them my present sorrow ceded some ground. And up behind came, I will not say other sorrows, but the makings of the same. For how had that sorrow so easily and profoundly come into me, unless I had poured out my soul upon the sand in loving a mortal man, as if he were immortal. To be sure, mostly the consolations of other friends repaired and restored me, with whom I began to love what I loved thereafter. And this was an enormous myth and a protracted lie. By its unclean tickling, my soul, itching in my ears, was polluted.

But that myth would not die for me, if any of my friends died. There were other matters which, among them, the more amply laid hold upon my mind – talking and laughing together, exchanging acts of goodwill, reading together pleasantly sounding books, at times lighthearted, at others serious, arguing occasionally but without spitefulness, as a man might with himself, and finding a multitude of agreements to outmatch our most rare disagreements, teaching and learning from each other, missing the absent with impatience, welcoming newcomers joyously ... By these and like self-expressions, out of the hearts of loving people and those who made love whole again, shown in countenance, words, eyes and in a thousand other reactions for our kindling, we set our souls on fire, and made one out of many.

IX

True Friendship

This is what is loved in friends – and loved in such a way that the human conscience feels guilty if a man fails to love him who loves him in return, or who does not return the love of one who first loved him, expecting nothing from his person but the demonstrations of goodwill. Hence the grief if a friend dies, the glooms of sorrows, sweetness turned to bitterness, the heart sodden with tears, and the death of the living from the lost life of those who die. Happy is the man who loves you, loves his friend in you, and loves his enemy for your sake, for he alone loses no dear one, since all are dear in him who cannot be lost. Who is this but our God, the God who made heaven and earth and fills them, because in so filling he created them? No one loses you unless it be he who lets you go. And because he lets you go is not his only path of flight and of escape from your loving, back to your angry presence? Where does he not find your law built into his punishment? And your law is truth, and you are truth.

X

The Fragility of All Things

God of all goodness, turn us and show us your face and we shall be saved, for whichever way the soul of man turns himself, unless it be towards you it is bound to troubles, notwithstanding that it can find preoccupation in lovely things outside of you and outside of itself. They are not truly lovely unless they are from you. They rise and set. By rising they acquire their first being. They grow to reach perfection, and when perfected die. All do not grow old but all die. So when they spring to life and struggle into being, the faster they grow in order to exist, the more they hurry, in order to die. This is their way. So much have you given them because they are fragments of things which are not simultaneously alive but by whose going and coming the universe consists. They are its parts. See, so does our speech proceed by sounds which have significance. There will never be a whole sentence unless one word cedes its place when it has made its contribution of sound and allows another to take its place. And by such means let my soul praise you, God, creator of all things. But do not let my soul be bound to words, by the glue of love through the body's senses. For they go where they were going to exist no more, and they tear the soul apart with pestilential lusts, for the soul itself desires and loves to rest in them because it loved them. But there is no resting place in them, because they have no permanence. They flee and who can follow with the body's sense. Who indeed can grasp them even when they are beside him?

The sense of our flesh is slow by its very nature. It is its own measure, sufficient for the end it was made for, but not to halt the stream of events running from its appointed beginning to its appointed end. For in your word, from which they came, they hear: 'Thus far and no further.'

XI

Mutable Creation, Immutable God

Do not be foolish, my soul, and do not let the ear of your heart grow deaf in the din of folly. And listen! The Word itself bids you come back, and there is the place of rest beyond disturbance where love is not forsaken unless it forsakes itself. See, these things recede that others may step into their place, so that this basic universe may stand complete with all its parts. 'Do I ever go away?' asks the Word of God. Set up there your dwelling-place. Establish there whatever you have taken from it, my soul, at least worn out with deceptions. Commit to truth whatever truth you have and you will lose nothing. Your decayed parts will bloom again, your lassitudes will heal, your weaknesses will be set right, renewed and made again a firm part of you. They will not bring you down to the place where they go, but will stand with you and will go on with you to the God who ever stands and endures.

Why, perverted one, do you go on following your flesh? Let it rather follow you now that you have turned. Whatever you apprehend by it is partial. You do not know the whole of which these are the parts, and yet they content you. But if your bodily sense had been capable of comprehending the whole, and had not, for your punishment, justly received only a part of the whole, you would be wishing all present creation to pass away, so that the total would please you more. For what we speak you also hear by means of a bodily sense, and assuredly do not wish the syllables to pause, but fly on, that others may come and you may hear the whole. So always, when any given thing is made up of many, all of which do not exist together, it delights more fully as a whole than in its several parts. But far better than these is the one who made them all. He is our God and does not depart and has no successor.

XII

The Love of God

If bodies are a pleasure, thank God for them and bend your love to their Maker, lest you displease him in the very area where you please yourself. If souls are a pleasure, let them be loved in God, for they themselves are changeful but in him find fixed stability. Otherwise they go to death. Therefore let them be loved in him and draw to him along with you such souls as you can, and say to them: 'Him let us love. He made these things and is not far away.' He did not make them and depart. They are of him and in him. See where he is, where truth is a savour. He is deep in the heart, yet the heart has strayed from him. Return, transgressors, to your heart, and cling to him who made you. Stand with him, and you will stand indeed. Rest in him and you will be at peace. Whither are you going into the rough places? The good which you love is from him, and it is good and sweet because of that very fact. It will naturally turn bitter, because whatever is from him is improperly loved apart from him. Whither are you travelling on and on by paths both hard and toilsome? Rest is not where you are looking for it. Seek it, by all means, but it is not where you are seeking it. You are looking for the blessed life in the realms of death. It is not there. How can there be a blessed life where there is no life at all.

But our life came down here and took away our death, and out of his own life's abundance he killed it, and with voice of thunder calls us to return to him in that secret place whence he came out to us, first into the Virgin's womb, where humanity was wed to him, mortal flesh not for ever mortal. And thence 'like a bridegroom proceeding from his chamber, he leaped like a mighty man about to run a race.' He delayed not, but ran, with his message proclaimed in deeds, words, death, life, descent, ascent, to return to him. And he withdrew from our eyes, that we might return to our hearts to discover him. For he went away, and yet, see, he is still here. He would not long be with us, but he has not left us. He went away to the place whence he never departed, because the world was made by him and he was in the world, into which he came to save sinners. To him my soul confesses, and he heals it because it sinned against him. Sons of men, how long will you be slow of heart? Will you not now, after life has come down to you, rise up and live! But whither ascend, since you are already uplifted, your head set against the heavens? Come down, that you may rise up, even up to God, for you have fallen in your rising against God. Tell them this, that they may lament in this vale of lamentation, and so snatch them with you to God, for it is by his Spirit you speak thus to them, if you speak ablaze with the fire of love.

XIII

The Theory of Beauty

Of these matters I was ignorant then, and loved lesser beauties. I was going down into the abyss and saying to my friends, 'Do we love anything that is not beautiful? What therefore is the beautiful? What is Beauty in its essence? What is it that draws and unites us to that which we love? For unless there is grace and splendour in it, in no way could they draw us to it.' And I marked and saw that in any given entity there was a beauty as it were of the whole, and something else which owed its beauty to a proper relationship to something else, as for example a part of the body to the whole body, a shoe to a foot, and such like. And this thought bubbled up into my mind out of the depths of my heart and I wrote, I think, two or three books 'on the Beautiful and the Fitting'. You know, God. They have slipped my memory. I do not possess them now, and I do not know where they are gone.

XIV

The Tangles of Love and Praise

What prompted me, Lord my God, to dedicate those books to Hierius, the Roman orator, whom I did not know personally? I loved the man for the fame of his teaching, which was brilliant, and some words of his which I had heard which delighted me, and more because of his general reputation. People extolled him with amazement, for, though born a Syrian and trained first in Greek eloquence, he had turned out to be a Latin orator of wondrous distinction, and most deeply versed in all knowledge that had to do with the study of wisdom. The man was praised and regarded even when he was not there. Does then such love penetrate the heart of the hearer from the lips of the one who offers praise? Indeed, no. One lover is fired by another. For this reason is one who is praised loved, provided it is believed that the praise comes from an unfeigned heart, as it does when one who loves praises.

Thus then I esteemed men on others' judgment, not on yours, my God, in whom no man is deceived. Why would I not like to be acclaimed (even on a less vulgar and loftier plane) as the charioteer or circus beast-slayer is extolled by the mob? I should not like to be praised and loved as actors are (though I myself have given such praise and love). I should rather live obscurely than so be known. I should rather be hated than loved in this way. Where are the masses of loves so varied and diverse stored in the soul? Why, since both of us are men, should I love in another that which, if I did not actually hate it, I should not reject and expel from myself? It is not like a good horse being loved by someone who would not want to be that horse even if he could be. We must talk about an actor who shares our humanity. So then, do I love in a man what I hate to be, since I am a man? Man is a great deep, Lord, whose very hairs you have numbered, nor are they lessened in your hands. Yet it is easier to number his hairs than the emotions and passions of his heart.

But that orator was of that breed whom I loved enough to want to be like him. I erred out of pride, blown about as I was by every wind. I was steered by you in a most subtle way. How does it come about, and how do I on sure ground confess to you, that I loved that man rather through love of those who praised him than for the real grounds of his praise? For if those same people had reviled the one they praised, and in their reviling and rejection had used the very same facts about him, I should never have been so fired and stirred. Yet certainly everything would have been the same, and the man himself no different. The difference would have been only in those who spoke to me. Observe how prostrate is the feeble soul, not yet stayed by truth's solidity. Just as the windy tongues blow from the breasts of those who profess to know, so is the soul borne along, twirled, twisted and twisted back again, the light is clouded over and truth undiscerned. Yet it stares us in the face. Something mighty it seemed to me, if my speech and meditations should become known to that man! If he approved of them, the more I should be fired. If he disapproved, my vain heart, empty of your stability would have been wounded. Yet that book on 'the Beautiful and the Fitting', which I had dedicated to him, I gladly turned over in my mind with admiration, and approved it with none to share my satisfaction.

XV

The Wanderings of Self-Willed Error

Yet in my profession I was not yet aware on what it is that so great a matter turns, omnipotent one, who alone does marvels. My mind was working in the realm of corporeal things. That is why I defined and distinguished the Beautiful as that which is beautiful in its own right, and the Fitting as that which owes the quality to something else to which it is attached, and I illustrated from corporeal things. Then I turned to the nature of the mind, but the false view I held of spiritual things prevented me from discerning the truth. And yet the very force of truth pressed upon my sight, but I turned my throbbing thought from the incorporeal to that which had outline, colour and solid mass, and because I could envisage none of these in my soul, I thought it was impossible to see it. And since in virtue I esteemed peace and in vice loathed discord, in the former I postulated unity, and division in the latter. In that unity, it seemed to me, lay rational intelligence and the nature of truth and the highest good, while in that division the ground, as it were, of irrational living, and the nature of ultimate evil. And this 'ground', fool that I was, I thought could be a way of life itself yet one divorced from you, my God, source of all that is. That unity I called a 'monad', a sexless intelligence, that division a 'duad' manifesting itself as rage in criminality, lust in impurities, not knowing what I was talking about. For I did not know and had not learned that evil had no essential being and that our intelligence was not the final, immutable good.

For just as crimes emerge, if that emotion of the soul in which the urge arises is vicious, and flaunts itself in unruly and insolent fashion; and just as lusts show themselves, when that movement of the soul where carnal pleasures are absorbed lacks discipline, so do errors and false ideas pollute the life if the intelligence where reason dwells itself is corrupted. Such was my situation, for I did not know that intelligence must itself be enlightened by another light, if it is to be a partaker in the truth, and you will light my lamp, Lord. My God, you will lighten my darkness, and 'of your fullness have we all received'. For you are 'the true light which lightens every man who comes into this world', for 'in you is no variableness, nor shadow of change'.

And there I was striving towards you and being at the same time pushed back from you, that I might get the taste of death, for you 'resist the proud'. And could anything be more arrogant than my wondrously mad asseveration that I was by nature what you are. I was subject to change (a matter obvious enough, since assuredly I was anxious to be wise, that is proceed from worse to better), and yet I chose rather to think of you as mutable than that I should not be what you are. So I was pushed back; you resisted my inconstant obstinacy; and I was imagining bodily shapes, and flesh though I was accusing flesh. A wandering spirit, I was not turning to you but was lost and went on drifting towards things which have no existence in you, me or in anybody, nor were created for me by your truth, but, out of my own conceit, and were phantasised in bodily terms. And I would say to your faithful little ones, my fellow citizens, from whom without awareness of the fact, I was in exile, I would say to them, wordy idiot that I was: 'Why does the soul which God made err?' But I did not want anyone to say to me: 'Why, therefore, does God err?' And I maintained that your unchangeable substance erred under compulsion rather than confess that my changeable substance went astray by its own free will, and that my error was my punishment.

At that time I was about twenty-six or seven years old, when I wrote those books, rolling around in my mind those corporeal fictions which deafened my heart's ears, when, in fact, sweet truth, I was straining to catch your inward melody. Preoccupied with my 'Beautiful and Fitting', I was really wanting to stand and hear, and find exceeding joy in the voice of your Espoused. I did not succeed, because I was snatched away by the clamour of error, and under the weight of my pride I sank to the depths. You did not 'make me to hear joy and gladness', nor did 'my bones rejoice'. They were not yet humbled.

XVI

Encounter with Aristotle

What advantage did it bring to me when, almost twenty years old, I came across something of Aristotle called the Ten Categories? At the name of this book, my Carthaginian professor of rhetoric, along with other reputable scholars, popped his cheeks with swelling commendation. For me I hung breathless upon it, as if it were something mighty and divine. Did I read and understand it unaided? I conferred with others who said that they had found the book difficult to understand, even with the most learned teachers, using both words and diagrams. They were not able to tell me more than I had acquired by my unaided reading. It seemed clear enough to me that the books spoke of basic realities, such, for example, 'man', of what he consists; what is meant by his appearance or kind, shape, height, his relationships, whose brother he is, his dwelling, birthplace, whether he stands or sits, is shod or armed, does anything or has anything done to him – and all the other numberless details which might fall into these nine types of which I have listed some by way of illustration – or which, beyond computation, are discovered in the Essential Substance itself.

What advantage, I repeat, did it bring to me (it even hindered me) when I was striving to understand you, my God, wondrously simple and changeless as you are, and at the same time thinking that all which exists is comprehended under those ten 'categories' – as if you yourself were subjected to your own greatness or beauty, those qualities being in you, as qualities are variously in what displays them, in a body, for example. In fact you yourself are your greatness and beauty. A body is not great or beautiful in proportion as it is a body, because, though it be less big or beautiful, it remains, none the less a body, does it not? It was falsehood that I had in mind about you and not the truth, phantasies of my wretchedness, not the foundations of your blessedness. For this you had decreed should befall me, that my soil should bring forth for me thorns and thistles, and that with toil I should win my bread.

What advantage, I say again, did it bring me, that I, the wickedest bondslave then of evil desires, should read and understand all I could find to read, of those books they call the liberal arts? I took joy in them but did not know whence came whatever of truth or certainty they contained. I had my back to the light, and my face towards that upon which the light shone. My face, in consequence, by which I discerned what was illuminated, received no light itself. Without great difficulty, and without a teacher, I grasped rhetoric, logic, geometry, music, mathematics, as you know, Lord God, because speed of understanding and acuteness of discernment are your gift. Yet I sacrificed none of it to you, and so it weighed not for my usefulness but for my destruction. I was eager to keep in my own power, so good a portion of my person. I guarded not my strength for you but 'departed into a far country to waste it in riotous living'. For what advantage was a good thing to me if I did not put it to good use? For I did not realise that those arts were most difficult to acquire even by the studious and intelligent, unless I should go about expounding them to others, among whom that person proved the most outstanding who lagged the least behind my exposition.

But what advantage did it bring me while I went on thinking that you, Lord God of truth, were a bright, enormous body, and I a fragment of it? Outrageous perversity! But that was I? And I do not blush, my God, to confess your mercies to me, and to call upon you, I who at that time blushed not to profess before men my blasphemies, and yap against you. Of what use, therefore, my nimble wit, nimble in those disciplines, and of what use the unravelling of all those knotty volumes without the slightest help from man's instruction, while in the teaching of godliness, I wandered on disgracefully and amid impious uncleanness? What hindrance was a far slower wit to your little ones, for they did not straggle far from you, and grew their feathers safe in the nest of your Church, and made strong the wings of love by the food of a healthy faith? Lord, our God, let us hope in the shadow of your wings. Protect and carry us. You will, both when we are small and on to our white hairs. Our strength is only strength when it is yourself. Our good lives with you. Only when we turn away, do we turn aside. Let us at last return, God, lest we be overturned. Our good lives with you, unblemished. And you are our good. We fear not that there shall be no place of return because we fell from it. However long we are away, our home falls not to ruin. It is your eternity.

BOOK FIVE

Escape to Italy

Introduction

The confusions of Book Four covered almost a decade. The
province had only four more to live. The millennium was
ending for Rome, and we should have been glad to know
more of what life was like in the province carved from the
territories of her ancient rival Carthage in the half century
before the Western Empire fell. 'As in the days of Noah',
people continued with their daily work, burdened by
imperial bureaucracy, overgoverned, but screened by the
Mediterranean from the more violent movements of history.
Men saved to educate their sons, the riotous students of
Carthage wasted their own and their teachers' time, all
unaware that their middle age was to see the Vandal
warbands ravaging their land. Their early manhood was to
see the Goths sack Rome, though, to be sure, that portent
had long been high in the northern heavens.

Augustine emigrated to Rome in 383. A restlessness was
upon him. Student indiscipline was one reason. Another
may have been the pressure of Monica on his life. Augustine
always moved slowly and cautiously. The weight of her
dominance is illustrated by the disgraceful way in which he
tricked her when he sailed for Rome. He was, in fact,
disillusioned with the Manichaeans, and she needed only to
follow the old bishop's advice, and keep her hands off, to see
her most earnest prayers fulfilled. The last thing Monica
could do was precisely that, and her son fled.

Faustus, the great leader of the Manichaeans, had finally
opened Augustine's eyes. He was a kindly person, a humble
but eloquent man. Augustine describes him well, as he
always does when he introduces a vital character. Faustus
could not clear up the intellectual difficulties which the
young African found in the sect's cosmology and doctrine.

He made no impulsive rejection but came to Rome no more than 'a vagrant follower'.

He was uncertain about Catholic doctrine, and found Mani's teaching about sin, temptation and responsibility a convenience of conscience for one who could never dissociate sex from sin. The Manichaean community, probably a close-knit body, were good to him at Rome. It was a Manichaean host who nursed him back to health when Rome's notoriously unhealthy climate struck him down immediately after his arrival, and it appears to have been the same sect's influence which secured him a civic post in Milan as teacher of rhetoric in 384. The evidence for Milan's strong tradition of education goes back to Pliny's letters of three centuries before.

Book Five, covering Augustine's twenty-ninth year, closes with this success. But in Milan he found Bishop Ambrose, a man of learning and eloquence, to whose sermons he listened rather as exhibitions of rhetoric and persuasive speaking than as expositions of Christian truth. This same year he had discovered in translation some of what the Academy was saying. Like some 'academics' of another age, the school made a cult of doubt. Doubt can cleanse the ground for truth, but is not an end in itself. Augustine never thought it was, but it helped him loosen some of the last tangles of error. The story quickens. The pursuer came closer.

I

Invocation of Praise

Accept the sacrifice of my confessions from the hand of my
tongue, a tongue which you have made and prompted to
confess in your name. Heal all my bones and let them say:
'Lord who is like you?' No one who confesses to you is
teaching you what goes on within him. A closed heart does
not shut out your eye, nor can man's hardness push away
your hand. In mercy and in judgment you open it when you
will and nothing can escape your warmth. Let my soul praise
you that it may love you; let it confess your mercies that it
may praise you. Your whole creation never ceases to praise
you, nor does the spirit of any man whose lips have been
turned to you, nor anything which has soul or body, through
the lips of all who think upon these things. So it is that our
soul may rise to you from its weariness, leaning upon what
you have made, and moving on to you who so wonderfully
created. There dwell refreshment and true strength.

II

The Unavoidable God

Let the restless wicked go and flee from you. You see them
and mark their shadows. Look, all is fair around them, while
they themselves are vile. How have they harmed you or
brought dishonour on your rule, which is just and perfect to
the boundaries of heaven and earth? To what place have they
fled in their flight from your face? Where do you not discover

them? They fled in order not to see you watching them only in their blindness to run into you ('You abandon nothing which you have made') . . . Yes, to run into you, the evil ones, and be justly afflicted! They snatch themselves from your mercy, collide with your righteousness, and stumble over your severity. They appear not to know that you are everywhere, that no place contains you, and that you alone are with them who withdraw far from you. Let them, therefore, return and look for you, for though they have abandoned their creator, you have not abandoned your creation. Let them return and, see, you are there in their heart, in the heart of those who call upon your name, cast themselves upon you, and weep upon your bosom after their hard wanderings. You gently dry their tears, while they weep the more and rejoice in their weeping, for you, Lord, are not a man of flesh and blood, but their creator who can refresh and comfort them. Where was I when I began to look for you? You were right in front of me, but I had drawn back and could not find myself, much less you.

III

Faustus the Manichaean

I expose to my God's sight that twenty-ninth year of my age. There arrived in Carthage one Faustus, a bishop of the Manichaeans. A great snare of the devil was he, and many were entangled in it by the bait of his smooth eloquence. Though I admired it, I was able to distinguish it from the truth of those matters about which I was most eager to learn, and my eye was not on the quality of the wordy dish, but what true knowledge their notable Faustus served me at table. His reputation had reached me ahead of him, to wit that he was a man most skilled in every sphere of sound teaching, and especially learned in all liberal disciplines.

Since I had read much of the philosophers and had much of what they said firmly in my memory, I began to set some

of it beside those endless myths of the Manichaeans. And
what the philosophers said (for all that they could only speak
of the world about us, and could by no means discover its
Lord) seemed to me the more capable of proof. For you are
great, Lord, and regard the humble but look distantly upon
the proud. You come near only to the contrite in heart and
are not found by the proud, not even if, by their careful skill,
they should number the stars and the sands, set bounds to
the constellations and track the pathways of the planets. For
by their wit and intellect they seek out these facts, and you
gave them both, and they have indeed discovered much.
They have foretold by many a year the eclipses of those
luminaries, the sun and the moon, the day, the hour, the
extent, and their calculations have proved accurate. Hence
their predictions; and they have written down the rules they
have discovered and those writings we can read today. From
them it is stated in advance in what year, in what month of
the year, on what day of the month, and on what hour of the
day, and to what portion of its light, the moon or sun will
undergo eclipse. It will come about as it is foretold. At such
matters men wonder and are astonished, if they do not know
how it is done, while those who do know boast and praise
themselves. Turning back from you in wicked pride, and
falling out of your light, they see an eclipse of the sun far
ahead, and fail to see their own present eclipse, for they do
not in piety seek the origin of the intelligence whereby they
make their investigations. Even if they discover that you
made them, they do not commit themselves to you, so that
you can preserve your own creation. They do not put to
death for you what they have made themselves to be, nor slay
like sacrificial birds their boastings, nor like the fishes of the
sea their researches, by which they walk the hidden pathways
of the deep, nor sacrifice like the cattle of the field their self-
indulgences – so that you, Lord, should, like a devouring
fire, consume their dead cares and bring them to newborn
immortality.

But they do not know that way, your Word, by which you
made that which they calculate, made those who calculate,
and the understanding by which they discern what they
calculate, and the mind, the source of their calculations –

and thy wisdom is beyond calculation. But the Only
Begotten is himself made Wisdom, Righteousness and
Sanctification for us. He was numbered among us and paid
tribute to Caesar. They do not know the way by which they
climb down from themselves to him, and by him ascend to
him. They do not know this way, and think themselves
uplifted bright among the stars. See, they have fallen to the
earth and their foolish heart is darkened. About the creature
they have much that is true to say, and Truth, the creature's
Maker, they do not humbly seek, and therefore do not find
it. Or, if they do so, and acknowledge God, it is not as God
that they honour him or thank him. They disappear in
speculations, calling themselves 'the Wise', and attributing
your works to themselves. Thus they struggle in perverted
blindness, to assign to you what is theirs, preferring their lies
to you who are Truth, and changing the glory of the
incorruptible God into the likeness of corruptible man, of
birds, quadrupeds, and creeping things, turning your truth
into a lie, devoting their service to the thing created rather
than to the one who created it.

Many true statements about the natural world from these
people I nevertheless remembered, and I seemed to find
reason in their chronological teachings and the visible
astronomical phenomena. I compared them with what
Manichaeus said on these subjects, on which he wrote
copiously and idiotically. I found in his writings no
reasonable explanation of solstices, equinoxes and eclipses
nor any such material as I had culled from works on secular
science. In his books I was bidden to believe what was far
different from any which my own calculations and observa-
tions approved.

IV

Here is True Wisdom

Lord God of Truth, does anyone who knows these matters please you for no other reason than that? He is an unhappy man who knows them all and does not know you, but happy is he who knows you yet does not know them. He who knows both is not the happier for knowing them. He is happy because of you alone – with this one proviso that, knowing you, he honours and thanks you and does not get lost in his own speculations. For example, he is the better man who knows how to own a tree and thanks you for its usefulness, though he does not know how many cubits high it is, or how broad its spread, than the man who measures it, counts its branches, but never calls it his own or esteems the one who made it. So is the faithful man who owns all this rich world, and possessing nothing yet possesses all, because he cleaves to you the Master of All, and knows nothing of the 'circles of the north'. Folly, indeed, it is to doubt that he is better than one who measures the sky, numbers the stars, weighs the elements, but passes you by who have ordered the universe in measure, number and weight.

V

Manichaean Arrogance

But who prompted one Manichaeus even to write of those things, skill in which was irrelevant to the learning of godliness? You told man: 'Look, godliness is wisdom'. Of this he might know nothing, for all his expertise in the rest. Most impudently daring to teach what he did not know, it naturally followed that he could not know the godliness of which we speak. To profess these worldly things, even from knowledge, is vanity. To confess to you is godliness. Thus straying, he had much to say on these matters, so that, refuted by those who truly knew their subjects, his understanding in matters even more difficult, was shown clearly for what it was. The man would not accept a small estimation of himself, but tried to make people believe that the Holy Spirit, Comforter and Enricher of your faithful, dwelt in full power and person within him. Thus, when he was convicted of false teaching about the heavenly constellations and the movements of sun and moon (little though these matters have to do with theology, and his presumptions being obviously profane) and when in mad, proud conceit he spoke not only ignorantly but falsely, he would claim that it was the person of the deity which spoke in him.

When I hear some Christian brother, speaking ignorantly and mixing up his facts, I listen patiently to his dogmatism. I do not think it harms him much, so long as he does not believe what is unworthy of you, Lord and Creator of all, if he does not know the shape and fashion of material creation. But it does harm him, if he thinks this is part of the very essence of theology, and arrogantly dogmatises about what he does not know. Such weakness in the cradles of faith is borne by Mother Love until the newborn being grows up to the status of full manhood, no longer to be blown about by every gust of teaching. But that man, teacher, authority, leader and chief for his dupes, laid it down that any follower must consider that it was not some human being but your Holy Spirit which he followed. Who would not judge that such lunacy, once convicted of its mendacity, should be abhorred and utterly cast aside? I had not yet positively concluded whether what he said explained the variations of day and night between the seasons, or the length of each day and night, eclipses, and other such matters I had read in books. Even such a conclusion could not exclude its elements of uncertainty, but I could, on the strength of his reputed sanctity, rest my faith on his authority.

VI

Faustus in Person

So through a space of almost nine years in which I was a vagrant hearer of the Manichaeans, I was waiting in impatient longing for the coming of Faustus in person. For the rest of them I had chanced upon, and who had proved wanting before the probing questions I put to them on these themes, promised me the man himself, at whose coming and conversation, not only these enquiries but even greater ones which I might find, would most easily, and with the utmost simplicity, be explained to me. He came, and I found him to be a gracious and pleasantly spoken man, and able to chat, much more delightfully than his followers, on the matters in question. But of what use was the most pleasing of butlers before my thirst for those more precious cups? My ears were clogged with such teaching which seemed no better because it was in better words, nor true because well said, nor the soul wise because the countenance was agreeable and the language graceful. They who had made their promises to me about him, were not good judges of the facts. He seemed to them sagacious and wise because his speech delighted them.

I felt there was another sort of people, too, who hold truth suspect, and refuse to accept it if it is offered in rich and ornamented speech. But you, my God, had taught me already by wondrous, hidden ways, that the truth is that none other than you can teach the truth, wherever he is, and whatever his origin. I believe that because you taught me and I had already learned from you that nothing should be deemed truly spoken because it is eloquently spoken, nor false because the indications of the lips are ill-arranged. Conversely, uncouth expression does not make something true, nor polished delivery make truth false. As with wholesome and unwholesome food, so it is with wisdom and folly, and as with adorned and unadorned language, so good food and bad can be served up in elegant or rustic dishes.

That is why the extreme eagerness with which for so long I

had awaited the man was delighted with his carriage and manner of argument, and by the apt speech and flowing words with which he clothed his thoughts. I was delighted, and along with many, indeed, more than many, I lauded and extolled him. I was annoyed that, in the press of his hearers, I was not allowed to meet him face to face and to share with him the questions which troubled me in friendly conversation and exchange of speech. When I did get the opportunity, and, along with my companions claimed a hearing at such time as he might properly engage in dialogue, when I brought forward matters which concerned me, I found him to be a man unversed in all liberal disciplines save grammar, and not extraordinary in that. Because he had read a few of Cicero's orations, and one or two of Seneca's books, a little poetry, and a few volumes of his own sect which happened to be written in good Latin, and because he had daily practice in preaching, eloquence came naturally to him, an eloquence made more acceptable and persuasive by a dexterity of wit and a certain inborn graciousness. Is it not thus, my God, judge of my conscience that I remember him? Heart and memory are in your hands. Obscurely and in secret, your Providence was dealing with me then. You were facing me with those shameful wanderings of mine, so that I should see and loathe them.

VII

Disillusionment

When it became clear enough to me that the man was ignorant of those subjects in which I had assumed he excelled, I began to lose hope that he could expose and resolve those questions which weighed with me. Even though ignorant in such areas, and even without being a Manichaean, a man could hold religious truth. In fact, their books were full of endless fables about the sky and the stars

and the sun and the moon. I was no longer able to believe
that he could accurately explain to me what I assuredly
desired, when I came to compare the calculations I had read
about elsewhere, or how the Manichaeans' books contained
the truth or a reasonable approach to it. When I brought
forward these subjects for investigation and discussion,
Faustus with all modesty was not bold enough to undertake
the burden. He knew his ignorance and was not ashamed to
confess it. He was not one of those chatterers of whom I had
met many, who, trying to teach me, said nothing at all. For
this man's personality, though not directed towards you, was
not immodest in itself. He was not generally ignorant of his
own ignorance. He was not willing to be involved rashly in
an argument in which he could not see a way through, nor an
easy retreat. I liked him the better for this, for the
moderation of a humble mind is a finer quality than the
knowledge which I sought. Thus I found him to be in face of
all the more difficult and subtle questions.

With the study I had directed towards Manichaean
literature thus crippled, and despairing of other teachers
since the very founder had turned out as he had in the
matters which interested me, I began to busy myself with him
in the study in which he was deeply preoccupied, the kind of
literature in which, as a Carthaginian teacher of rhetoric, I
taught my pupils. I read with him the books he was eager to
hear, or which I judged compatible with such a mind. But all
the efforts by which I had determined to advance in that sect,
collapsed when I came to know that man – not to the point of
a complete break with them, but deciding that, in the event
of my finding nothing better than that into which I had
plunged, meanwhile to be content, unless something more
attractive should chance to appear. So it was that the man
Faustus, who proved a snare of death to many, had already
begun to loosen the coils in which he held me without
knowing or wishing that to be. Your hands, my God, in the
secret of your Providence, were not abandoning my soul. By
the blood of my mother's heart, through her tears day and
night, sacrifice was being made for me to you, and you dealt
with me in strange ways. This was your doing my God, for
the steps of a man are directed by the Lord, and he will

choose his way. How win salvation apart from your hand which is always repairing your creation?

VIII

To Rome

In your dealings with me, you implanted the urge to proceed to Rome, and there teach what I taught in Carthage. I will not fail to confess to you how I came so to be persuaded, because in this context your profoundest movements and most outstanding mercy towards us can be considered and set forth. I did not wish to go to Rome for the reason that a greater income or higher standing were promised there. My friends argued thus, and the fact had some influence upon me. This was the greatest, almost my only reason: I heard that young men pursued their studies more earnestly there, and were kept under a more ordered bond of discipline, and did not in random and disorderly fashion rush in and out of schools under whose master they are not enrolled, and indeed were not allowed in without his permission.

At Carthage, on the other hand, pupils showed a disgusting and unruly lack of discipline. They burst in impertinently, and looking almost like madmen, upset such ordered proceedings as any master may have arranged for his students' progress. They do much that is outrageous, indeed punishable by law, with amazing stupidity. Custom is their pretext, revealing them as the more wretched in that they do under its cover of right what will never be sanctioned by your eternal law. They think they do it with impunity, though they are punished by their very blindness to their deeds, and suffer beyond all measure of what they do. That is why I took no part in such conduct in my own student days, but when I was a teacher I was compelled to endure it from others. I therefore decided to go where all who knew assured me such conduct was not tolerated. But you, my hope and portion in the land of the living, who were thrusting me to going abroad for the salvation of my soul, applied the goads of Carthage so that I might be driven away from them, and offered the allurements of Rome to draw me thither, and that through men who love a life that is death, now acting madly, then promising vain things. For straightening my path you secretly used both their waywardness and mine. For both they who disturbed my rest were blind with a base madness, and those who enticed me to another mode of life, tasted of the earth. I who in Carthage hated genuine unhappiness, in Rome sought a spurious felicity.

But you knew, God, why I left one place and sought the other, and revealed it neither to me nor to my mother who shockingly lamented my departure and followed me to the waterfront. I deceived her as she clung wildly to me, begging that I should go back with her or she should come with me. I pretended I had a friend I could not desert until he was under sail on a good wind. I lied to my mother, and such a mother too, until I got away from her. This also you have in mercy pardoned, and preserved me, filled full of the most execrable defilements, from the waters of the sea, through to the water of your grace. When I was washed in this, the floods of my mother's tears would be dried from her eyes, those tears by which each day on my account she watered the earth beneath her face. When she refused to go back without me, I persuaded her to spend the night in a chapel of Saint Cyprian, close by our ship. During the night in great secrecy I set out without her. She stayed behind in prayer and tears. She only begged of you, my God, with tears so plentiful that you would stop my sailing, but deeply planning and hearing afar the real core of her longing, you disregarded the prayer of the moment, in order to make me what she always prayed that I should be. The wind blew and filled our sails and the shore vanished from our sight. In the morning she was mad with grief, and with complaints and lamentation she filled your ears, which took no notice of them because you were tearing me away by my own desires, precisely in order to put an end to those same desires, and also that her carnal affection for me should be scourged by sorrows. As mothers do, but more than most mothers, she loved to have me near her, and she did not know what joy you were about to build for her out of my absence. That is why she wept and wailed, and by those same torments showed what remnants of Eve were still in her, as with sorrow she sought that which by sorrow she had brought to birth. After accusing me of treachery and cruelty she turned again to prayer for me and went home. And I to Rome.

IX

Illness in Rome

Amazingly, I was received in Rome with the lash of bodily illness. I was on my way to hell, loaded with all the sins I had committed against you, against myself and others, sins heavy, many, and beyond the bondage of original sin by which in Adam we all die. You had pardoned none of them for me in Christ, nor had he by his cross resolved those hostilities which in your sight I had brought upon myself by my sins. How could he do so by the crucifixion of a phantom, for that is what I believed about him? So true, then, was the death of my soul as the death of his flesh seemed false to me. Yet as true as was the death of his flesh, so false was the life of my soul, which did not believe in the death of his flesh. In deepening fever I was moving on to death. Where would I have gone, had I gone then, but to the fire and torments my deeds deserved, by the truth of your decree? My mother knew nothing of this, but in my absence prayed for me. But you, present everywhere, heard her where she was, and had pity for me where I was, so that I should recover my body's health, crazed though I still was in my unholy heart. In that deep peril I had not longed for your baptism. I was better when, as a child, I begged for it of my mother's love, as I have remembered and confessed. But I had grown in shame, and like a madman, I laughed at the prescriptions of your medicine who twice did not suffer me, in the state I was in, to die. If my mother's heart had been struck with such a wound, it could never have been healed. I cannot find words to express what her love for me was, and with what greater travail she brought me to birth in the spirit, than she had at my birth in the flesh. I cannot then see how she would have been healed, if a death like that had struck through the heart of her love. And where would be those mighty prayers, so importunate, unbroken? And always to you. But would you, God of mercies, spurn the contrite, humbled heart of a chaste, devoted widow, ceaseless in her works of mercy, attentive and obedient towards your saints, passing no day without an offering at your altar, coming twice a day, morning and evening to your church, always, every day, not to hear empty tales and old wives' chattering, but your voice in what was spoken, as you heard her in her prayers? Would you despise and reject without aid the tears of such a one who sought from you neither gold nor silver nor any trivial and fleeting blessing but the salvation of her son's soul? It was by your gift that she thus prayed. Indeed, no, Lord. You were listening, and doing everything in its predestined sequence. Banish the thought that you were deceiving her in those visions and your answers to prayer which I have mentioned – and in others I have passed over, and which she held in her faithful heart. Like a signed document she kept pressing them upon you. Because your mercy is everlasting, you grant to those whose debts you have wholly forgiven, even to become their debtor by virtue of your promises.

X

Intellectual Confusion

So you restored me from that illness, and made your handmaid's son well in body. Your purpose was to give me a better and more certain health. Even then at Rome I joined those deceived and deceiving 'saints' – not only their rank and file, one of which was the man in whose house I had fallen ill and recovered, but associating even with those they call 'the elect'. I still believed that it is not we who sin, but some undefined 'nature' within us, and to be thus faultless was joy to my pride, as it was not to confess some evil I had done that you might heal my soul when I had sinned in your sight. I loved to excuse myself and blame something else which was with me, but not I. But truly it was wholly I, and my wickedness had divided me against myself. That sin was more incurable in which I did not consider myself a sinner. God Almighty, it was accursed iniquity to prefer that you should be overcome in my person to my destruction, than that I should be overcome in you for my salvation.

Not yet had you placed a guard upon my mouth, and a door of control about my lips, so that I should not bend my heart to evil words which make excuses for sins along with men that work iniquity (I was still linked with their 'elect'). Losing hope, however, of making progress in that false doctrine, for all that I had decided to continue in it for want of something better, I was becoming more remiss and careless in my adherence to it.

In fact the notion had occurred to me that the so-called 'Academics' were wiser than other philosophers, for they had laid it down that doubt should be the general attitude, and that no truth could be grasped by man. Such seemed to me to be clearly their opinion, and my belief was generally shared, though their ultimate purpose I did not yet understand. I openly discouraged the host whom I have mentioned from the excessive faith he had, as I saw it, in the fictions with which Manichaean books are filled. And yet I was much more friendly with them than I was with other folk who were not involved with that sect. Many of them were quietly working in Rome and I did not defend them with my one-time spirit. Still my association with them made me more slack in looking for something else, especially since, Lord of heaven and earth, Creator of all things seen and unseen, I despaired of finding the truth in your Church, from which they had alienated me. It seemed most revolting to me that you should have the form of human flesh, and be bounded by the bodily limits of our members. And because, when I wanted to think of my God, I did not know how to do so save as a mass of bodies – for I could not conceive anything existing in any other terms – there lay the chief and almost the only cause of my inevitable wandering.

That is why I believed the essence of evil to be something like this, endowed with bulk, foul, ugly, gross which they call earth, or else thin and subtle like the body of air. They conceive of this to be a malicious intelligence creeping through the earth. Some sort of piety compelled me to believe that a good God did not create any evil nature, so I postulated two confronting masses, both infinite, but with the evil one lesser, the good one larger. From this diseased beginning other unholy notions followed. When my mind endeavoured to retreat into the Catholic Faith, it was beaten back because that was not the Catholic Faith which I had in mind. And I thought it more reverent of me, my God (to whom your mercies are acknowledged by me) to believe you infinite in every direction save where the mass of evil blocked you in, where I was forced to postulate limitation, rather than to hold the opinion that you are in all respects confined by the limitations of a human body. It seemed to me better to believe that you created nothing bad – and badness to my ignorance seemed not only some essence but a bodily reality (I could think of a mind, in fact, only as a refined body, diffused through much space) than to believe that anything could come from you of the sort I imagined the essence of evil to be. Our Saviour himself, your Only-begotten, I would think of as thrust forth for our salvation from the bulk of your brightest mass. So I could believe nothing more about him, save what by my own proud thinking I was able to imagine. I considered that such a substance could not have been born of the Virgin Mary without being mingled with her flesh. I could not see how such a mingling could take place without contamination. So it seemed to me. I was afraid therefore to believe in the incarnation lest I should be forced to believe him defiled by the flesh. Now will your spiritual ones laugh gently and lovingly at me, if they should read of these confusions. Yet that was the sort of man I was.

XI

Manichaeans and Catholics

Further, I thought that what these people found to criticise in your Scriptures, could not be defended. But occasionally I had a genuine desire to confer with someone who really knew about those books, and find out, point by point, what he thought. A certain Elpidius, speaking and arguing with those Manichaeans at Carthage, had made an initial impression on me. He produced from the Scriptures matters not easy to confute. The answer of the Manichaeans seemed to me to be a very feeble one, an answer, in fact, which they did not care to use in public, but only privately among their own. They would say that the New Testament Scriptures had been corrupted by unnamed revisers with the aim of inserting the Jewish law into the Christian faith, but offered no copies of the uncorrupted text. Somehow those 'masses' they talked about held me firmly down a suffocated prisoner, my mind full of 'corporeal' concepts. Underneath, gasping for the breath of your truth, I was unable to breathe it in its pure simplicity.

XII

Dishonesty in Rome

Diligently, therefore, I began to practise that for which I had come to Rome – the teaching of Rhetoric. The first step was to gather at my residence some with whom and through whom I began to build a reputation. I forthwith became aware that things were done in Rome which I had not to endure in Africa. Indeed those 'overturnings' by abandoned young men were not, I was assured, practised here. But, my informants said, 'to avoid payment to their teacher, many

students band together to betake themselves to some other
teacher, breaking good faith and for love of money making
justice cheap.' My heart detested them, though not with
perfect hatred. I suppose I hated them more for what I was
likely to suffer from them than for the wrong they committed
in general. Certainly such folk are vile and basely false to
you, loving the ephemeral trivialities of the day, and its
polluted gold which stains the hand even when it is grasped.
They embrace this fleeting world and despise you who ever
await and call them back, and who indeed forgive the
adulterous soul of a man who returns to you. And now I
hate such bent and twisted beings, well though I might love
them should they seek salvation, and set what they learn
ahead of money, and what they learn indeed count less than
you, our God, the truth and fullness of all certain good and
purest peace. But at the time it was more for my own sake
that I was unwilling to endure such wicked people, rather
than that for your sake they should be made good.

XIII

To Milan and Ambrose

A message came to the prefect of the city from Milan to
Rome, asking for a professor of Rhetoric for that city,
offering even travel at public expense. I made application
through those very folk drunken with their Manichaean
frivolities, to get rid of whom I was to go (though neither I
nor they were aware of the fact). The result was that the
prefect Symmachus appointed me, after I had passed
scrutiny by a set oration. I came to Milan and Bishop
Ambrose, known the world over among the best of men,
your devout worshipper, whose polished speech dispensed
to all the people the fatness of your corn, the joy of your oil
and of your wine, the drunkenness which makes not drunk.
All unknowing, I was led by you to him, that through him,

with my full knowledge, I should be led to you. Like a father that man of God received me, and like a bishop approved enough of my migration. I began to love him, not indeed at first as a teacher of the truth, for I had despaired of discovering truth in your Church, but as a man who was kind to me. I listened closely to his public preaching, not with the attention I owed, but examining in a fashion his eloquence, to see whether it came up to his reputation, or whether it flowed higher or lower than was said of him. I weighed his every word attentively, but cared little for or held lightly what he had to say. I was delighted with the sweetness of his discourse. Although it was the discourse of a more learned man, it was not, as mere oratory, as persuasive and inveigling as that of Faustus was. In content there was no comparison. Faustus roved amid his Manichaean fallacies. Ambrose, with the utmost soundness, taught salvation. But salvation is far from sinners such as I was at the time. Yet, though I did not know it, I was drawing gradually nearer.

XIV

Nearer and Nearer

Heedless enough though I was to learn what he was teaching but only to listen to the manner of his speech – this vain care stayed with me, despairing though I was that a way was open to you for man – still, along with the words which I loved, their content too, which I held lightly, slipped into my mind. I did not know how to separate them. When I opened my heart to receive the eloquence of his speech, there came in alongside, however slowly, the truth of what he said. It first began to dawn on me that it could be defended, and that the Catholic faith, for which I had thought nothing could be said in answer to the Manichaean assault, might well, I began to think, be proclaimed without absurdity, especially when I often heard this or another puzzling passage from the Old

Testament explained, where a literal interpretation had overthrown me. So when I had heard many places in those books spiritually explained, I began to blame my own hopelessness, in so far as this had led to my belief that the law and the prophets could in no way be upheld against those that loathed and ridiculed them. Yet I did not for all that feel that the Catholic way could be held by me, because it, too, could have its learned apologists, who, with ample and reasonable arguments, might refute objections to it. Nor did I consider what I held condemned because the arguments for and against were in balance. So it was that in my judgment Catholicism did not appear beaten, but was not the obvious victor. Then indeed I gave most earnest thought to discover whether in some way and by certain proofs, I could convict the Manichaeans of falsehood. But if I could have brought myself to think of a spiritual ground of being, all their strongholds would have been forthwith dismantled and cast from my mind, but I was not able.

However concerning the body of this world and all nature which bodily perception can reach, more and more seriously considering and comparing, I judged some of the philosophers to be nearer the truth. So, after the manner of the Academics, doubting everything and tossed this way and that, I decided that I had to leave the Manichaeans. I did not think, in that same period of my doubt, that I could continue in that sect, to which I now preferred some of the philosophers. And yet, to those philosophers, because they were without the saving name of Christ I quite refused to commit the curing of my sickness of soul. I determined therefore to be an enquirer in the Catholic Church, which had my parents' commendation, until some certainty should shine out for me to which I might direct my course.

BOOK SIX

Monica and Alypius Arrive

Introduction

Inevitably Monica arrived, pursuing her prodigal over sea and land. It says much for the continued order of the Imperial world and its systems of communications, glimpsed long before in the story of Saint Paul, that a woman could thus journey from Africa to Milan without difficulty. There had been a storm in the Sicilian strait in which the good lady had taken occasion to play Paul on the Alexandrian grain-ship, before the crew.

Monica found her son deeply under the influence of Ambrose who was answering his moral difficulties about the Old Testament, perhaps by some resort to Eastern Church allegorising. Ambrose was a leader, an orator, a churchman of note, who, more than any one man, led Augustine to surrender. Monica at first found him a little difficult to adapt to, but ended by complete obedience and surrender of her African (charismatic?) ways. Ambrose, a man of superb common sense, watched and waited.

Augustine still under the Academics' influence 'kept his heart from all commitment, fearing a headlong fall.' His firm theism gave him a head start. His delays over minor points of doctrine and expression are exasperating, until it is remembered that conversion, as Augustine saw it, involved a demanding monasticism.

Alypius reinforced this conviction. He arrived in Milan in 384, a one-time pupil of Augustine in Carthage, whose addiction to the chariot races and later the gladiatorial shows was healed by Augustine. Augustine's flair for telling a good story gives a live and attractive picture of Alypius, his adventure in the circus, his mistaken arrest in the silversmiths' market, his integrity in office, his friendship and asceticism. Augustine's capacity for friendship almost led to the formation of a commune at this time, a project promptly put down by one or two of the wives of the participants, in whom the idea evoked no enthusiasm.

I

Monica Arrives

My Hope from my youth, where were you and to what place
had you withdrawn? Had you not, in truth, created me and
set me apart from the beasts and the birds of the air, making
me more wise than they? Yet was I walking through
darkness, and over slippery ground. I was seeking you
outside myself, and finding not the God of my heart. I had
touched the sea's abyss, had no faith, indeed despaired of
discovering the truth. My mother had come to me, strong in
her godliness, following me by land and sea, in all dangers
unperturbed in you. In perils on the sea she even encouraged
the sailors, whose common rôle it is to encourage the
anxious and inexperienced on the deep. She promised them
a safe arrival, because you had promised her this in a vision.
She found me in grave danger, and in despair of finding out
the truth. Yet when I told her that I was no longer a
Manichaean, but not yet a Catholic Christian, she did not
jump for joy, as if she had heard some unexpected news.
Concerning that part of my wretchedness, which made her
plead with tears before you for my resurrection from some
sort of death, she had become confident. She carried me, as it
were, on the bier of her thought, so that you might say to the
son of the widow: 'Young man, I say to you, Arise' – and the
young man would come back to life and begin to speak, and
you would restore him to his mother. So it was that her heart
did not pant with any wild rejoicing when she heard that so
much was already accomplished of that which she daily
prayed with tears should come about, to wit, that, though I
had not yet received the truth, I had been snatched from
falsehood. Indeed she was confident that you would grant
the rest because you had promised the whole. With perfect

peace and a heart full of assurance, she replied to me that she
believed in Christ, that before she left this life she would see
me a faithful Catholic. This much she said to me. But to you,
fountain of mercies, she poured out more and more prayers
and tears, for you to speed your aid, and lighten my
darkness. She would rush more eagerly to church, and hang
on Ambrose's words as if they were 'a fountain of water
springing up to life eternal.' She loved that man as if he were
an angel of God, because she had heard that it was through
him I had meanwhile been brought to my state of doubtful
hesitation, through which I was destined to pass from
sickness into health, with some sharper danger intervening,
the 'critical climax', as the doctors say. Of this she felt sure.

II

Monica Abandons Old Ways

It had been her custom in Africa to bring to the shrines of the
saints oatcakes, bread and wine. She was forbidden by the
doorkeeper to do this. When she learned that the bishop had
forbidden the practice, so dutifully and submissively did she
comply that I was amazed how easily she was persuaded
rather to blame her custom, than to question the
prohibition. No fondness for wine laid siege to her spirit, or
provoked her to turn against the truth, as it is with many men
and women who are as disgusted at 'the hymn of sobriety' as
drunkards are at a watered drink. As for her, when she had
brought along her basket of ritual foods, to be just tasted and
then given away, she never served herself more than one little
cup, watered to her abstemious taste, to be taken for
politeness' sake. And if there were a number of shrines of the
dead to be similarly honoured, she took around the same
little cup. She would share this in small sips with those about
her, not only very diluted but very warm. She was seeking
worship not pleasure.

So when she discovered that this practice had been countermanded by the famous preacher and priest, even for those who used it with discipline, lest occasion for guzzling should be given to drunkards, and because those feasts for the dead were very similar to the superstition of the Gentiles, she most gladly gave it up. Instead of a basket full of what earth produces, she had learned to bring to the martyrs' memorials a breast full of purifying prayers, so that she might give what she could to those in need, and that the communion of the Lord's body might be celebrated at the places where, in the manner of his suffering, the martyrs were sacrificed and crowned.

And yet, my Lord God, my heart which you can see, tells me that my mother would perhaps not easily have abandoned this custom, if it had been banned by any other than the Ambrose whom she so loved. That deep love was because of my salvation. And he, indeed, loved her for the intense piety of her way of life, by which, amid good works, and 'fervent in spirit', she was always in his church. When he saw me he often broke forth into praise of her, and congratulated me on having such a mother. He little knew what a son she had in me, who doubted everything and thought the path to life was beyond finding.

III

Ambrose

I was not yet agonising in prayer for your help. My restless mind was given rather to learning and debate. I judged Ambrose himself to be a happy man in the estimation of society, honoured as he was by such important authorities. Yet his celibacy seemed a painful state to me. What hope he cherished, what sort of fight he fought against the temptations of his very eminence, and what sweet joys his heart tasted from your sustenance -- at such matters I did not know how to guess, nor had I personally known them. Nor did he know of the tides which tossed me, nor the pit of my peril. For I could not ask of him what I wanted, in the way I wanted to do so, for the hordes of busy folk whose weaknesses he served kept me from all conversation with him. For the very brief time he was not occupied with them, he was refreshing his body with the barest of necessities, or his mind with reading. When he was reading, his eyes scanned the pages, and his heart searched the sense, but his voice and tongue were still. Often when we were together, for everyone had free access to him and could come without announcement, we saw him reading silently in this way, and no other. Sitting in long silence (for who would dare to burden one so absorbed?) we might rise and go. It occurred to us that for that brief time of vacation, which he had won from the din of others' business for the renewing of his mind, he did not want to be distracted. Perhaps, too, he was taking care lest, if a puzzled and attentive person heard some difficult passage from the author he was reading, he might be compelled to explain it, or to discuss some of the more difficult questions. Giving time to such a task, he would read less volumes than he desired. Yet the need to conserve his voice, which easily grew hoarse, could have been the truer reason for his silent reading. Whatever intention he had, in that man it was a good one.

But certain it was that I had no opportunity of enquiring about what I sought from your holy oracle, that man's heart, unless it were something which could be briefly heard. But those tides within me, if I were to pour them out to him, needed to find him truly unpreoccupied. I could never find him so. Yet every Sunday I would hear him before the people 'rightly expounding the word of truth.' And it became more and more clear to me, that all those knots of cunning criticism, which our deceivers had woven against the holy books, could be untied. But when I came to understand that man, created in your image, was not so understood by your spiritual sons whom, through our Catholic Mother, you have brought to rebirth by your grace, to the point that they believed and imagined you to be bounded by a human shape, (although I had not the slightest riddle of a notion of what a spiritual essence might be) yet I blushed with joy that my yapping of so many years had not been against the Catholic Faith but against the fictions of fleshly imaginings. In this indeed I had been wickedly rash, because I had spoken in condemnation of what I should have discovered by inquiry. But you, most high and most near, most set apart and most present, whose members are not greater and smaller, seeing that you are wholly everywhere, and not located in space, and are not in bodily shape, have yet made man in your image, though, see, he from head to foot is in space.

IV

Letter and Spirit

Therefore, since I was ignorant of how this 'image' was to be conceived, I should have hammered the question of how it was to be believed, rather than have insolently opposed it, as if it was so believed. And so anxiety about what certainty I must hold the more sharply gnawed my heart as my shame increased that for so long, fooled and tricked by the promise of certainties, in childish error and vehemence I had gabbled about so many uncertainties as if they were sure. That they were false was later clear to me. It was certain, none the less that, uncertain though they were, I had held them for certain, when in blind contentiousness on many points I accused your Catholic Church. I had not yet found that it was teaching the truth, but I had found it was not teaching that of which I gravely accused it. And so I was astounded and changed my mind. I was also glad, my God, because your only Church, the body of your only son, in which the name of Christ was first put upon me, did not relish these childish trifles, nor contained in her sound doctrine the notion of packing together the Creator of all, in the similitude of human members into a measurable space, great, as you will, and large, but still finite all around.

I was also glad that the old Scriptures of the Law and the Prophets were set before me to be read, and not with that eye by which previously they were made to seem ridiculous, when I censured your holy ones for thinking this or that – which in truth they did not think. I was glad to hear Ambrose saying in his sermons to the people what he assiduously commended as a basic rule: 'The letter kills, the spirit gives life', and he would draw aside the veil from what, according to the letter, seemed to teach wrong doctrine, and show the spiritual truth. He said nothing to which I might take exception, though he might say what I could not yet accept as true. I kept my heart from all commitment, fearing a headlong fall, all of which made my suspended judgment more truly the way to death. In fact I wanted to be as assured about the unseen as I was that seven and three make ten. I was not so mad as to imagine that even this could not be understood, but I wanted everything else to be as clear as this, whether it was something corporeal not present to my senses, or something spiritual which I was able to conceive only in corporeal terms. By believing I could have been healed, so that the cleansed eyesight of my mind could somehow be directed to your truth, eternally abiding and in no point falling short. But it often happens that one who has had experience with a bad doctor is afraid to entrust himself to a good one, and so it was with the health of my soul. It could only be healed by believing, but for fear of believing falsehoods it refused to be cured, and resisted your hands which had prepared the medicines of faith, applied them to the whole world's diseases, and given them authority so great.

V

The Authority of Scripture

From this point I began to give first place to the Catholic

teaching, feeling that less presumptuously, and quite without deceit, it called for belief in what could not be proved – both in the nature of that belief, and its limitations of acceptance and substance. In the contrary doctrine I saw that credulity, based on a rash promise of knowledge, was ridiculous, along with its high command to believe a host of utterly absurd stories because they could not be proved. Then, Lord, little by little, with most gentle and merciful hand, you touched and quietened my heart, as I thought of the countless beliefs I held about things I could not see, nor had seen when they occurred. There are, for example, so many events in world history, so much about places and cities, which I had not seen, so much, indeed, concerning friends, physicians, these people or those, which, if we did not accept their truth, would cut us off from life. Finally, with what unshaken faith I held my parental origin, which I could not know without believing what I heard. You brought me at last to the conclusion that it was not those who believed your writings, which with such authority you had set fast among all nations, but those who did not believe, who were to be blamed, and that they should not be heard who might say: 'How do you know that those books were given to the human race by the Spirit of the one true and truthful God?' For this was my chief article of faith, and no contentiousness of conflicting philosophers which had crowded my reading could wrench it from me, that you are, whatever it is that you are (something beyond my knowledge), and that the government of man's affairs is yours.

But this I believed, at one time more sturdily, at another more feebly, that you lived, and had a care for us. I did not know what I ought to believe about your essence, or what way led to you or led back to you. And so since we are too weak to discover the truth by pure reason, and for this reason needed the authority of the holy Scriptures, the conviction was growing in me, that you were in no way likely to endow those Scriptures the world over with authority so pre-eminent, unless it had been your will that by that authority you should both be believed and sought after. For now the 'absurdity' which used to trouble me in those

writings, when I had heard much of it satisfactorily
explained, I set down to the profundity of their mystery.
Thus it was that their authority seemed to me the more
venerable, and worthier of religious faith, in accordance as it
was readier to hand for all to read, in the clearest words and
most unpretentious style, while it reserved the majesty of its
hidden meaning for those of a deeper understanding, and
engaged the attention of those of a serious turn of mind.
Thus it might receive all in its common bosom, and through
narrow paths draw a few to you, yet many more than if it had
not stood apart with authority so lofty, nor drawn the
multitudes into the lap of its holy humility. I would ponder
these matters, and you were by my side. I sighed and you
heard me. I was stormtossed, and you took the helm. I trod
the broad way of the world, but you did not forsake me.

VI

Vain Quest for Happiness

I panted after honours, gains, marriage, and you laughed at
me. In those desires I suffered the bitterest of trials. And you
were the more gracious to me in that you did not allow
anything that was not yourself to grow sweet to me. Look at
my heart, Lord, for it was your will that I should remember
this, and confess it to you. Now let my soul hold fast to you
for you have freed it from that binding bird-lime death. How
unhappy it was! And you pricked the rawness of its wound,
so that abandoning all else it should be converted to you,
who are above all, and without whom nothing else would be,
yes, converted to you and so find healing. How unhappy
then was I, and how you worked to make me conscious of my
unhappiness, on that very day when I was preparing to recite
an oration in praise of the emperor. Many a lie I had in it,
and those who knew I lied cheered the liar. My heart was
panting with these anxieties, and tossing in the wasting

fevers of my thoughts. Passing along a Milan street I saw a poor beggar, his stomach full, I suppose, joking and chaffing. I groaned, and remarked to my friends who were with me on the host of sorrows which arise from our own mad ways, because in all such endeavours of ours all we want is to attain a carefree happiness. To that goal, which we should probably never reach, the beggar had come before us. Such endeavours were bearing me down. Dragging the pack of my own unhappiness, and increasing its weight in the act, I was spurred on by my desires. What the beggar had won by a few bits of money (begged at that), I was now scheming for by sorrowful twistings and turnings. My goal? The joy of a passing happiness!

Indeed the beggar had no real joy. Yet I, with those ambitions, was in search of a joy much more unreal. To be sure, he was happy, and I was troubled with care. He was without care, while I was afraid. If anyone should ask me whether I should prefer to be glad than to be afraid, I should answer: 'To be glad'. Again if he should enquire whether I should rather be in the beggar's place, than in my own at that moment, I should choose my own, worn out though I was with anxieties and fears – but I should choose perversely, for was it at all a true choice? I ought not to put myself ahead of him, because I was better educated than he was, though I got no joy out of that, and only sought to please men by it, please them I say, but not instruct them. That is why you broke my bones with the stick of your discipline.

Away then from my soul those who say: 'What matters is the source of a man's happiness.' The beggar was glad in his drunkenness, you my soul, in your glory. What glory, Lord? That which is not in you. For just as the beggar's was no true joy, so was yours not true glory. And it subverted my mind the more. That night the beggar would digest his drunkenness. I had slept with mine and risen with it, and was like to do both again, for how many days! I know, indeed, that the source of a man's happiness does make a difference, and the joy of a faithful hope lies incomparably far from such emptiness. At the moment, he and I were far apart. In very truth he was the happier man, not only because he was soused in mirth, and I disembowelled with anxieties, but because he, by hoping for the best, had acquired wine, while I, by lying, had won a gust of pride. I said much in this vein to my good friends, and in them I saw reflected my own condition, and discovered that it went ill with me. I grieved over it, and found it twice as bad, and if any prosperity smiled on me, I was too weary to lay hold of it, for almost before I could get my hands on it, it was off in flight.

VII

Alypius and the Races

We joined in moaning about this, we who boarded as friends together, but I discussed matters most freely with Alypius and Nebridius. The former was a fellow townsman, son of a leading family and younger than I was. He had also been my pupil, first when I began to teach in our own town, and later at Carthage. He was devoted to me because he thought me good and learned, and I to him because of his strong inclination to virtue which was obvious in spite of his youth. But that whirlpool of Carthaginian morals, in which such trifling shows blaze, had sucked him into racing madness. He was miserably involved in this, when I, pursuing my rhetorical profession, set up a public school there. He did not attend my classes because of some quarrel which had broken out between our fathers. I had found out that his love for the racecourse was ruining him, and I was deeply concerned that he was on the way to destroying his high hopes, if, as I was beginning to think, he had not already done so. But I had no chance of warning him, or by any form of restraint, reclaiming him, either on the grounds of friendship or the authority of a teacher, for I thought he shared his father's opinion of me. This, in fact, was not the case. Dismissing what his father desired in this matter, he began to greet me, and occasionally slip in and out of my lecture room.

It had, however, dropped out of my mind to put it to him that, by his blind, undisciplined zeal for empty sport, he might destroy so good an intelligence. But you, Lord, who govern the helm of all you have created, had not forgotten him, because he was destined to be among your sons and the dispenser of your sacrament. That his redemption should be openly ascribed to you, you worked indeed through me, but without my knowing it. One day, when I was sitting in my usual place with my students in attendance, he came, greeted me, took a seat, and gave his attention to the subject before us. While I was expounding the text I had in hand, an illustration from the racecourse occurred to me by which to make what I was seeking to implant more readily clear, along with a biting comment on those whom that madness had enthralled. God, you know, that at the time I had no thought of curing Alypius of his infection. But he took it to himself, and believed that it was said on his account alone, and that which someone else might have made an occasion of anger against me, that honourable young man made an occasion of anger against himself, and of deeper esteem towards me. Long since you had woven it into your Scriptures: 'Rebuke a wise man, and he will love you.'

For my part, I had no such rebuke in mind, but you, who use all men, whether they know it or not in the sequence you know (and it is just), made burning coals of my heart and tongue, to set on fire a mind of which much good was hoped, and heal its wasting. Let him who does not bear your mercies in mind not utter your praises. I make confession of them to you from my inmost heart. After hearing those words, he dragged himself out of that deep pit, into which, blinded by the wondrous pleasure it gave him, he had chosen to be plunged. With strong self-control he stirred up his spirit. All those smuts of horse-racing fell away from him and he never went back to them. At this he overcame his father's reluctance and became one of my students. He retreated and gave leave. Beginning to listen to me again, Alypius was tangled with me in superstition, loving the Manichaean show of continence which he thought true and genuine. It was in fact a mad, seductive continence, snaring precious souls, unable yet to reach the height of virtue, souls open to deception by the outward appearance of a virtue shadowed and pretended.

VIII

Alypius and the Gladiators

Alypius, not abandoning that earthly way of life, drummed
into him by his parents, had gone ahead of me to Rome
to study law. There he was snatched up with an incredible enthusiasm for the gladiatorial shows. Though he
avoided and loathed such sports, some of his friends and
fellow-students, meeting him on the way home from dinner,
in spite of his strong refusal and resistance, dragged him off
by friendly force to the amphitheatre, at a time when these
cruel and deadly shows were on. This is what he said at the
time: 'Though you drag my body to that place, can you make
me turn mind and eyes to those shows? I shall be there and
yet not be there, and shall thus overcome both you and
them.' They heard this but none the less took him along with
them, perhaps to try out that very thing, whether he could
carry it out. When they arrived and were seated where they
could, the whole place grew hot with those most monstrous
pleasures. Closing the doors of his eyes, Alypius forbade his
mind to go out to such evils. If he could only have stopped
his ears too! For upon the fall of someone in combat, when a
mighty shout of the whole throng had strongly beaten on
him, overcome by curiosity, and in a way ready, whatever it
might be, to despise and conquer it, even if it should be seen,
he opened his eyes, and was wounded in his soul more
seriously than the other man, whom he wanted to see, was
wounded in body, and fell more wretchedly than he did at
whose fall the cheer was raised. The noise entered through
his ears and unlocked his eyes, and brought it about that a
soul which, up till then, was bold rather than strong, should
be struck and beaten down. It was the feebler, too, because it
had relied on its own strength, when it should have relied on
you. The sight of the blood was like drinking barbarity. He
did not turn away but fixed his eyes on it. Unknowing he
gulped down the Fiends of Hell. He was thrilled with the
crime of that fight, and intoxicated with a bloody joy. He
was not the man he was when he had arrived, but one of the

mob he had joined, the complete companion of those by
whom he had been brought there. What more? He watched,
cheered, took fire, and carried away a madness which drove
him back again, not only along with those who had first
carried him off, but even leading them and dragging others
in. It was from this with most mighty and merciful hand that
you plucked him, and taught him not to have confidence in
himself but in you. But this was a long time afterwards.

IX

Alypius Arrested

But this Alypius stored away in his memory for future
medicine. There was this, too, which happened in the
market-place of Carthage while he was still studying under
me. In the middle of the day, he was in the market-place,
thinking over, as scholars train themselves to do, a theme
which he was going to recite. You allowed him to be arrested
by the market-police as a thief, and for no other reason I
think you permitted it, our God, than that he who was later
to be a man of such eminence, should begin to learn how, in
court hearings, a man should not be readily condemned by
another out of a reckless credulity. He had, in fact, been
strolling alone before the judges' platform with his note-
book and pen when, look, another young member of the
school, the real thief, came in unobserved by Alypius,
secretly carrying a hatchet. He began to cut through the lead
of the leaden gratings which fence over the street of the
silversmiths. There was a stir of attention among the
tradesmen beneath at the sound of the hatchet, and they sent
someone to lay hold of anyone they might find. The thief,
hearing their voices, went off in fear, leaving his tool behind,
so that he should not be caught with it. Alypius, who had not
seen him come in, was aware of his going out, and the speed
with which he was off. Wanting to find what it was all about,

he entered the place. He found the hatchet, and was standing wondering about it and thinking, when, see, those who had been sent discover him alone, and in his hands the tool whose noise had alerted them to come. They arrest him, drag him off, and to their market neighbours, who had gathered round, they boast that they had taken the thief redhanded. He was taken off to appear in court. To this point was Alypius to learn his lesson. Promptly, however, Lord, you were there to aid his innocence, of which you were the sole witness. While he was being taken off, to prison or execution, a certain architect who was in charge of public buildings met them. They were especially glad to encounter him, for they would commonly fall under his suspicion over missing goods lost from the market-place. Now, at last, he could see who the real culprits were! But the man had often seen Alypius at the house of a senator to whom he frequently went to pay his respects. He recognised him immediately, and taking his hand, drew him out of the crowd, enquiring the cause for such a catastrophe. He heard what had been done, and ordered all the brawling, threatening rabble there to accompany him. They came to the house of the young man who had committed the misdeed. There was a boy at the door, too small to fear any harm to his master from the occasion, who was easily able to make it all plain. He had actually been with his master in the market-place. As soon as Alypius recollected this, he told the architect. He showed the boy the hatchet, asking whose it was. He immediately answered: 'Ours', and on being questioned disclosed everything. So was the charge transferred to that house, and the mob, which had already begun to triumph over him, put to confusion, for Alypius was destined to be the dispenser of your Word, the judge of many cases in your Church. He went home with better experience and instruction.

X

Alypius' Integrity and Nebridius' Arrival

I found him in Rome, and he was bound to me by the strongest ties, accompanied me to Milan, both to keep by my side and to practise some of the law that he had learned, rather to meet his parents' wishes than his own. Three times he had sat as an assessor there, with an integrity which amazed the rest – though he, for his part, was amazed rather at them who ranked gold ahead of integrity. His character was also tested, not only by the lure of greed but also by the goad of fear. At Rome he was the assessor to the Commissioner of the Italian Treasury. There was at the time a very powerful senator, by whose favours many were bound, and by fear of whom many were tamed. This man, after the fashion of his influence, sought some personal concession which was contrary to law. Alypius stood out. A bribe was promised. He scorned it in his heart. Threats were offered. He trod them under foot, with everyone amazed at so rare a spirit which neither coveted as friend, nor feared as foe, so considerable a person, and one mightily well known for the numberless ways he had of doing favour or harm. The judge himself, whose assessor Alypius was, although he did not want the request granted, still did not openly oppose it, but blamed the matter on Alypius, saying that he was the impediment – which was, in fact, true, for if the judge had done it, Alypius would have resigned. By one thing alone he was almost tempted, and that through his love of learning, to wit, that he might get books copied at prices available to praetors. Considering justice, however, he thought better of it, judging the equity by which he was restrained more profitable than the power by which he was allowed. A small matter, but 'he who is faithful in little is faithful too in much.' In no way will that be vain which has come from your lips of truth: 'If you have not been faithful in the Mammon of Unrighteousness, who will entrust true riches to you?' And, 'if you have not been faithful in what belongs to another, who will give you what is your own?' Such was the one who was my close friend, and who shared my wavering purpose as to what way of life should be chosen.

Nebridius, too, who left the place of his birth near Carthage, and Carthage itself (where he had lived for the most part), leaving too his father's rich country estate, his home, and a mother who was not likely to follow him, had come to Milan for no other reason than to live with me, in a burning zeal for truth and wisdom. Together he sighed with me, and along with me was tossed about, an ardent searcher for the blessed life, and a sharp examiner of the most difficult questions. There were the mouths of three needy ones, gasping out their mutual poverty and waiting upon you 'to give them their food in due season.' And in all bitterness, which by your mercy followed all our worldly doings, we envisaged the end, and the reason for our sufferings. Darkness overwhelmed us and we would turn away with groaning and ask: 'How long are these things to be?' We often talked like this, but for all our words did not forsake those things, for there was nothing sharp and clear for us to lay hold of, if we did forsake them.

XI

Decade of Bewilderment

Busily turning it all over in my mind, what most amazed me was how long a time it was since my nineteenth year, when I had first begun my passionate interest in the study of wisdom, determined, when that was found, to abandon the empty hopes and lying insanities of vain desires. But, see, I was now in my thirtieth year, stuck in the same bog, by my greed to enjoy what was to my hand, ephemeral and destructive though that was. I kept on saying: 'Tomorrow I shall find it. It will appear plainly and I shall grasp it. See, Faustus will come, and he will make everything clear! Oh, great men of the Academics! Can nothing certain for the conduct of our lives be understood? No, let us search more carefully, and not lose hope. See, those matters in the writings of the Church which once seemed absurd to us, no longer seem like that, and can honestly be understood in another way. I will fix my feet in that step where I was placed by my parents, till such time as transparent truth is found. But where, when, shall it be sought? Ambrose has no time. There is no time to read. Where do we find the very books? Where, when, do we buy them? From whom do we borrow them? Let times be appointed, hours spaced, for the salvation of the soul. A great hope bursts forth. The Catholic Faith does not teach what we thought it did, and of which we ignorantly accused it. Its learned men consider it sin to believe God to be bounded by the limitations of a human body. Do we hesitate to knock, that the other doors may be opened? My students fill all my mornings. What shall we do with the rest of the day? Why do we not do this? But when are we to visit our important friends, of whose support we have need? When are we to write something scholars will buy? When are we to take a rest, relaxing the mind from the intensity of our cares? Away with everything, and let us have done with these empty trivialities, devoting ourselves to the search for truth and nothing else. Life is wretched, death uncertain. Should it steal upon us suddenly, in what case shall we make our departure, and where are we to learn those things we have neglected here? And shall we not rather suffer the penalty for this negligence? What if death itself shall cut off and end all care along with feeling? And so another theme for enquiry! Banish the thought that it should be so. It is not without purpose or meaning that the sublimity of the authority of the Christian Faith is spread worldwide. Never would things so great and of such fashion be wrought by God for us, if, with the body's death, the life of the soul should also vanish. Why then do we delay, abandoning worldly hope, to devote ourselves completely to the quest for God and the blessed life? But wait: even these things are pleasant; they have no little sweetness. Our interest in them must not be lightly cut off, because it is a shame, having done so, to go back again. See how much it means to win some distinction. What more is there here to be desired? We have a host of influential friends. Without striving for much more, even a governor's post could be given us. And a wife could come our way, with some money so as not to increase our expenses, and this will be the end of our ambition. Many great men, men most deserving our imitation, have been dedicated to the study of wisdom, although they were married.'

Such were the words I used to say, and meanwhile those winds were pushing my heart this way and that. And time was passing, and I was delaying my conversion to the Lord. Day after day I put off living in you. I did not put off my daily dying in myself. I loved the blessed life, but was afraid of finding it where it was to be found. In flight from it, I sought it. I thought I should be too miserable if I were deprived of a woman's embraces, and I never considered the medicine of your mercy for the curing of that same weakness, for I had no experience of it. As for continence, I supposed it to be a matter of our own strength, strength of which I knew nothing. I was so foolish that I did not know that no man can be continent unless you give him the power. Assuredly you would have given it, if, with groaning of spirit, I had beaten on your ears, and with firm faith I had cast my care on you.

XII

Argument on Marriage

Alypius, in fact, was the one who kept me from marrying. He was always harping on the theme that, if I did, it would in no way be possible for us to live together in undisturbed leisure and love of wisdom, as we had long desired. He himself in that regard was most chaste, indeed astonishingly so. He had had a measure of sexual experience in early youth, but had not been captivated by it, indeed he regretted and rejected it, and thenceforth lived in the most complete continence. I opposed him with instances of men who, though married, cultivated wisdom, served God acceptably, and were faithful and loving towards their friends, men from whose loftiness of spirit I myself fell far short. Bound with the disease of the flesh and its deadly sweetness, I dragged my chain along, afraid to be set free, and as if my wound had been struck afresh, I pushed back the words of one who advised me well, as if they were the hand of one who would unchain me.

Moreover, it was also by me that the serpent spoke to Alypius, too, through my tongue weaving and planting pleasant snares in his path, to tangle his honourable and unfettered feet. Having no small regard for me, he wondered that I was stuck so fast in the birdlime of that pleasure, that I would pronounce a single life impossible to live, whenever the question rose between us. He wondered too that I should defend myself, when I noted his amazement, by stressing the great difference between his occasional, furtive and almost forgotten experiences, easy enough therefore to despise, and the pleasures of my continuous custom. And, I would add that, if the honourable name of marriage should be added to them, he ought not to wonder why I could not reject that course of life. Alypius himself began to desire marriage, by no means captivated by a lust for such pleasure, but by a desire to find out about it. He would say that he wanted to know whatever it might be, without which my life, which pleased him so, would not seem life, but an ordeal to me. For his mind, free from that bondage, was amazed at my servitude, and from that amazement grew a desire to experiment. The experience itself was likely to follow, and thence perhaps the fall into the bondage which amazed him – seeing he wanted to 'make a covenant with death', and 'he who loves danger will fall into it.' Any honour there may be in the task of managing marriage and rearing children moved neither of us much. What did most strongly move me, and held me a tormented slave, was the custom of sating an insatiable lust. Wonder was leading him into captivity. In such case were we, until you, Most High, not forsaking our earthiness, pitying us in our pitiable state, came to our aid in wondrous hidden ways.

XIII

Monica Plans his Marriage

Relentless pressure was on me to marry. I searched personally, and promises were made, my mother taking the leading part. Her object was that, once I was married the baptism of salvation would wash me clean. She rejoiced to see me daily fitting myself for it, observing that her prayers, and your promises, were finding fulfilment in my faith. It was then that, both at my request, and through her own desire, with the strong crying of her heart, she daily sought of you, through a vision to give some indication about my future marriage. It was never your will. She saw some meaningless figments of her imagination to which the thrust of an eager human spirit drove her. She told me of these, but not with the confidence she commonly displayed, when you made some message clear to her, but rather treating them lightly. For she used to say that there was a kind of savour which she found it difficult to describe, between your revealing something to her and her own soul's dreamings. Yet she pressed on, and a girl was proposed who was almost two years under marriageable age. She pleased me, so the delay was agreed upon.

XIV

Scheme for a Commune

Many of our group of friends who loathed the stormy troubles of human life had discussed the matter together, and had almost reached the firm conclusion to withdraw from the multitudes and live at leisure. This state we would bring about if we brought together our several resources and made one common household of it all, so that, through the trust of friendship, this should not belong to one and that to another, but that which should be made one out of all, should wholly belong to each and all to all. There would probably, we thought, be ten of us in this community, some among us very rich men, chiefly my fellow townsman Romanianus. He had been my very close friend since early life. Serious disturbances in his affairs had brought him up to court. He was most eager for this project and promoted it with great authority, because his solid wealth put him far ahead of the rest of us. We had set it down that two officers should be annually appointed to look after all necessary arrangements, the rest being left unencumbered. But after we began to consider whether our wives would permit this (for some of us were already married, others had marriage in view) all the plan which we had shaped so well, broke up in our hands, was shattered and abandoned. So we were back to our sighing and moaning, and wanderings, and to following the broad, beaten tracks of the world. Many thoughts were in our hearts 'but your counsel abides for ever.' By this counsel, you ridiculed ours, and prepared your own for us, intending to 'give us meat in due season, to open your hand and fill our souls with blessing.'

XV

Lost Love

Meanwhile my sins were multiplying, and the woman I used to live with was torn from my side as a hindrance to marriage. My heart, which clave to her, was cut, wounded and bleeding. She went back to Africa, vowing to you to know no other man, and leaving behind the son she had borne to me. But I, unhappy man, who could not do what a woman had done, impatient of delay, seeing it was two years before I would possess the one I sought, and because I was a slave to lust rather than a devotee of marriage, took another woman, though not as a wife. Thus the sickness of my soul was to be fed and prolonged, intact or stronger, into the dominion of marriage, under the conduct of enduring custom. Nor was the wound which was made by the amputation I had already suffered, healed. It was inflamed, acutely painful and festered, the pain more dull, but aching more hopelessly.

XVI

God Closes In

Praise to you and glory, fount of mercies! I became more unhappy, but you more near. Your right hand was more and more ready. It was to snatch me from the mire and wash me, but I did not know. It was only the fear of death and your judgment to come which kept me from a deeper gulf of fleshly pleasures. That fear, amid all my changing opinions, never left my heart. I would argue with my friends, Alypius and Nebridius, about the limits of good and evil. In my mind I would have given the prize to Epicurus, save that I believed that the life of the soul survived death and found a place it had deserved. This Epicurus would not concede. And I asked: 'Suppose we were immortal, and should live in endless carnal pleasure, without any fear of losing it, why should we not be happy, or what else should we look for?' I did not recognise that this very thing had much to do with my great unhappiness. I was so submerged and blind that I could not see the light of a virtue and beauty to be embraced for their own sake, which the eye of the flesh cannot see. It is discerned in the heart. Nor, unhappy man, did I take thought about the source from which it flowed. Yet I pleasantly discussed ideas so foul with my friends! I was not able to be happy without friends, whatever the abundance of my carnal pleasures. Such was my disposition at the time. Assuredly I loved those friends for their own sake, and in return I felt I

was loved by them for my own sake, too. O twisted paths!
Alas for my bold soul, which hoped that, while forsaking
you it would find something better! It has turned and turned
again on its back, its sides, its belly, found all things hard and
you alone its rest. And, look, you are near at hand! You
deliver us from our wretched wanderings and establish us in
your way. You comfort us and say these words to us: 'Run
on, I shall carry you. I will bring you through and there, too,
I will carry you.'

BOOK SEVEN

Last Impediments

Introduction

It was Augustine's thirty-first year and still one of delay. He was quite unable to rise above his inability to apprehend the spiritual save in material terms, or to comprehend evil and its origin at all. It was as difficult to do so then as it still is today. It was at this point that, through some intelligent Milanese, Augustine met some of the writings of the Neoplatonic school, in the translated works of the Roman Victorinus, an African like himself. Neoplatonism led back to Plato, Christianity's 'old loving nurse', as the Cambridge Platonists of three centuries ago called the great Greek, and Platonism formed a link between the old world and the new in Christian thought, a theme which need not detain us here.

It did not detain Augustine long. How much, or how well Victorinus translated, is again not known, but it was the influence of the Platonists which brought Victorinus to Christ in 364, and through him impressed Augustine, seemingly alleviating his problems over God, good and evil. A progress can be traced through all the seventh book. The encounter with the Platonists was an event in the pilgrimage and the *Confessions* are a biography of events rather than circumstances.

One passage in Book Seven illustrates Augustine's inquisitive and undisciplined mind. He tells of some 'research' into astrology, and the determined experiments of a scientifically-minded friend to find the truth about our master stars and constellations. Curiously it was Esau and Jacob which finally convinced our author. Perhaps he needed, as a largely self-taught man, to clear such rubble from his path as he struggled back to the Catholic Faith. Christian thinkers were admitting that the Neoplatonists had an inkling of Christian truth.

I

Envisaging God

Now my unutterably wicked youth was dead, and I was on
my way into young manhood, older in years, but by the same
token the more foul in vanity. I was unable to conceive any
kind of substance which could not be seen by our eyes. I did
not think of you, God, in the shape of a human body. I had
always avoided that notion since I began to hear anything of
philosophy, and I was glad to have found this much in the
faith of our spiritual mother, your Catholic Church, but
what else to think of you I could not conceive. And being a
man (such a man too) I sought with all my heart to believe
you to be the sovereign and only true God, beyond
corruption, damage or change. I did not know whence or in
what way, yet plainly saw and was certain that what can be
corrupted was inferior to that which cannot be, and I
unhesitatingly set ahead that which could not be damaged
to that which could be, and knew that what is beyond change
is better than that which is subject to change. My heart
protested wildly against all my 'phantoms', and at one blow I
sought to drive away from my mind's eye that troop of
uncleanness which flitted about it. Scarce were they
banished than with the flick of an eye, look at them
thronging back again, rushing on my sight and beclouding it,
so that I was constrained to think of you, not indeed in
human shape, but something bodily all the same, extended
through vast space, either infused into the sum of things or
diffused infinitely beyond it – yes, that incorruptible being,
beyond damage or change, which I preferred to that which
can be corrupted, suffer harm, or know change! And

whatever I took away from such spaces seemed nothing to me, completely nothing, not even void. It was just as if a body were removed from a place, and the place should remain unoccupied by any body at all, earthly, of water, of air or heavenly, but yet should be an empty space, a spacious nothingness.

So I, made gross in heart, and not quite clear even to myself, conceived as nothingness, that which was not extended over certain distances, thinly spread or bulked together or distended, or which did not nor could partake of such dimensions. My heart was ranging over such forms as my eyes were accustomed to see, but I did not see that this very application of the mind, by which I shaped those images, was not of that kind, and yet could not have shaped them had it not been some great thing. So, too, I thought of you, life of my life, as vast, penetrating through infinite space, the whole mass of the universe and beyond it in every direction, through immeasurable boundlessness, so that the earth, the sky, the universe should hold you, and find their bounds in you, but you find bounds nowhere. For just as the body of this air which is above the earth does not impede the transit through it of the sun's light, which penetrates it, not by bursting through or cutting a path, but by filling it, so I thought that the body, not only of heaven and air and sea but even of the earth, was pervious to you, so that in all its parts, greatest and smallest, it was penetrable to admit your presence by a hidden inward and outward inspiration directing all your creation. So I surmised, unable to comprehend aught else – yet it was not true. For thus a greater portion of earth would hold a greater portion of you, and a smaller portion a smaller. Thus all things would be full of you, so that in proportion to its larger size, and the larger space it occupied, the body of an elephant would contain more of you than the body of a sparrow. So would you make parts of yourself present to parts of the world, proportionately, in fragments, large to large and small to small. But you are not like this. But you had not yet made light my darkness.

II

Nebridius Refutes Manichaeism

What Nebridius used to argue long since at Carthage to our great acceptance, was sufficient answer for me to those deluded charlatans and wordy mutes (your word did not ring in what they said) . . . Nebridius had answer enough: 'What,' he would ask, 'was that imaginary tribe of darkness, set, as it were, in a confronting battleline, likely to do to you, had you declined to oppose it?' If the answer should be that they would have done you some harm, then you would be vulnerable to violence and corruption. But if the answer should be that they would in no wise hurt you, then there would be adduced no reason for your fighting them, and in so fighting that same portion or member of you, or offspring of your very substance, would be mingled with opposing powers and natures not of your creation. So far would it have been polluted by them and changed for the worse, that it would be turned from happiness to unhappiness, and would need help to be rescued and purified. And this 'offspring of your substance' was this soul of ours, which, enslaved and polluted and corrupted, your Word, free, pure, and undefiled, might aid – that Word itself being subject to corruption because it was the offspring of one and the same substance. So, should they affirm that you, whatever you are and of whatever substance, are incorruptible, then all these doctrines are false and accursed. But if the answer should be that you are subject to corruption, that very statement is immediately false, and at first utterance to be execrated. This argument therefore was sufficient refutation of those who should be totally vomited out, as if from an overloaded stomach. They had no way out, save by dreadful blasphemy of heart and tongue, in thinking and speaking thus of you.

III

Free Will and Sin

But up to this time, though I both said and believed that you, our Lord God and true God, who made not only our souls but our bodies, all beings and all that is, were beyond defilement and change of any sort, I could not clearly and without difficulty grasp the cause of evil. I could see that it must be so sought, whatever it might be, that I should not in the process be constrained to think a changeless God subject to change, for thus I should become what I was looking for. So with some sense of security I went about my search, convinced that what those said whom I shunned with all my soul was not true. I could see that in their search for the cause of evil they were filled full of evil themselves in believing that your essence suffered evil rather than that their own committed it. So I concentrated on understanding what I now was hearing, that free will was the cause of our sinning and that suffering was your judgment. However, I could not see it clearly. Thus in trying to draw my intelligence from out that depth, I was plunged back into it. As often as I tried, this was repeated. This raised me up a little into your light, for I was as conscious of having a will as I was of living. So when I willed, or by my will rejected anything, I was positive that it was only I who exercised my will in this way or in that, and I glimpsed that here was the cause of sin. But what I did against my will, I seemed to suffer rather than to do, and I counted that not as fault but punishment, and since I considered you just, I promptly confessed that I was not unjustly punished. But again I would say: 'Who made me? Was it not my God, who is not only good but goodness itself? How then does it happen that I can will evil and not will good? So that there might be cause for just punishment? Who was it that set and ingrafted into me this shoot of bitterness when I was wholly made by my sweetest God? If the devil was the doer, whence the devil? And if he himself, by his own rebellious will, became the devil from being once a good angel, whence in him that evil will which made him devil, when by the most excellent creator he had been wholly made a good angel?' By these thoughts I was once more depressed and stifled. Yet was I not reduced to that hell of error, in which you are rather thought to suffer evil than man to do evil, and where no one makes confession to you.

IV

The Incorruptible God

Thus did I now struggle to find out the rest, since I had already concluded that the incorruptible is better than the corruptible, and confessed, in consequence, that you, whatever you are, are incorruptible. For no soul has ever been able or will be able to conceive of anything better than you who are the highest and best good. But since most truly and certainly the incorruptible is to be preferred to the corruptible (the concept I now favoured) I might well, in my thoughts, have touched on something better than my God, had you not been incorruptible. Therefore when I perceived that the incorruptible must be preferred to the corruptible, at that point I should have looked for you, and from that point observe where evil lies, that is whence rises corruption itself, by which your essence can in no way be harmed. Corruption simply does not mar our God – by no will, necessity nor unforeseen event, because he is God, and what he wills is good, and he, he himself is that good, but to be corrupted is not good. Nor are you, against your will, forced to do anything because your will is not greater than your power, but it would be greater if you were greater than yourself, for the will and power of God is God himself. What is unforeseen to you who know all things? There is nothing created which you do not know. What more are we to say why that essence which is God should not be corruptible, when, if this were not the case, it would not be God?

V

Envisaging Omnipresence

I was looking for the source of evil, and in an evil way I looked for it, and failed to see the evil in the very quest. I set out in my mind's eye the whole creation – I mean, first, what can be discerned in it. sea, earth, air, stars, mortal creatures, and then what eludes sight, heaven's firmament above with all the angels and its spiritual denizens (but even these, as though they were bodies, set in this place or that as my imagination chose). Of your creation I made one mighty mass, its constituents marked each from each by their varied bodies, those that in fact were bodies, and those which, instead of spirits, I had imagined to be bodies. And this mass I made enormous, not as great as it was, a matter beyond comprehension, but as large as the mind could grasp it, and nevertheless on all sides finite. But you, Lord, I imagined on every side environing and permeating it, but in every way infinite – as if one should imagine a sea, everywhere and in all directions through unmeasured space extending, one only boundless sea, and yet a sea, containing in itself a sponge, vast as can be imagined but none the less finite and yet everywhere and on all sides filled with that infinite sea. So, thought I, with your creation. Though finite, it is filled with your infinitude. I would say: 'Look, there is God and what God has created.' And God is good, most mightily and incomparably better than these. Being good he has created what is good, and see how he surrounds and permeates it. Where then is evil, and whence and by what path did it insinuate itself? What is the root and the seed of it? Does it simply not exist? Why then fear and beware of what has no being? And if we vainly fear, fear itself is evil, which to no purpose goads and torments the heart. And it is a greater evil to the extent that what we fear has no existence – yet we go on fearing. Whence comes it then, since God, good himself, made all these things good. That is, the greater and highest good made lesser goods, and yet the one creating and the

things created are all good. Whence, then, evil? Was there
some blemish in the raw material from which he shaped and
ordered everything, some of which he left remaining without
transmuting it into good? But why? Was he unable in such
fashion so to change and transform the whole that nothing
evil should be left behind, when he is able to do everything?
Finally, why did he choose to make anything out of it, or
why rather, by that same omnipotence, did he not bring it
about that there should be no such evil material at all? Was it
able, in fact, to exist against his will? And if it was eternal,
why for so long, for eternal aeons of backward time, did he
suffer it to continue, and after so long decide to make
something out of it? Or, if he suddenly made up his mind to
do something, why, being able to do everything, did he not
rather do this, that nothing should exist save only he himself,
the whole of truth, the highest and infinite good? Or, if it
were not well that he who is good should not also construct
and found something good, that raw material which was evil
having been removed and annihilated, why did he not
establish some good material, out of which to create all
things? For he would not himself be omnipotent, if he could
not create something good without the help of material not
of his own creating. Such were the thoughts I churned in my
unhappy breast, weighed down by gnawing cares about the
fears of death and my inability to discover the truth. Yet did
the faith of your Christ. our Lord and Saviour of the
Catholic Church, abide firm in my heart, shapeless, to be
sure, in many ways, and fluctuating from the straight rule of
doctrine. Nevertheless my soul did not abandon it. Indeed,
daily, more and more, it drank it in.

VI

The Astrologers

By this time I had rejected the deceitful fortune-telling and wicked lunacies of the astrologers. My God, let your mercies, from out of my soul's inner being, confess to you about this too. You, you and only you – for who is it that calls us back from the death that is in all error but the life which knows not how to die, and the wisdom which, needing no light itself, lightens minds which need it and governs the world to the very fluttering leaves of the trees – you, I say, took care of the obstinacy which made me argue with Vindicianus, that shrewd old man, and with Nebridius, that young man of admirable spirit, when the former emphatically affirmed, and the latter, not without some hesitation often said, that there is no way of foreseeing what is yet to be, but that man's conjectures were like a game of chance, and, by talking much, some things to come were spoken about, those who spoke not knowing them, but stumbling upon them by continually talking. You also took care that I should have a friend, a frequent visitor to the astrologers. He was not skilled in their literature, but a curious client of theirs. He had some knowledge, he said, picked up from his father, but did not know how far that knowledge went to refute astrology. This man, Firminus by name, liberally educated and of polished speech, asked advice of me as a very dear friend, on certain matters which concerned him, and in which his worldly hopes were intimately involved. What did I think, he asked, about his so-called 'constellations'. In such matters I was at the time veering towards Nebridius' opinion, and did not quite refuse an opinion and tell him what my wavering conjecture was. I did, however, add that I had almost concluded that such matters were empty folly. It was then that he told me that his father had been most curious about those treatises, and had a friend who equally pursued such studies along with him. By joint study and pooling of information they were intensely devoted to these bits of nonsense. It was like a fire inside them. They would observe down to the minutes the birthtimes of even dumb animals about the house, and relate the position of the heavens to them in order to collect experimental details of the so-called art. He said he had heard from his father that, at the time when his mother was carrying the same Firminus, a maid-servant of his father's friend was also pregnant. This did not escape the master's notice, for he took care with the most exact attention to mark the birthtimes of his very dogs. It thus came about that one man was noting with the most careful attention the days, hours, and even smaller divisions of the hours of his wife, and the other of his servant-girl. Both began labour at the same time. Thus, to the very minutes, both were compelled to follow the same constellations, in giving birth, one to a son, the other to a baby slave. As soon as the two women fell into labour, each reported to the other what was happening in the two houses, and organised mutual interchange of information as soon as the birth took place. This they could each do promptly, each, as it were, in his own sphere of control. The messengers of the respective households, met, he said, halfway between so that neither of them was in a better position to observe any position of the stars, or other precise timing than the other. Yet Firminus was born to high estate in his parents' home, traversed the brighter paths of life, increased with riches and exalted with honours. The slave on the other hand went on serving his masters, the yoke of his condition in no way lightened. Firminus knew him and so told the story.

When, on the authority of such a person this was heard and accepted as true, all my reluctance crumbled, I first sought to reclaim Firminus himself from that inquisitiveness. I said that, at the outset, on examining his horoscope, for a true forecast I should have seen his parents there as first among their peers, a noble family in their own city, freeborn, with an honourable and liberal education. But if that slave with an identical horoscope had consulted me in search of a true forecast, I should have seen in it, on the contrary, the basest of family background, the status of slaves, and other details, remotely different and far removed from the former prognosis. It follows that, if I told the truth, I should draw contrary conclusions from the examination of the same phenomena, and that I should be a liar if I pronounced them identical. It most certainly follows that whatever truth emerges from the consideration of the same star patterns, is uttered by chance, and not by logic, and whatever is falsely said, reveals not unskilfulness in the art but the falsehood of the chance.

So, accepting this approach, and turning such matters over in my mind, in case any one of those same dolts who seek such gains, and whom now I longed to assail and refute with derision, should confront me with the charge that either Firminus had misinformed me or his father had misinformed him, I turned my investigation to those born twins, both of whom emerge from the womb in such close sequence that whatever significance the small interval of time may have (however great it may be in those fellows' contentions) is beyond human measurement, and cannot be written into the charts which the astrologer is to examine, if he is to pronounce the truth.

And it will not be the truth because, with the same charts before him, he must have made identical pronouncement on Esau and Jacob. Their fortunes nevertheless were different. So he would be a liar, or, if he told the truth, it would not be for both. Yet his data for examination were the same. For you, Lord, most righteous ruler of the universe, for all that the forecasters, and those who seek their forecasting, do not know, work through a wisdom beyond our knowing, so that he who consults the forecaster hears what out of the depths of your just judgment he ought to hear, according to the unseen deservings of the souls of men. To him no man should say: 'What is this?' 'What is that?' Let him not say anything – for he is only a man.

VII

Agony over Evil's Origin

And now, my helper, you had freed me from those chains and I was beginning again to ask where evil came from and found no way out. You did not allow me to be swept away by the billows of those thoughts from the faith by which I believed in your existence, and that your essence was unchangeable, and that you loved and judged mankind;

further, that in Christ, your son, our Lord, and in the holy
Scriptures which the authority of your Church pressed upon
me, you had laid down the way of man's salvation to that life
which lies beyond this. With these thoughts intact and
unshakeably strengthened in my mind, I was feverishly
looking for the origin of evil. What torments came from the
travail of my heart, what groans, my God. Yet you heard,
without my knowing it. When in silence I sought earnestly,
the dumb contritions of my soul were great cries for your
mercy. You knew what I was suffering, though no man did,
for what portion was channelled through my tongue into the
ears of my closest friends? Did the tumult of my soul, for
which neither time nor words sufficed, have a voice for
them? Yet the whole of it reached your ears. I cried aloud
with the groaning of my heart, and my longing was before
you though 'the light of my eyes was gone from me'. That
was within, and I without. That was not in space, and I was
reaching out for that which is bounded in space. I was
finding no resting-place there, nor did those regions receive
me so that I could say: 'It is enough, it is well' – yet they
suffered no returning to that which might have been well
enough. To these things I was superior, inferior though I was
to you. To me, your subject, you are true joy to me, and to
me you have made subordinate which you have created
inferior to me. This was the true meaning and the middle
region of my salvation, that I might remain comformable to
your image, and in serving you become master of my body.
When I rose in pride against you and 'ran upon the Lord with
the thick boss of my shield', it was then that those lower things
prevailed over me and kept me down, and left no relief or
breathing-space. They charged upon me from all sides as I
looked upon them. And in my thoughts these very carnal
images pressed upon my efforts to return, and seemed to say:
'Where are you going, unworthy one and base?' But they had
sprung from my wound, because you have humbled the
proud like a wounded man, and I was barred from you by my
bruising, and my swollen face was closing up my eyes.

VIII

The Relief of God's Mercy

You, Lord, abide for ever but are not for ever angry with us, because you pity dust and ashes and it pleased you to reshape my distortions. You stirred me with your goads within so that I should not be at peace until you should be manifest to my inward sight. And by the hidden hand of your healing my swelling abated, and the dimmed and darkened eyesight of my mind was daily healed by the stinging balm of healthy sorrows.

IX

Platonism and Christianity

Since you first of all desired to show me how you 'resist the proud and give grace to the humble', and with what mercy on your part the way of humility was made clear to men in that your 'Word was made flesh and dwelt among us', you provided for me through a certain man, swollen with the most monstrous pride, some books of the Platonists translated from Greek into Latin. There it was that I read, not indeed in the very words, but to the same purpose, and reinforced by manifold reasons, that 'in the beginning was the Word, and the Word was with God, and the Word was God. That same Word was in the beginning and was God. All things were made by him and without him nothing was made. In that which was made was light and the light was the light of men. And the light shines in darkness and the darkness did not overtake it.' Further I read that the soul of man, though it may bear witness to the light, is not in itself that light, but that the Word, God himself, is the true light, 'which lights every man who comes into the world. And though he was in the world and though the world was made by him, the world did not recognise him. He came to what was his own and his own people did not receive him. But to as many as did receive him, he gave to them the power to become the sons of God, to those who believed in his name.' To be sure I did not read this there in so many words. But I did read there that the Word, God, 'was not born of flesh and blood, nor of the will of a man, nor of the will of the flesh, but was born of God.' But I did not read in the Platonists that 'the Word was made flesh and dwelt among us.'

I also discovered in those books, though put differently in many ways, that the Son, being in the likeness of the Father, thought that equality with the Father not something to snatch, because he was by nature the same, but 'he emptied himself, receiving the body of a slave, and, thus discovered in human form, he humbled himself, obedient to death, and that death on the cross. That is why God lifted him high from the dead, and gave him a name which is above every name, so that at the name of Jesus every knee should bend, of beings above, on earth and below the earth, and every tongue should confess that Jesus is Lord to the glory of God the Father.' Those books did not contain those words. Nor that, before all times and beyond all times, the 'only begotten Son' remains unchangeably co-eternal with you, and 'of his fulness' all souls receive, that they may be blessed, and that they are reborn to wisdom by their sharing in the wisdom of the one who remains in them. All this is in those books, but not that he 'in due time died for the ungodly', and that 'you did not spare your only Son, but gave him up for all of us.' But 'you hid these matters from the wise and made them known to little ones', that all they 'which labour and are burdened might come to him' for refreshment, because 'he is gentle and quiet of heart and he directs the gentle in judgment, teaching them his ways, with an eye to our humility and toil, forgiving all our sins.' But those who walk high in the actor's boots of a loftier learning do not hear him saying: 'Learn of me for I am gentle and quiet of heart and you will find rest for your souls.' And 'if they know God, it is not as God that they honour him, nor are grateful to him, but fade away in their thoughts. Their foolish heart is darkened.

Calling themselves wise, they turn out to be fools.'

It was in the same books that I read too of your 'unchangeable glory changed into images and other representations of corruptible man, birds, animals, reptiles', for example into the Egyptian food for which Esau lost his birthright, for the nation which was your firstborn worshipped instead of you the head of a four-footed animal, turning in heart back to Egypt, and bending your image, their soul, before the image of a hay-eating calf. I discovered these things in those books but did not feed on them. It was your pleasure, Lord, to take away the reproach of humbling from Jacob and make the older serve the younger, and you called the Gentiles into your inheritance. From them I had come to you, and I set my mind upon the gold which you directed your people to take away from Egypt. It was yours, wherever it was. You said by your apostle to the Athenians (it was from Athens that these books came): 'In you we live and move, indeed, exist' just as some of their own poets had said. But I did not set my mind on the idols of Egypt which they served with your gold, they who 'changed God's truth into a lie and served the creature rather than the Creator.'

X

Mystic Musings

Thus bidden return to myself, I made my way under your leadership, into my inner being, as I could, with you becoming thus my guide. I entered, and by some vision of the soul I saw, above soul and mind the Lord's unchanging light – not this common light, visible to all flesh, nor yet a greater light, but of the same kind. It was something which shone much, much more brilliantly and filled all space. It was not light as we know it, but totally distinct. Nor was it above my mind, as oil lies on water, nor as the sky is over the earth, but above my soul because it made me, and I am less than it because I was made by it. He who knows the truth knows that light, and he who knows it knows eternity. Love knows it, O eternal truth, and true love, and loved eternity! You are my true God. For you I sigh day and night. When first I knew you, you raised me up to see what I might see, though I was not yet such as could see. You beat back the weakness of my sight, pouring your light strongly upon me, while I trembled with love and awe. I discovered I was far removed from you in the matter of unlikeness, as if I heard you say this from heaven: 'I am the food of grown men. Grow, and you shall feed on me. But you shall not change me like the food of your flesh into you, but you shall be changed into me.' And I knew that, 'because you have taught man because of iniquity, you made my soul consume away like a spider's web.' I said: 'Is truth nothing at all because it is not diffused through space defined or infinite?' And you called from afar: 'I am that I am.' And I heard as the heart may hear, and there was no reason at all that I should doubt it. I should rather doubt my own existence than that of truth, 'which is clearly seen, understood by those things which are made.'

XI

The Nature of Being

And I looked at things beneath you, and saw that they neither exist completely nor were completely non-existent. They exist for they are from you, yet do not exist because they are not what you are. For only truly does that exist which remains unchanging. To cling fast to God is therefore good for me, because, if I do not remain in him, I shall not be able to remain in myself. But he, 'remaining in himself makes everything new', and 'you are my God because you do not need my goodness.'

XII

Tormented Thought on Good and Evil

It became clear to me that those things are good which yet are corrupted, for neither, if they were supremely good, could they be corrupted, nor, unless they were good, could they be corrupted, for, if they were supremely good, they would be incorruptible, and if they were not good at all, there would be nothing in them which could be corrupted. Corruption harms, but could not harm unless it made goodness less. Therefore either corruption does no harm, which is impossible, or, which is utterly certain, all which is corrupted is robbed of goodness. If they were robbed of all good, they would altogether cease to be. If they are to continue to exist, but so as no longer be able to suffer corruption, they will be better, for they will continue on incorruptibly. But what is more monstrous than to affirm that things which have lost all their goodness are made better? So if they are going to be robbed of all their goodness, they will altogether cease to exist. Therefore while they exist they are good. Therefore whatever exists is good, and that evil whose origin I looked for, is not a substance, for, were it so, it would be good. Either it would be an incorruptible substance and so a chief good, or a corruptible substance which could not be corrupted unless it were good. And so I saw, and it became clear to me, that you have made all things good, and there is not any substance that you have not made. And since you did not make all things equal, therefore such are all things, for individual things are good, and at the same time are all things together very good, because our God made all things very good.

XIII

The Theme Continued

To you nothing at all is evil, not only to you but to your creation at large, because there is nothing outside to break in and upset the order you have imposed on it. But in parts of it some things do not harmonise with other parts, and are considered evil for that reason. But with other parts they do harmonise and are good, good in themselves. And all these things which do not mutually harmonise together, do harmonise with nature's lower part, which we call earth, with its cloudy and windy sky which befits it. Let it be far from me to say: 'These things should not be', for if these were the only things I could see, I should still long for the better, and should be bound to praise you for these alone, for the creatures of earth call for your praise – creeping things, deep seas, fire, hail, snow, ice and stormy winds, which do your bidding, mountains and all hills, fruit-trees and all cedars, beasts and all cattle, that which crawls and that which flies with wings, kings of earth and all peoples, chiefs and all judges of earth, young men and maids, old men and children, let them praise your name. And since those of the heavens praise you too, our God, in the heights let all your angels praise you, sun and moon, all the stars and light, the heaven of heavens and the waters above the heavens, let them praise your name. I did not now long for better things because I had thought it all out, and with sounder judgment I understood that the things above were better than the things below, but all together better than those above taken by themselves.

XIV

Nothing in Creation to be Rejected

Those to whom anything which you have made is displeasing
are not sane, just as I was when much displeased me, but
because my soul was not bold enough to find my God
displeasing, I wanted nothing which was displeasing to me to
belong to you. That is how my soul had formed the notion of
two substances, found no rest, and talked nonsense. It
retreated and made for itself a God, which occupied infinite
tracts of all space, counting him to be you. Him he located in
its heart, and again became the temple of its own idol,
something which was abominable to you. But when you had
calmed my head without my knowing it and 'closed my eyes
lest they should look on vanity', I was saved a little from
myself, and my madness was put to sleep. I awoke in you,
and saw that you were infinite in another way. This sight did
not come from the flesh.

XV

God and His Creation

I looked around and observed that all things owed their
being to you, that all finite things are in you but differently,
not as it were in space, but because you hold all in your hand
in truth. And all things are true, so far as they have being,
and falsehood is not anything except when something is
thought to exist which does not. I saw that everything was
adapted to its place and time. I saw, too that you who are
eternal, did not begin to work after innumerable tracts of
time past, for all tracts of time which have been and are to be,
neither go nor come without your working and remaining.

XVI

The True Nature of Evil

I found by experience that it is nothing strange that bread which is pleasant to a healthy palate is revolting to the unhealthy, as light which is hateful to sick eyes is delightful to the clear. Your justice displeases the wicked, much more the viper and the maggot, both of which you created good, and adapted to lower parts of your creation, as are the wicked themselves, the more so in proportion as they are unlike you. The opposite likewise applies. I sought what wickedness might be and found it not to be a substance but a bending of the will away from you, from God, towards lower things, casting away its inner life and making a blown-up outward show.

XVII

The Struggle to Understand

And I wondered that I now loved you, and not a phantasm in place of you. I did not hold back from enjoying my God. I was enraptured by your beauty. Yet I was soon torn back by my own weight, and fell with a groan into those other things. The weight was the habit of the flesh. But the memory of you was mine, and in no way did I doubt that there was one to whom I could cling, only that I was not yet the person who could cling. The corrupted body weighs down the soul and the earthly dwelling-place presses down the mind with its multitude of thoughts. I was, however, convinced that 'the things not seen from the world's foundation, understood by the things created, are visible, even your eternal power and divinity.' Seeking why it was that I approved corporeal beauty, celestial or of the earth, and why I judged soundly on changing things and pronounced that this should be thus, this not – enquiring in this way, I say, whence came such faculty of judgment, I had discovered the unchangeable and real eternity of truth above my changeable mind. So step by step I passed from bodies to the soul, which perceives through the body, and from that point to its inward faculty to which the body's senses announce external things (even animals go this far); from there I went on to the reasoning faculty to which the data from the senses of the body are referred for judgment. This also, finding itself to be a changeable part of me, responded to its own understanding and emancipated my thoughts from their common habit, withdrawing from those troops of contrary phantasms, and so to discover the light which bathed it. At this, beyond doubt, it cried: 'The unchangeable is better than the changeable.' But by the one it had reached the other. Otherwise it would have had no reason for its preference. Thus in the twinkling of an eye, it reached 'that which is'. Then I saw 'the invisible things known through things created'. But I could not gaze fixedly upon them, and, weakly beaten back, I resumed my old cast of thought, and carried with me only a dear memory, and a longing, like that of the odour of a food one has not yet been able to feed upon.

XVIII

Only One Way

I began to look for a way of gathering enough strength to enjoy you, and did not find it till I embraced 'the mediator between God and men, the Man Christ Jesus, who is above all, blessed of God for ever'. He called me and said: 'I am the way, the truth and the life.' He mixed that food which I was too weak to receive with our flesh, for the Word was made flesh that by your wisdom, through which you made the universe, he might suckle our infancy. I could not hold fast my Lord Jesus Christ, the humbled, the Humble One, nor yet did I know what that humility would teach us. Your Word, truth eternal, high raised above creation's highest, lifts the humbled to itself. It has built for itself here below a lowly house out of our clay, by which to bring down from their high esteem those who should be humbled and draw them to himself, healing their swollen pride and nourishing their love, so that they might go no further in self-confidence, but rather be reft of strength, and seeing before their feet deity made weak in putting on our 'coat of skin', might cast themselves wearily upon it, so that it, in rising, might lift them up.

XIX

God in Flesh Appearing

I had indeed held a different opinion. I thought only of my Lord Christ as a man without equal, of surpassing wisdom, especially because, being wondrously born of a virgin, he seemed, by divine provision for us, to have deserved so great an eminence of authority – offering thus an example of despising temporal things for the winning of immortality. But I could not grasp what mystery lay in the verse: 'The Word was made flesh.' This much I had understood from the written tradition – that he ate and drank, slept, walked, knew joy and sadness and preached, so that the flesh which was bound to your Word held a human soul and mind. Everyone knows this who knows that your Word does not change. As far as I was able, I, too, knew this and found no grounds for doubting there. For to move the limbs, as he chose, or chose not to do so, now to be stirred by some emotion or not, now to utter wise sayings in words, or to keep silence, all these belong to soul and mind and are subject to change. And if such things should be written falsely of him, the rest, too, would fall under suspicion of falsehood, and there would remain no saving faith in those scriptures for man. So, since they were true, I acknowledged that in Christ was perfect man, not a mere body of a man, or with the body a soul without a mind, but a true man, not a representation of truth, but a man whom, for some extraordinary excellence of human nature, and a more perfect share of wisdom, I judged to be set before all others.

Alypius thought that Catholics believed God to be thus clothed with flesh, and that besides God and flesh there was no soul in Christ, and that they did not think that a human mind was ascribed to him. And because he was firmly persuaded that the actions recorded of him could have been done only by a living, rational being, he was moving more slowly towards a true Christian faith. Later, perceiving this to be an error of the heretic followers of Apollinarius, he became a satisfied conformist to the Catholic faith. For my part, I confess that it was rather later that I learned how, in the phrase 'the Word made flesh', Catholic truth is distinguished from Photinus' falsehood. The rejection of the heretics makes the opinion of your Church, and the content of sound doctrine, stand out. For 'heresies must arise that the approved may be made obvious in the midst of the weak.'

XX

Platonism is no Substitute

Having by then read the Platonists' books I mentioned, and been persuaded by them to seek for incorporeal truth, I got a sight of your 'invisible things which are understood by what you have made.' Though I was pushed back, I saw what it was that, through the murk of my own mind, I was not able to contemplate: I became sure that you exist, and are infinite, yet not dispersed over finite and infinite space, that you truly exist who are the same for ever, varying in no part or movement, and that all things derive from you by this one sure proof that they do exist. Of such matters I was certain, yet too weak to enjoy you. I talked volubly, to be sure, as if I were an expert, but had I not sought your way in Christ, our Saviour, I was an expert bound for extinction. I had begun to covet the reputation of a philosopher, which carries its own punishment. For this I had no tears, for I was above all blown up with knowledge, for where was that upbuilding love on a foundation of humility, which is Christ Jesus? When would these books teach me it? Yet these books, I believe, it was your will that I should encounter, before considering your Scriptures, and that I should fix in memory how those books affected me, and that when later I should find my peace in your Scriptures, my wounds touched by your healing fingers, I should learn and see the difference between presumption and confession, between those who see the goal but not the way to it, and the road that leads to the blessed homeland, not only to be seen but dwelt in. For had I first been shaped in your holy Scriptures, and in the constant use of them you had grown sweet to me, and only afterwards fallen in with those books, they might, perhaps, have torn me from the solid ground of holiness. Or even if I had continued in that healthy frame of mind I had acquired, I might be thinking, that if one had studied these alone, he could have obtained it in those Platonist writings alone.

XXI

The Reasons for This

With strongest hunger then I laid hands on the venerable writings of your Spirit, above all the apostle Paul. Those questions died in which he seemed to me to be at conflict with himself, and in which the text of his argument seemed to contradict the testimonies of the Law, and there appeared to me the single face of that pure speech. I learned to 'rejoice with trembling'. I began and found that whatever I had read in the Platonists was said in Paul's writings along with the praise of your grace, that whoever sees may 'not so glory as if he had not received' not only what he sees but also that he may see ('for what has he that he has not received?'), and that he may not only be urged to look upon you who are always the same, but also to be so healed that he may hold you, and that the one who is too far off to see you, yet may walk the path both to seeing and to holding. For though a man may delight in the law of God 'after the inner man', what shall he do with that 'other law in his members which wars against the law of his mind, and brings him into captivity to the law of his sin which is in his members?' For 'you are righteous, Lord, but we have sinned, committed iniquity, and done wickedly', and your hand has been made heavy upon us, and we are justly handed over to that ancient sinner, the king of death, who has persuaded our will to take on the likeness of his, which stood not in your truth. 'What shall wretched man do? Who will free him from this dead body, save by your grace, through Jesus Christ our Lord?' Him you begat, co-eternal with yourself, and 'formed in the beginning of your ways', and in whom the prince of this world found nothing worthy of death, yet killed him, and 'the document written to condemn us was erased.' – The Platonists contained none of this. Those pages do not hold the face of holiness, the tears of confession, 'your sacrifice, a troubled spirit, a broken and a contrite heart', the salvation of your people, 'the bridal city', 'the earnest of the Holy Spirit', 'the cup of our salvation'. No one sings in those books: 'Shall not my soul be subject to God? Of him comes my redemption, for he is my God and my salvation, my guardian. I shall no more be moved.' In the Platonist writings no one hears him call: 'Come to me all that labour'. They scorn 'to learn of him because he is gentle and quiet in heart', 'for these things you have hid from the wise and revealed them to babes'. It is one thing to see from a wooded peak the homeland of peace and not to step out on the road to it, and in vain to try through pathless ways, besieged and infested by fugitive slaves and soldiers, under their chief, the lion and the serpent, another thing to keep the path that leads that way, garrisoned by the care of the heavenly commander where no deserters from God's army play the brigand. They avoid it like a torment. Such truths permeated my being when I read 'the least of your apostles', considered your works, and was overwhelmed with awe.

BOOK EIGHT

'Pick It Up and Read It'

Introduction

It is as well to remember that Augustine had begged in prayer to be allowed to 'wind and wind round and round in present memory the spirals of his errors.' The century was drawing to its end. He was in the forties of his age, and was recollecting over a decade the significance of certain events in his pilgrimage to Christ. The course is often better seen from a higher summit of the years, in the sixties, perhaps, or in the seventies if such a height is won.

Seven books lie behind. The eighth brings climax but it is only when the twisted path of a tormented man has been followed thus far, that Augustine's conversion can be adequately understood. Perhaps a decade later he might have looked back with greater comprehension and clarity. He might have spared his readers much rhetoric and convoluted thought.

Book Eight, perhaps with greater unity than the other seven, brings the story to the famous event which finalised a spiritual journey. Ambrose was a stronger force in Augustine's life than he is prepared to admit. Weaker men admire stronger men, and there were elements of weakness in Augustine's personality. Witness his escape from the unruly schoolboys of Carthage, his deception of Monica, his inability to break with the Manichaeans, his domination by Alypius...

Ambrose defied an empress, and this moved Augustine, and gave weight to his teaching on theology. He was an orthodox Catholic. He believed in the Incarnation, anathema to the Manichaeans. On the Church and the Old Testament he impressed Augustine with the reason of his beliefs. Indeed Ambrose was a reasonable man and believed, as an 'informed conservative', that no one was required to sacrifice his God-given reason to accept the tenets of Christian belief.

Meanwhile his readings in the books of the Neoplatonists cleared Augustine's mind about a transcendental God. Plotinus, from whose works Victorinus had translated, believed in 'the Word', of which Heraclitus had spoken nine hundred years before, and which was a common Greek idea. Hence the attraction of the neoplatonic writings for well-read Christians. 'In the beginning was the Word,' said John, and it needed only one more step to Christ, '. . . and the Word was made flesh.' Was not one of the last recorded words of Socrates as Plato reported him: 'How can I say more unless I have the word of some divinity?' The notion is as fruitful today: 'In the beginning was a Mind which spoke.'

Wise old Simplicianus, Ambrose's assistant, shrewdly picked up the point when Augustine sought his counsel, and mentioned that he had been reading Victorinus' translations. He told vividly the story of the great Roman rhetorician's confession of Christ. Augustine's strong flair for story-telling leaves us with two vivid vignettes of Simplicianus and Victorinus, two men of choice quality adorning this last half-century of Rome.

Full of 'fightings and fears without within', Augustine was carried on as though by some tide of events from this point onward. A fellow countryman from Africa, one Potitianus, called in, and launched into a discussion on monastic living. He told of the conversion of two public officials. The tale of Saint Antony which had captured the two men on an afternoon's walk, deeply stirred Augustine with whom surrender to God had come to mean, quite unnecessarily, the renunciation of all secular living.

It was, he said, as if God was 'turning me round toward myself, taking me from behind my back, where, unwilling to look myself in the face, I had placed myself. He set me before my face.' There followed the famous story of the garden and the child's chant from over the wall. He is unable to tell it in one piece. He intrudes a long passage about the will. Why does it obey immediately if it is a case of tearing his hair and beating his brow, but, when bidden surrender itself, it has wondrous powers of resistance? But such was the tormented saint. He could not come to an act of committal without tortures of introspection. Mani was still playing the imp in his mind. It is a grand conclusion, and would have been more striking as literature could he have reached it with greater promptitude. But would it then have been as true an autobiography?

I

Last Hesitations

Grant to me, O God, to remember with gratitude to you, and to acknowledge your mercies to me. Let my bones be bathed in your love and say: 'Lord, who is like to you? You have torn my chains apart. Let me offer you the sacrifice of praise. I will tell you how you tore them apart.' And all who worship you when they hear, will say: 'Blessed be the Lord in heaven and earth. Great and wondrous is his name.' Your words had stuck fast to my inner heart, and I was walled around by you on every side. Of your life eternal I was now convinced, though I saw it blurred as in a mirror. Yet I had wholly ceased to doubt about an incorruptible substance from which all other substance came, nor did I desire to be made more certain of you, but more steadfast in you. In my daily life, all was flux, and my heart had to be purged from the old leaven. The Way, my Saviour himself, pleased me, but I still shrank from penetrating its narrow places. You put into my mind, and it seemed good in your sight, to go to Simplicianus, whom I thought a good servant of yours, and your grace was a light in him. I had heard that, from his youth, he was a devout Christian. He had now grown old. By reason of a long life spent to good purpose in following your way, he seemed to me to have experienced and learned much. So indeed he had. From such store, I wanted him to advise me, as I told him of my anxieties, what might be the proper way for one so troubled as I was to walk in your path.

I saw that the Church was full, and that one went this way and another that. I was concerned that I was living a worldly life, and a heavy load it was, now that those desires no longer fired me, as they used to do, with hope of honour and gain, so that I should endure so heavy a bondage. For beside your sweetness and the beauty of your house, which I loved, those thoughts no longer delighted me. But I was still enslaved by the love of woman, and the apostle did not forbid me to marry, though he did advise me to do better, wishing 'that all men were as he was.' But I, a weaker man, chose the softer place. Because of this alone I was in general confusion, weary and wasted with withering cares, constrained, as I was, against my will, to conform to a married life to which I was given up and bound. From the mouth of Truth itself I had heard that there were 'eunuchs who had made themselves thus for the kingdom of heaven's sake', but, said the Word, 'let him receive it who can.' Surely all men are vain in whom is not the knowledge of God, and who have not been able, 'from the good things which are visible to discover him who is good indeed.' But I was no longer in that vanity. I had risen above it, and by creation's universal witness, I had found you, our creator, and your Word, God together with you, and together one God, through whom you created all things. And there is another tribe of the wicked who, 'though they know God, have not honoured him as God, nor have shown gratitude.' Into this state also I had fallen, but your right hand upheld me, lifted me and placed me where I could grow healthy again. You said to man: 'See, the fear of the Lord is wisdom', and: 'Desire not to seem wise', because 'those who said they were wise turned out to be fools'. And I had now found the good pearl, and, with the sale of all I had, it should have been bought, but there I was hesitating.

II

Story of Victorinus

So I went to Simplicianus, the father in the faith of Bishop Ambrose, and loved by Ambrose as a father in the flesh. I

told him of the tangle of my wanderings. When I told him I
had read some Platonist books which Victorinus, once
a rhetorician of Rome, who 1 had heard had died a
Christian, had translated into Latin, he congratulated me for
not having fallen in with the writings of other philosophers,
'full of falsehoods and deceits after the fashion of this world's
thinking.' In the Platonists' books, he said, God and his
word are everywhere implied. Then, to urge me towards
Christ's humility (that which is 'hidden from the wise and
revealed to little ones') he mentioned Victorinus himself,
with whom, when he was in Rome, he had enjoyed a close
friendship. He told me a story about him which I must make
known, for it is greatly 'to the praise of your grace' and that
must be confessed to you. It tells how that most learned old
man, skilled supremely in all liberal learning, who had read
and judged so much philosophy, the teacher of so many
noble senators (as a mark of outstanding service, he had won
and received the honour this world's citizens count the
highest – a statue in the Roman forum), this man, right to the
time I mention, had been a worshipper of idols, a partaker in
sacrilegious ceremonial in common with almost all the
Roman nobility. Omens they breathed like the air and
'monstrosities of every kind, the barking Anubis who lifted
spear against Neptune, Venus and Minerva,' worshipping
the very ones Rome had once overcome... These cults the
aged Victorinus with his thundering eloquence had once
defended. But he did not blush to become a child of your
Christ, a newborn babe at your fount, submitting his neck to
the yoke of humility, and bending his brow to the reproach
of the cross. O Lord, you who 'have bowed the heavens,
come down, touched the mountains till they smoked', how
did you penetrate that breast? He read the Scriptures, said
Simplicianus, and most diligently sought out and perused all
Christian literature, and often said to Simplicianus, not in
public but in private and more as a friend: 'Understand that I
am already a Christian.' Simplicianus would reply: 'I shall
not believe it, nor number you among Christians until I see
you in Christ's church.' At this he would laugh and say: 'So
walls make Christians?' He often said that he was a
Christian, and Simplicianus always made the same reply,

while the quip about the walls was as frequently repeated. He was sensitive about offending his friends, arrogant demon-worshippers. He imagined that from their Babylonian dignity, as if 'from Lebanon's cedars which the Lord had not yet beaten down', hostility would avalanche upon him. Later, with reading and earnest thought, he gathered strength. He began to fear being denied by Christ 'before his holy angels if he feared to confess him before men.' He stood guilty in his own eyes of a grievous crime, that of being ashamed of the humbling sacraments of your Word. He had not, he reflected, been so ashamed of the blasphemous rites of arrogant demons, whom he had accepted along with all their arrogance. And so, abashed before the truth, he lost his shame before vanity. Suddenly and unexpectedly he said to Simplicianus: 'Let us go to church, I want to be made a Christian.' Simplicianus, not able to contain his joy, went with him. There he received his first instruction in the mysteries of the faith, and not long afterwards submitted his name for the regeneration of baptism, to Rome's astonishment and the joy of the Church. The proud saw it and were enraged. They 'gnashed their teeth and melted away.' But the Lord God was his servant's hope, and he paid no regard to empty, lying manifestations of madness.

At last when the hour was come for making open profession of faith (in Rome the custom was for those about to come into your grace to make it, in prescribed and memorised words, from a raised position in full view of the people) the priests offered Victorinus the opportunity to do so in greater privacy, as sometimes was allowed to those feeling nervous or fearful. He preferred, however, to make his profession of salvation in full view of the holy congregation. It was not salvation he taught, when he taught the art of speech, he said, but he proclaimed that profession publicly. How much less, therefore, should he fear your gentle flock, when he uttered your word, who in uttering his own words had not feared mad crowds. So when he rose up to make pronouncement, all who knew him (and who did not?) whispered his name to each other with a buzz of congratulation. There ran a suppressed murmur through all the congregation who rejoiced as one: 'Victorinus,

Victorinus.' Quickly they voiced their exultation when they saw him, and as quickly fell silent to hear him. He made profession of the true faith with outstanding boldness, and everyone would have drawn him to their heart. By their love and joy, that is what they did, and love and joy were the hands they used.

III

Pleasure and Pain

Good God! What goes on in a man that he should rejoice the more about the salvation of a soul despaired of, and freed from greater danger, than if hope had always been about him or his danger had been less? Indeed, you, too, merciful father, rejoice more about one who repents than over ninety and nine good people who have no need to repent. And it is always with joy that we hear of the wandering lamb brought home on the shepherd's rejoicing shoulders, and when the lost drachma is returned to your treasury, her neighbours sharing the rejoicing of the woman who found it. And the joy of a solemn church service makes for tears when the parable of the younger son is read aloud. 'He was dead and was alive again, lost and was found.' You rejoice over us and over your angels with holy love, for you are always the same, for you know in the same way all things, though they neither continue the same, nor follow the same pattern. What then goes on in the soul, when it is more delighted at finding or getting back what it loves than if it had always possessed it? So it always is with other things, too, and everything testifies loudly that so it is. The conquering general triumphs but he would not have won had he not fought, and the greater the peril in the battle, the greater the joy in the triumph. The storm tosses the sailors and threatens shipwreck. Sky and sea grow calm, and they rejoice greatly, because they were greatly afraid. A loved one is ill, and his pulse gives an ominous report. All who desire his recovery are sick at heart along with him. He recovers but does not yet walk with the strength he had. Yet there is joy such as there was not when earlier he walked in health and vigour. Men win by difficulty the very pleasures of human life, not only those which fall on us unexpectedly and without our planning, but also those set up by us and sought. There is no pleasure in eating and drinking, unless the discomfort of hunger and thirst precedes. Drunkards eat salt savouries to bring on an uncomfortable heat. Drinking quenches this with pleasure. It is also the custom that betrothed girls are not handed over forthwith, lest the husband holds cheap the bride given him for whom, held back, he has not sighed as a wooer. This holds true in base and contemptible joy, as well as in that which is lawful and permitted, in the sincerest honour of friendship and in the case of one who 'was dead and came back to life, was lost and found' – the greater the joy, the greater the preceding painfulness. What does this mean, O Lord, my God, when you are eternal joy to yourself, and some things around you continually rejoice in you? What does it signify that this one part of creation alternates between failure and success, manifold alienation and equal conciliation? Is this the way with them, and is this their lot, from the highest things of heaven to the lowest of earth, from angel to worm, from the first movement to the last – you have set in place all manner of good things, and all your holy works, each where it should be, accomplishing everything in its due season. Alas, for me, how high are you in the highest, how deep in the deepest! You never depart, yet scarce do we return to you!

IV

The Force of High Example

Come, Lord, act, stir us, call us back, kindle and seize us, be fragrant and sweet. Let us love and hasten. Do not many, out of a deeper hell of blindness than Victorinus was in, approach and return to you, and find enlightenment as they receive the light which, with its acceptance, gives 'power to become your sons'. If they be less well known abroad even they who do know them rejoice less with them, for when joy is shared with many, joy is fuller in each. They grow ardent and are fired each by the other. Then because they are known to many, to many also they are an influence for salvation, and many will follow the way they lead. Therefore those who have gone before, rejoice much in them because they do not rejoice with them alone. But banish the thought that in your habitation the persons of the rich should be received before the poor, or the noble before the ignoble. For 'you have chosen the weak things of the world to disconcert the strong, and the base things of this world and the despised you have chosen, and those things which are not, to reduce to nothing those which are.' Yet even that same 'least of your apostles' himself, through whose tongue those words were uttered, when Paulus the Proconsul, his pride conquered by the apostle's warfare, was put under the gentle yoke of your Christ and made a subject of the great king, he also, called Saul up till then, was pleased to be named Paul, in testimony of a victory so great. For the enemy is more truly overcome in one he holds more strongly, and through whom he holds many more. How much the more gratefully then was the heart of Victorinus valued, which the devil had held as an impregnable stronghold, and Victorinus' tongue by which mighty and sharp weapon he had put down many. So much the more abundantly was it fitting that your children should exult, because our king had bound the strong man, and because they saw his vessels taken from him and cleaned and made fit to honour you and 'serviceable to the Lord for every good work.'

V

Hindrances

As soon as your man Simplicianus had told me about Victorinus, I was all afire to do what he had done. This, in fact, was why Simplicianus told the story. And after he had added how, in the days of the Emperor Julian, Christians were forbidden to teach literature and rhetoric, a law which Victorinus obeyed, choosing rather to give up his wordy lecture-room than your word by which you make eloquent the tongues of the dumb, he seemed to me rather more fortunate than resolute, because he found thus an opportunity to be free only for you. For this I sighed, bound as I was, not by another's iron bond, but by my own iron will. My willingness the enemy held, and out of it had made a chain and bound me. Of a stubborn will is a lust made. When a lust is served, a custom is made, and when a custom is not resisted a necessity is made. It was as though link was bound to link (hence what I called a chain) and hard bondage held me bound. But a new will which was born in me to wish to worship and enjoy you, the only assured pleasure, was not yet strong enough to overcome the old will, strengthened as it was by age. So my two wills, one old, one new, one carnal, one spiritual, strove together, and by their discord tore my soul to shreds.

So I began to understand in my own experience what I had read, how 'the flesh lusts after the spirit and the spirit lusts after the flesh.' I was in both, though rather in that which I approved in myself than in that which I disapproved, for in the second I was less myself. Mostly I suffered it against my will, than acted willingly. Yet it was through me that custom had been made a stronger battler against me, because I had come willingly whither I should not have come. Who has a right to speak against it, if just punishment follows the sinner? Nor had I that excuse I used to make, that I was no longer forsaking the world to serve you because the knowledge of the truth was uncertain to me, for the truth was already certain. Still, in bondage to earth, I refused to fight for you and feared as much to be stripped of my encumbrances as one should fear to be bound by them.

So, as happens in a drowsiness, was I pleasantly loaded with the baggage of this world, and the thoughts I had in mind of you were like the struggles of those who want to wake up, but overcome by deep sleep are drowned in it again. And just as there is no one who wants to go on sleeping for ever (for in any sane man's judgment it is better to stay awake), still a man does often postpone shaking off sleep, when he feels a heavy lethargy through all his limbs, and in spite of himself is prone to doze again, when often it is time to rise, in just such a fashion, I was certain that it was better to surrender to your love than to give in to my desire. The former course pleased and convinced me; the latter seduced me and held me prisoner. I had no answer when you said: 'Sleeper arise. Stand up from the dead, and Christ will give you light.' Though you showed me on every side that what you said was true, though convinced of that truth, I had nothing at all to answer other than some dull and drowsy words: 'Soon', 'Coming soon', 'Leave me just a little'. But my 'little while' stretched on and on. In vain I delighted in your law 'after the inward man, while another law in my members rebelled against the law of my mind and led me captive under the law of sin which was in my members.' That law of sin is the violence of custom, by which the mind of man is dragged prisoner even against its will, but deservedly because willingly it slides into it. 'Wretched man, then, who should deliver me from this dead body, save it be by your grace through Jesus Christ our Lord?'

VI

Ponticianus on Antonius

And how you delivered me from the bondage of sexual desire, by which I was held in tightest servitude, and from the slavery of worldly business, I will now narrate, with confession to your name, my helper and redeemer. I was doing my common tasks with growing tension, daily sighing to you. I would go to church whenever I was free from those tasks under whose burden I groaned. Alypius was with me, free now from his legal business after a third term as assessor, and awaiting a new clientele – just as I made a business of my rhetorician's skills, if indeed they can be taught. Nebridius had agreed to our friendly requests to lecture for Verecundus, a very close friend of all of us, a citizen and teacher of literature in Milan. On the score of friendship he asked urgently for loyal aid from our number, and he stood in great need of it. So no desire for advantage drew Nebridius to this task, for, had he so wished, he might have made more by literature, but being a very kind and gentle friend, as a duty of kindness, he was amenable to our request. He did so with the utmost discretion, wary of reputation among those called great in this world and avoiding what is found with them, disquiet of mind. He wanted his mind to be free, and at leisure for as many hours as possible for seeking, reading, hearing about wisdom.

And so one day (I do not recall why Nebridius was absent) one Ponticianus, our countryman, as an African, a man in high office in the imperial court, called on Alypius and me. I forget his reason. We sat down together to talk. It happened that, upon a gaming table before us, he noticed a book. He took it and opened it, quite unexpectedly finding it to be the apostle Paul. He had thought it would be one of the books I was wearing myself out teaching. Smiling and looking intently at me, he expressed pleasure and wonder that he had come upon that book only in my reach. He was a Christian and a faithful one too, who was often on his face before God in long and frequent prayers. When I told him I was spending much time in the study of those writings, he told the story of Antonius, the Egyptian monk, whose name shone brightly among your servants, but was unknown to us until that hour. When he discovered this, he prolonged the conversation, informing us about so great a man and wondering at our ignorance of him. We were astonished to hear of your wonderful works, so amply attested within

recent memory, indeed, near our own times, in the true faith
and the Catholic Church. We all wondered – we, to hear that
those works were so remarkable, he, because we had never
heard of them.

The conversation moved on to the monastery congregations and their ways, a sweet savour to you, and the fruitful
deserts of the wilderness of which we knew nothing. At the
time there was a monastery at Milan, full of good brethren,
outside the city walls under the supervision of Ambrose, and
we did not know about it. He went on with his tale at length,
and we listened with silent attention. He told us then how,
one afternoon at Trier, when the emperor was watching the
chariot races, he and three companions had gone out for a
walk in the gardens close to the city walls. There, as they
chanced to stroll in pairs, one walking apart with him and
the other two likewise together, they chanced upon a
cottage, where lived some of your servants 'poor in spirit, of
whom is the kingdom of heaven.' There they found a little
book on the life of Antonius. One of them began to read it in
wonder and excitement, and while he was reading to
consider laying hold of such a life himself, and leaving his
secular employment, to serve you. These men were officers
called 'civil servants'. Then, on a sudden, filled with holy love
and sober shame, angry with himself, he looked at his friend
and said: 'Tell me, please, what goal do we wish to attain by
all these labours of ours? What are we seeking? What are we
striving for? Can our hope in Court rise higher than to be the
emperor's friends? And in that place what is there that is not
brittle and full of danger? And through how many dangers
do we reach the greater danger? How long will that take? But
if I so will, see, now I can become the friend of God.' So he
spoke and travailing with the birth of his new life, he turned
his eyes to the book again. He read on and was transformed
in that inner part where you can see. His mind was stripping
off the world, as soon became apparent. While he read and
storm raged in his heart, he groaned, and with clear vision
determined on better things. Now yours, he said to his
friend: 'Now I have torn myself free from that hope we had,
and I have decided to serve God. This, from this hour, in this
place, I undertake. For you, if you do not care to imitate me,

do not oppose me.' The other replied that he would join him
to share such great reward, such great service. Both, now
yours, began to build a tower at the cost such a tower costs,
that of leaving their all behind and following you. Then
Ponticianus and his companion, who were wandering in
other parts of the garden, came looking for them. They
found them and suggested going home, for the afternoon
was passing. The others, telling of their resolution and
decision, and how such a desire had grown and taken root in
them, begged that they would not be annoyed with them if
they refused to accompany them. Ponticianus and his friend,
unchanged though they were from their former ways, yet
wept for them, he said, congratulated them, and commended
themselves to their prayers. Drawing their hearts earthward
they went back to Court. The other two lifting their hearts
heavenward stayed in the cottage. Both were engaged to be
married. Their intended wives, when they heard the story,
also dedicated their virginity to you.

VII

The Effect of the Story

This was Ponticianus' story. But you, Lord, while he was
speaking, were twisting me round to look at myself, taking
me from behind my back, where I had set myself, when I had
no wish to see what I looked like. You planted me face to face
with myself to make me see how vile I was, bent, dirty,
bespattered and full of sores. I looked and loathed myself
but there was nowhere where I could escape myself. And as I
tried to turn my eyes from myself, he went on and on telling
his tale. Upon this again you put me face to face with myself,
and pressed me upon my own eyes, that I might find iniquity
and loathe it. I knew it, pretended not to see it, held back and
forgot.

Then, indeed, the more warmly I approved those about

whose healthy emotions I was hearing, for they had handed themselves over to you to be healed, so much the more did I detest and hate myself in comparison with them. Many of my years (some twelve, I think) had flowed away since my nineteenth year, when, after reading Cicero's 'Hortensius', I had been stirred to the study of wisdom. And I was still postponing the rejection of earthly happiness, and the giving of myself to the search for that, whose mere pursuit, not necessarily its finding, is to be preferred to all the treasures and kingdoms of men ever found, and all the pleasures of the body though flowing round me at a word of command. But I, most wretched youth, and more wretched at my youth's beginning, had even sought chastity at your hands and said: 'Give me chastity and self-control but not yet', for I was afraid you might quickly hear me from afar, and swiftly heal me from the malady of lust, which I preferred to be sated rather than extinguished. And I had wandered along wicked ways through an unholy superstition, not, indeed, assured that it was right, but preferring it to the others which I did not honourably seek, indeed which I maliciously opposed.

I thought I was deferring from day to day the despising of this world's aspiration and the wholehearted following of you, because there did not appear to be any certain goal to which to direct my course. But now came the day when I was to be stripped bare before my eyes, and my conscience was to rebuke me: 'Where is your tongue? Assuredly you used to say that it was because of uncertainty about the truth that you were unwilling to throw off the pack of vanity. Look, certainty has now appeared, and the pack is still on your back. Those who have not so worn themselves out with seeking, nor spent a decade or more in thinking it over, with freer shoulders are receiving wings.' Thus was my heart gnawed, and I was strongly confounded with an awful shame, while Ponticianus was saying these things. When he had finished the story, and concluded the business for which he had come, he left, and for me what did I not say to myself? With what scourges of condemnation did I not lash my soul, to make it follow me, as I strove to follow you. It dragged back, refused, but gave no excuse. All its arguments were spent and refuted. Only a silent trembling was left, and it feared like death to be restrained from that way of life by which it was wasting away to death.

VIII

Strife in The Garden

Then in that mighty conflict of my inner dwelling place, which I had strongly stirred up in the chamber of my heart, troubled in both face and mind, I assailed Alypius. I cried: 'What is wrong with us? What is this you have heard? The unlearned rise and take heaven by storm, and we, with our learning, see where we wallow in flesh and blood. Are we ashamed to follow because others have gone ahead, and not ashamed not to follow at all?' Some such words I said, and my fever tore me away from him while he, looking at me with astonishment, said nothing. I did not sound like myself. Forehead, cheeks, eyes, colour, the level of my voice gave expression to my mind more than the words I uttered. A small garden was attached to our dwelling, and we had freedom to use it, as indeed, the whole house, for the master of the house, our host, did not live on the premises. To the garden, the tempest in my breast snatched me. There no one would hinder the fiery disputation I had begun against myself until its consummation, known already to you, but not to me. I was only healthily mad, dying in order to live, knowing what an evil thing I was, but not knowing what good thing I was about to be. So I went off into the garden with Alypius following close behind. His presence did not make my privacy the less, and how could he desert me in so disturbed a state? We sat as far away from the house as we could. I groaned in spirit, tempestuously indignant that I was not surrendering to your will and covenant, my God, and which all my bones, praising it to high heaven, called out to me to do. Not only to go there, but also to arrive, asked for no more than the will to go. The way was not by ships, carriages or feet. It was not so far from the house as the place to which we had gone where we were sitting. It required no more than the will to go there, a resolute and thorough act of will, not to toss and turn this way and that, a half-maimed will, struggling, one half rising, one half sinking.

In the wild passions of my irresolution, I did with my body what people sometimes want to do but cannot, either lacking the limbs, their limbs in chains, weakened by weariness, or otherwise impeded. If I tore my hair, beat my brow, clasped my knee with knitted fingers, it was because I wanted to do so. Yet I could have wanted to, and not done so, if my limbs had not been pliable enough to do my will. So much then I did when to will was not in itself to be able. And I did not what I both longed immeasurably more to do, and which soon, when I should will, I should be able to do, because soon, when I should will, I should will thoroughly. In such case power and will coincide, and willing is forthwith doing. And yet it was not done, and my body obeyed more easily the weakest willing of my mind, moving limbs as it directed, than my soul obeyed itself to carry out in the will alone, this great will which should be done.

IX

The Problem of the Will

What causes this appalling situation? And why? Let your mercy but give me light, and I should put the question, if it so be that the hidden punishments of men and the darkest tribulations of Adam's sons should chance to have an answer for me. Whence and why this monstrosity, say I? The mind commands the body and the body forthwith obeys. The mind commands itself and is resisted. The mind commands that the hand move itself and such is its readiness that there is scarce a break between the command and its execution. Yet the mind is mind and the hand is body. The mind commands the mind to will. It is the same thing, but it does not. Whence and why again? It commands I say, that it will and would not command unless it willed, and yet what it commands is not done. But it wills not entirely, and so it follows that it does not command entirely. It commands to the extent that it wills, and the command is not done in so far as the will falls short. The will commands that there be a will, not another, but itself. But it does not command fully, and so the thing it commanded is not done. For if the will were fully engaged it would not command it to be, it would be already. It is not, therefore, a monstrosity partly to will and partly not to will, but a malady of the mind? It does not wholly rise, but is uplifted by truth, borne down by habit. Therefore there are two wills: one of them is not whole, and what the one lacks the other has.

X

More on the Will

Let them perish from your sight, God, as indeed they do, those empty talkers and seducers of the mind, who, because they have observed that in an act of deliberation two wills operate, assert that there are two minds in us of two kinds, one good, one evil. Truly, they are evil, when they hold these evil ideas. And the same people shall become good if they hold the truth and consent to it, that the apostle's words may apply to them: 'You were once darkness but are now light in the Lord.' For those people, in their desire to be light, in themselves but not in the Lord, supposing the nature of the soul to be what God is, are thus made darkness more dense by the shocking arrogance of their withdrawal from you – from you, 'the true light that lights every man who comes into the world.' Take heed what you say and blush for it. Draw near to him and be enlightened, and your faces will not show your shame. When I deliberated about serving my

Lord God, as I had long had in mind to do, it was I, I myself, who willed and who willed not. I neither willed wholly nor wholly willed not. So I strove with myself and was torn apart by myself. And that rending came about against my will, but demonstrated not the presence of another mind, but the punishment of my own. So 'it was no more I that worked it but sin which dwells in me', the punishment of a sin more willingly committed, because I was a son of Adam.

For if there are as many contrary natures in man as there are contesting wills, there will be not merely two but many. Suppose a man should be turning over in his mind whether he should go to the Manichaean chapel or to the theatre, they cry: 'Look, two natures, a good one pulling this way, the other, a bad one, pulling that. Whence else this hesitation between conflicting wills?' My answer is that both these wills are bad, both that which pulls in their direction, and that which drags back to the theatre. They do not believe that to be other than a good will which leads to them. Suppose one of us should be turning it over in his mind, tossed about by the strife of two contesting wills, whether he should go to the theatre or to our church, will they not be in difficulties about the answer? Either they must confess (which they have no desire to do) that the good will prompts the visit to our church, as it is in them who, as partakers in their sacraments and held by them, go to their church meeting, or else they must suppose two evil natures and two evil souls at conflict in one man, and their customary affirmation that there be one good, another bad, will not be true. Otherwise they must be converted to the truth and not deny, that in the act of deliberation one soul is distracted between two contrary wills.

Let them no more say then that, when they are conscious of two conflicting wills in one man, there are two contrary minds made of two contrary substances, derived from two contrary principles, one good, one bad, in strife. For you, true God, refute, contradict, convict them – as when, both wills being bad, a man deliberates whether he should kill another by poison or the knife, whether he should seize this estate or that belonging to someone else when he cannot seize both, whether he should buy pleasure by extravagance or greedily keep his cash, whether he should go to the races or the theatre if both be available on the same day. I add a third example, to rob another's house if the chance offers, or fourthly to commit adultery if the opportunity simultaneously appears, if all these situations came at exactly the same time and all are equally desired, but cannot at the same time be done ... Four different wills or, in the vast variety of things desirable, even more, are in conflict each with each and tear the mind apart, yet they do not commonly say that there are four different substances. So, too, in the case of good wills. I ask them whether it is a good thing to take delight in reading the apostle, to be delighted by a solemn psalm or to expound the gospel. To each question they will answer: 'Yes'. What if all these give equal pleasure, and all at the same time? Do not different wills distract the heart of man while he is considering which he should rather lay hold of? All are good, yet stand in rivalry until one is chosen, by which act the whole will is set at rest though heretofore divided? So, too, when eternity delights us above, and when below the pleasure of earthly good holds us back, it is the same soul which wills neither with completeness. That is why it is pulled apart with heavy trouble, while, because of truth it puts one alternative first, but because of habit does not set the other aside.

XI

The Inner Conflict

So sick was I and in agony of mind, accusing myself much more sharply than my habit was, writhing and twisting in my chain until that should be broken which bound me. It still held me though its grip was weakening. Yet, Lord, you pressed upon my inner person, in severe mercy doubling the lashes of fear and shame, lest I should slip back again, and that small, thin fetter which remained should not be snapped, but should gather strength again and bind me more firmly. And I was murmuring to myself: 'Look, let it be done now, done now'. As I said the word I almost did it – almost did it, yet did it not. Yet I did not quite go back to that which was, but stood nearer and gathered breath. I tried again, and little by little got nearer and all but touched and laid hold of it. Yet I was not quite there to touch and hold, hesitating to die to death and live to life, and the ingrained worse was more powerful in me than the unaccustomed better. And that very instant of time on which I was to be something different, the nearer it drew to me, the greater dread did it beat into me, though it did not beat me back nor turn me aside. It only held me in suspense.

The trifles of trifles, the worthless amid the worthless, past objects of my affections, were what was holding me, pulling at the garment of my flesh and whispering: 'Are you sending us away? From this moment we shall not be with you for eternity? And from this moment you will not be permitted to do this and that for ever?' And what did they suggest by my 'this and that', my God? Let your mercy turn it away from your servant's soul. What impurities, what acts of shame they suggested. But by now I was much less than half hearing them, and they were not so openly meeting me on the path and contradicting me, but rather muttering behind my back, and furtively tugging at my cloak to make me look back, as I made away from them. Yet they did hold me back from tearing myself away and shaking them off, and leaping over to the place to which I was called, while a violent habit cried: 'Do you think you can live without them?'

It was speaking very faintly by now. For on that side to which I had set my face and which I trembled to approach appeared clear the chaste dignity of Continence. Serene was she, not carelessly merry, honourably alluring me to come and not to doubt, and stretching out to receive and to embrace me, holy hands, full of hosts of good examples. With her were so many boys and girls, a multitude of youth and every age, grave widows, aged virgins, and Continence herself in every one of them, by no means childless, but the fertile mother of children and of joys from you her husband, Lord. And she was smiling at me with an encouraging smile saying as it were: 'Will you not be able to do what these youths and maidens have done? And are any of these or those able so to do save it be in the Lord, their God? The Lord their God gave me to them. Why do you stand in your own strength, and so fail to stand? Cast yourself fearlessly on him. He will not pull back and let you fall. Cast yourself on him without a care. He will receive and heal you.' I was blushing the more for I still could hear the whisperings of those trifles, and I was hanging back. And again she seemed to say: 'Make yourself deaf to those unclean members of yours, and let them die. They tell you of delights but not according to the law of the Lord your God.' Such was the controversy in my heart, nothing but myself against myself. Alypius, sitting by my side, was silently awaiting the outcome of my extraordinary agitation.

XII

Climax

A strong surge of thought dredged from my secret depths and cast up all my misery in a heap before my inner eye. A mighty tempest arose bearing a great storm of tears. To shed it with befitting speech, for to be alone seemed the better state for weeping, I rose from Alypius' side, and withdrew some distance, so that even his presence should not be an embarrassment to me. Thus I thought, and he was sensitive. I think I had earlier said something in which the sound of my voice made it clear that I was heavy with tears. I thus arose, while he stayed where we had been sitting, greatly amazed. I flung myself carelessly down under some fig tree, and let the reins of weeping go. The streams of my eyes broke forth, a sacrifice acceptable to you. I said to you, in words something like these: 'And you, O Lord, how long, how long? Will you be angry for ever? Remember not past iniquities.' For I felt I was in their grip and I cried out in lamentation: 'How long, how long, tomorrow and tomorrow? Why not now? Why not an end to my vileness in this hour?'

Such were my words and I wept in the bitter contrition of my heart. And, see, I heard a voice from a neighbouring house chanting repeatedly, whether a boy's or a girl's voice I do not know: 'Pick it up and read it, pick it up and read it'. My countenance changed, and with the utmost concentration I began to wonder whether there was any sort of game in which children commonly used such a chant, but I could not remember having heard one anywhere. Restraining a rush of tears, I got up, concluding that I was bidden of heaven to open the book and read the first chapter I should come upon. I had heard of Antonius that from a public reading of the gospel he had chanced upon, he had been commanded as if what was read was said especially to him: 'Go, sell all that which you have, give it to the poor, and you shall have treasure in heaven, and come and follow me', and that by such a word from God, he had been immediately converted to you. Excitedly then I went back to the place where Alypius was sitting, for there I had put down the apostle's book when I got up. I seized it, opened it and immediately read in silence the paragraph on which my eyes first fell: '...not in the ways of banqueting and drunkenness, in immoral living and sensualities, passion and rivalry, but clothe yourself in the Lord Jesus Christ, and make no plans to glut the body's lusts...' I did not want to read on. There was no need. Instantly at the end of this sentence, as if a light of confidence had been poured into my heart, all the darkness of my doubt fled away.

Putting my finger or some other mark in the page, I shut the book and with a calm face now I told Alypius, and he thus made known to me what had taken place in his heart unknown to me. He asked to see what I had read. I showed him. He read on, and I did not know what followed. It was this: 'Let the weak in faith receive.' He took it to himself and showed it to me, and by such admonition he was given strength, and to that resolution and purpose without any stormy hesitation he applied himself along with me. This was most like him, for his was a character which had long been much, much better than mine. Then we went inside to my mother, and told her to her joy. We told her the course of events. She rejoiced triumphantly, and blessed your name, 'who are able to do above all that we ask or think.' She saw that you had given her so much more concerning me than she had sought with her pitiful and tearful lamentations. You converted me to yourself, so that I no longer sought a wife nor any hope in this world, standing on that rule of faith in which so many years before you had shown me to her. You changed her grief to joy, more richly than she had desired of you, and a joy more cherished and chaster than she sought from grandchildren of my body.

BOOK NINE

Requiem for Monica

Introduction

It followed from Augustine's view of conversion that he should abandon his profession of rhetoric. It crosses the reader's mind that rhetoric could well be taught by a Christian. Speech and logic are not immoral. It is a matter of how they are used. The suspicion lurks that the new convert sought a low profile. He would teach to the end of term in deference to his students. His increasing asthma, too, was making the classroom difficult. He disliked exhibitionism ... All perhaps true.

At any rate, Verecundus had a villa fifty miles away and Augustine and his friends borrowed it for a protracted house party. He became lost in admiration of the Psalms, thought and wrote much amid endless philosophical and theological discussion. It was a rich and invigorating experience. He gave a future public much over this productive period. King Alfred of England translated one of these books, the *Soliloquies*, a measure of the Latinity of the Wessex monarch.

It is clear from much of this writing that the neoplatonists had vitally penetrated Augustine's thought. And why not? Many a Christian classicist has taken delight in the outreaching for ultimate truth in Greek philosophy and especially in Plato. Truth is indivisible and Christ is Truth. Hence the mainspring of his anger against the Manichaeans which appears in this book.

Historically, Book Nine is an interesting glimpse into the Christian Church in the last half century of the Empire. Had it become predominantly middle class? Save for some philosophical reflections on the spurious happiness of a drunken beggar in Book Eight, Augustine's picture of life in the Church and amid the intelligentsia of Milan gives no

notion of the proletariat. Indeed, in all the writings of early
Christianity, apart from the New Testament itself, are the
people of the streets, the trades, the humbler business world
and the slums, to be seen clearly at all?

We learn a little of Monica, soon to die, of her childhood,
her unhappy married life up to Patricius' muted conversion,
and her counselling activities among similarly afflicted
matrons. She had set her heart on returning to Africa after
Augustine's baptism, along with Adeodatus and Alypius, by
Ambrose at Easter 387. The party was on its way and had
paused at Ostia. Here leaning on a window-sill Augustine
heard his mother confess her content. Life had at last given
her all she desired. She was ready to go.

There followed a curious neoplatonist vision of ultimate
beauty, which Monica allegedly shared with her son. It is not
likely that her formal and matter-of-fact mind rose to such
mystic ecstasies, but Augustine liked thus to remember that
brief hour of contemplative delight. A few days later she died
of some feverish illness. The main road traversed the
unhealthy lowlands of the coastal marches, and she no
doubt contracted some infection there. She was in her fifty-
sixth year.

Augustine, commonly quick to tears, is proud of the fact
that he went through her funeral dry-eyed. Adeodatus was
rebuked for weeping. Grief was no doubt considered a denial
of faith. Socrates checked some tearful lamentation at his
deathbed. The Stoics rose above such weakness. Jesus wept,
and Augustine might well have remembered it.

He concluded with a sombre prayer for Monica's soul.
True, she was a lifelong Christian. Hers had been a faithful
life. She was baptised and therefore 'born again'. But what of
the sins she had committed since that saving event?
Augustine had no 'assurance'.

Ostia is an important archaeological site, which has been
extensively investigated. Many wealthy nobles had villas
there, including it seems, the Anicii, one of the great
Christian families of Rome. Augustine, as a convert of the
great Ambrose, may have stayed in one of these seaside
houses. There are warehouses and baths (whither Augustine
went because of a superstition that a bath assuaged grief),

the church, and much else which leaves a vivid impression of the busy port. In 1945 a fragment of Monica's epitaph was found by accident. Two schoolboys were digging a hole for a goalpost.

I

Exordium of Praise

O Lord, I am your servant and the son of your handmaid.
You have torn my chains apart. I will offer you the sacrifice
of praise. Let my heart and tongue praise you and all my
bones cry out: 'Lord who is like you?' Let them cry out, and
do you answer me and say: 'I am your salvation.' Who am I,
and what manner of man? What evil have my deeds not been,
or, failing my deeds, my words, and, failing words, my will?
But you, Lord, are good and merciful. Your right hand
observing the depth of my death, drained to the bottom of
my heart the abyss of its corruption. This amounted to the
utter rejection of my own will and the acceptance of yours.
Where, through that span of years was my free will, and from
what deep, low hiding-place was it summoned up in a
moment of time, so that I should bow my neck to your light
yoke, and my shoulders to your easy burden, Christ Jesus,
my aid and my redeemer? How joyous it suddenly became to
me to forgo the varied sweetness of trifles I feared to lose,
and now was glad to fling aside. For you, true, supreme
sweetness, cast them out of me, and in their place came into
me, sweeter than all pleasure (though not to flesh and
blood), brighter than all light, deeper than all depths, higher
than all honour (though not to the high in their own conceit).
Now was my mind free from those gnawing anxieties of
seeking, getting, wallowing and scratching at the mange of
lust. And I babbled like a babe to you, my fame, my wealth
and health, my Lord God.

II

Abandonment of Rhetoric

I made up my mind, under your eye, gently to withdraw the service of my tongue from the loquacity trade. I preferred this to snatching it away in a wild hurry. Students – not students in your law, nor in your peace but of mad mendacity and courtroom strife – should no longer buy from my mouth the weapons of their recklessness. It happened most fortunately that there were very few days left till the autumn vacation. Those days I decided to endure in order to retire with dignity, and, bought out by you, no longer put myself up for sale. My purpose then was known to you, but not generally save to close friends with whom it was agreed not to publicise the matter. To me, climbing upwards in the valley of tears, and singing a 'song of degrees', you had given sharp arrows and coals of fire to arm me against any subtle tongue which, in guise of counselling, should speak against me, eating me up, as it were, by love, as one commonly eats food.

You had shot my heart through with the arrows of your love, and I carried your words thrust deep into my inner being. The examples of your servants, ones whom you had transformed from darkness to light, and from death to living, stored away in the depth of my thought, were burning and consuming the heavy torpor by which we might have slid down into the pit. They fired us with such heat that every blast of contradictory speech from a subtle tongue could only blow the flame to sharper heat, not put it out. However, since for the sake of your name which you had made holy throughout the earth, we had those who commended our wish and resolve, I judged it ostentatious not to wait for the vacation when it was so near, but immediately to abandon a public profession which everyone could see. The result would be that everyone, observing my resignation so near the end of term would have much to say about my desire for notoriety. What good would it have done me to have people thinking and arguing about what I had in mind, and to have what good I did evil spoken about?

There was this fact, too, that in that same summer, as a result of my literary toil, my lungs began to give out. I found breathing difficult, and pains in the chest told their own tale of damage, refusing clearer or more prolonged speaking. It had at first worried me because it was compelling me almost without option to put down the burden of my profession, or certainly to leave it for a while, if I was to recover my health. But as soon as the desire to abandon my work arose and became confirmed in me, and to see that you are Lord, you know, my God, how I began to be glad that this perfectly genuine excuse had come up, to moderate the general hostility of those who would never have me free for their sons' sake. So, filled with this satisfaction, I endured it until that span of time (some twenty days) ran out, courageously, because covetousness, which used to help me carry the heavy load, had ebbed, and I should have been deeply depressed had not patience taken its place. It is possible that some one of your servants, my brethren, would say I sinned in this that, now wholeheartedly committed to your warfare, I should have suffered myself to have occupied for even one hour, the chair of falsehood. I make no excuse. But, Lord most merciful, have you not pardoned and remitted this sin for me, among other atrocious and deadly ones, in the holy water?

III

Verecundus' Hospitality

Verecundus grew thin with stress over this our blessing, for being most firmly bound by his own impediments, he saw himself deprived of our fellowship. He was not yet a Christian, though his wife was a believer. Yet, in fact, it was by her, a tighter fetter than all the rest, that he was hindered from the journey that we had undertaken. And yet, he kept saying, that he would not be a Christian on any other terms than those he could not yet meet. Yet he kindly offered us the use of his country-house for as long as we wished. You will reward him, Lord, in the resurrection of the just. Indeed you have already give him that lot. In our absence in Rome he was seized with a sudden illness, during which he became a Christian and a believer, and departed this life. And so 'you had pity, not on him only but on us also', lest, remembering the lovingkindness of our friend towards us, and not numbering him among your flock, we should be tortured with grief intolerable. Thanks be to you our God. We are yours. So say your voices of encouragement and consolation. You, whose promises are true will repay Verecundus for his country house of Cassiciacum, where we found rest in you from the fever of the world, and the loveliness of your fresh green Paradise. You banished his earthly sins in that nourishing mountain of yours, the mountain of abundance.

So Verecundus, at that time, was troubled, but Nebridius shared our happiness. He was not yet himself a Christian, for he had fallen into the pit of that most destructive error, believing, as he did, that the flesh of your Son's truth was a phantasm. He was extricating himself from this, though he was not as yet initiated into the sacraments of your Church. He was, however, an eager seeker for the truth. Not long after our conversion and regeneration by your baptism, a faithful member now of the Catholic church, serving you in final chastity and continence among his own folk in Africa (his whole family had been made Christian through him) you released him from the flesh and now he lives 'in Abraham's bosom'. Whatever is meant by that phrase, there my Nebridius lives, my sweet friend, your adopted son, a son out of a freedman, there he lives. What other place is there for such a soul? There he lives, a place about which he often questioned me, poor creature though I was and ignorant. No longer is his ear open to my mouth, but his soul's mouth is at your fountain and he drinks in as much wisdom as he can thirst for – endlessly happy. Yet I do not think he can be so drunken with it that he forgets me, since you, Lord, of whom he drinks, are mindful of me. Such then we were consoling a

sorrowful Verecundus, our friendship still intact after our
conversion. We bade him continue to honour his married
state. We were waiting for Nebridius to follow us. Being so
near he was about to do so, when the days I wrote about soon
slipped by. Many and long they seemed to me beside my love
for freedom and liberty to sing to you from my heart of
hearts. 'My heart has said to you: I have sought your face,
your face, Lord, I will seek.'

IV

Musings at Cassiciacum

The day came for me to be released from my Chair of
Rhetoric, from which in spirit I was already free. It was
done. You delivered my tongue from that which you had
already delivered my heart, and joyously I blessed you on the
way to the villa with all my household. My books bear
witness to what I did there in letters – now in your service but
still breathing out the airs of the proud school, as though this
were but a vacation. There were books argued over with
those at hand, or between you and me alone. My letters bear
testimony to the part in them Nebridius had, even when he
was not there. When would I have enough time to note down
all your great blessings bestowed on us at that time,
especially since I am hurrying on to tell of greater ones. My
memory prompts me (and sweet it is to me, Lord, to confess
to you) by what stings in my heart you tamed me, how you
smoothed me down, 'making low the mountains and hills' of
my imaginations, and 'straightening my crooked places and
making the rough places smooth'; also by what means you
brought into subjection to the name of your only begotten
son, our Lord and Saviour Jesus Christ, the brother of my
heart, Alypius, a matter on which at first he would not allow
me to write. He preferred those writings to savour rather of
the 'lofty cedars' of the schools which the Lord had smashed,

than of the wholesome herbs of the Church, antidotes for snakes.

My God, what cries I lifted up to you when I read the Psalms of David, faithful songs, sounds of devotion which shut out the puffed up spirit. I was a beginner in genuine love to you, a pupil taking holiday in the villa with my fellow pupil, Alypius. My mother was still with us, clothed as a woman but with a manly faith, tranquil as befitted her age, with a mother's love and Christian holiness. How I cried to you in the words of those psalms and how I was fired by them with love towards you, burning to sound them forth if that were possible to the whole world against the pride of humankind. In truth they were already sung all over the world and no one can find shelter from your heat.

With what strong sharp pain was I enraged against the Manichaeans. Yet, on the other hand, I was sorry for them, because they knew nothing of those healing sacraments and were insanely rejecting the antidote which could have made them whole. I could wish that they had been somewhere near me without my being aware of their presence, and could have watched my face and heard my voice when I read the fourth psalm, during that time of leisure. What that psalm did for me! 'When I called, the God of my righteousness heard me. You made space around me in my trouble. Have mercy on me, Lord, and hear my prayer.' Would they could hear without my knowing they could hear, so that they would not think I was speaking because of them. Indeed, I would not speak those words, nor in the same way, if I knew I was heard and seen by them. Nor, if I were to do so would they so accept them, for I was speaking with myself before your face, out of the natural disposition of my soul.

I shuddered with fear, Father, and at the same time was fired with hope and rejoicing at your mercy. And all this found exit through my eyes and voice, when your good spirit turned and said to us: 'Sons of men, how long will you be heavy of heart? Why do you cherish vanity and seek falsehood?' That, in fact, I had done. And you, Lord, had already made great your holy one, raising him from the dead, and setting him at your right hand, whence from on high he should send your promise, the Comforter, the Spirit of Truth.' He had already sent him without my knowing it. He had already sent him for he was now exalted, rising from the dead and ascending to heaven, for till then the Holy Spirit was not yet given, because Jesus had not yet been clearly set forth. And the prophecy cries: 'How long will you be heavy of heart? Why do you cherish vanity and seek falsehood? Know that the Lord has made great his holy one.' He cries out: 'How long?' He cries out: 'Know this.' And I was so long in my ignorance cherishing vanity, and seeking falsehood, and that is why I heard and trembled, for it was addressed to such people as I remembered myself to have been. In those phantasms I had once held for truth, there was vanity and falsehood. I called aloud earnestly and strongly, grieving at what I remembered. I wish they had heard, those who still cherish vanity and seek falsehood. Perhaps they would have been troubled and cast it from them, and you would have heard them when they cried to you. He died a true death in the flesh for us, he who makes intercession for us.

I went on reading: 'Be angry, but sin not.' How moved was I, my God, who had now learned to be angry with myself for things past, that I might not sin in what was yet to be. Yes, to be justly angry for it was not the 'other nature' of the tribe of darkness which sinned on my behalf, as they say who are not angry with themselves and so stored up anger for themselves in the day of anger, and the revelation of your just judgment. What I held good was no longer outside myself, nor was it sought by the body's eyes in yonder sun. Those who would find their happiness outside themselves fade easily away and dissipate their persons on the ephemeral things before their eyes. Hungry of heart they lick their shadows. If only, wearied with hunger, they would say: 'Who will show us good?' We would answer and they would hear: 'The light of your face is marked upon us.' We are not 'that light that gives light to every man who comes into the world.' Yet we are given light by you, so that we who were once darkness might become light in you. If they could only see the eternity within their hearts. I had tasted it, and I raged that I could not make them see it, if they should come to me with their wandering

heart in their eyes and say to me: 'Who will show us good?'
There it was, there in my room alone, where my heart was
challenged, there where I had made my sacrifice, offering up
what once I was with the consciousness of my life's renewal
begun in me and hoping in you, there, I say, you began to be
sweet to me, and give joy in my heart. I cried out as I read this
aloud, and felt it in my heart. I did not want to acquire more
earthly possessions, wasting the hours, and wasted by them,
when I had in eternal simplicity other corn, other wine and
oil.

 With a loud shout from my heart, I cried aloud in words of
the next verse: 'In peace!' If I could have that peace! What
did the psalmist say: 'I will go to rest and take my sleep', for
who shall stand against us when that saying comes to pass:
'Death is swallowed up in victory'? You, above all are that
which does not change, and in you is the rest which forgets
all labours, for there is none beside you. You, Lord, have
appointed me in hope alone not to seek those things which
have no part in you. I read on and my heart burned, but did
not discover what I should do for the deaf and the dead, of
whose number I had been, a thing diseased, a bitter blind
snarler against the Scriptures sweet with heaven's honey,
bright with your light. I was eaten up with zeal against the
foes of these Scriptures.

 When shall I recall everything about those days of
holiday? But I have not forgotten, nor shall I fail to speak
about the sting of your lash and the swiftness of your mercy.
You tormented me at that time with toothache. When it grew
so bad I was not able to speak, it came into my heart to beg
all my friends who were there to pray to you for me, God of
all manner of salvation. I wrote the request on wax and gave
it them to read. As soon as with humble devotion we fell
upon our knees, the pain fled. What pain? How did it go? I
confess that I was afraid, my Lord and my God. Since life's
beginning I had never known anything like it. The
movements of your will were planted deep within me, and
rejoicing in faith I praised your name. But that faith would
not allow me to be at peace about bygone things which were
not yet forgiven me by your baptism.

V

Ambrose Prescribes Reading

The autumn vacation was over, and I gave out to the people of Milan, that they should find another word-merchant, because I had chosen your service. Nor was I equal to the profession because of my breathing difficulty, and chest-pain. I wrote and told your bishop, the godly Ambrose about my past wanderings and present resolution, so that he should tell me what I should chiefly read of your Scriptures, to make me the readier and fitter to receive a grace so great. He advised the prophet Isaiah, because, I think, that beyond the rest he was a clearer foreshadower of the gospel and the calling of the Gentiles. I, however, not understanding what I read in the earlier chapters, and judging the rest by these, put him aside for later reading, when I should be more practised in the Lord's language.

VI

Baptism at Milan

When the time came for me to give in my name, we left the country and returned to Milan. Alypius decided to be born again in you along with me. He was clothed now in a humility befitting your sacraments. He was the strongest tamer of his body. He even trod barefooted Italy's frosty soil, an uncommon venture. We took with us the boy, Adeodatus, born of my flesh in my sin. You had made him well. He was near fifteen years of age, and in mental power excelled many serious and learned men. I acknowledge your gifts to you, my Lord God, creator of all things, most potent to reform all our deformities, for apart from sin, I had no part in that boy. That he was brought up by us in your discipline, was your inspiration and of no other. Your gifts I acknowledge. There is a book of mine called 'The Master', a dialogue between him and me. The ideas are all his, and appear under the name of my companion in the discourse when he was about sixteen years old. I knew of many other astonishing facts about him. His intelligence was awesome to me. Who apart from you can be the designer of such wonders? Soon you plucked his life from the earth and I remember him without anxiety, for I fear for nothing in his childhood or youth or in his whole person. We took him along with us, the same age in grace, to be brought up in your teaching. We were baptised and anxiety over our former living fled. In those days I could not have enough of the wondrous sweetness of pondering the depth of your plan for man's salvation. How I wept over hymns and psalms, moved to the depths by the voices of your Church at song. Those voices flowed into my ears, truth seeped into my heart, the emotion of devotion surged up, my tears flowed and happy was I in that fellowship.

VII

Persecution Averted

The Milan congregation had not long begun this style of worship and devotion, with great zeal among the brethren singing with heart and voice together, when, after a year or so, Justina, the mother of the boy emperor, Valentinianus, began to persecute your servant, Ambrose. It concerned her particular heresy into which she was seduced by the Arians. The faithful congregation kept continuous watch in the church, ready to die with your servant the bishop. There your handmaid my mother, bearing a leading part in those anxieties and vigils, lived on her prayers. We, still unkindled by the heat of your spirit, were none the less deeply stirred by the disquieted and troubled city. It was then that the custom common in the eastern churches of singing hymns and psalms was established, so that the people should not grow faint, outwearied by sorrow. It has been kept up to this day with many, indeed almost all your congregations worldwide, doing the same.

It was at that time that you made known to your servant whom I have named, where the bodies of Protasius and Gervasius, the martyrs, lay. You had kept them secretly stored uncorrupted in your hiding-place for many years, to bring them out at the proper time to check the imperial dowager's madness. With due honour they were dug up and transferred to Ambrose's basilica. Not only were those troubled by unclean spirits healed, as the evil presences confessed themselves, but a well-known citizen who had been many years blind, asked and heard the reason for the popular excitement. He jumped up and asked his guide to take him there. Led there he begged and won permission to touch with his handkerchief the casket of your saints, whose death is precious in your sight. He did this, placed it to his eyes, and they were immediately opened. Your praises glowed and shone as the fame of it spread. Thus the mind of that hostile woman, though not brought to the health of faith, was checked from its rage of persecution. Thanks to you, my God. Whence and whither have you led my memory that I should thus confess to you great things which I might have forgetfully passed over? Yet then, when the odour of your ointments was so fragrant, we did not pursue you. So the more I wept at the singing of your hymns, then sighing for you and breathing you, as far as the air is free to breathe in this house of straw.

VIII

Monica's Upbringing

You who make men of one mind to live together, brought Euodius, a young man from our own provincial town, to be our guest. A civil servant, he was converted to you and baptised before we were. Leaving the world's warfare he donned your armour. We were together, and were intending to share our dwelling in our holy calling. We were looking for the place where we might most usefully serve you, and together we went back to Africa. When we were at Ostia-on-Tiber, my mother died. I pass over much for I am in a hurry. Accept my confessions and thanksgivings, my God, for numberless matters left unsaid, but I will not pass by whatever my soul brought forth from that handmaid of yours who brought forth me, both in the flesh into this world of time, and in the spirit so that I should be born into eternal light. I shall not speak about her gifts, but of yours in her, for she neither created nor reared herself. You created her, for neither mother nor father knew what sort of person should be made from them, and it was the sceptre of Christ, the rule of your only Son, which shaped her in a Christian home, a good member of your Church. Yet she commended for her Christian education, not so much her mother's care, as that of an aged serving-woman who had carried her father round as a baby as little boys used to be carried on the backs of older girls. That was why, because of her old age and excellent character, she was held in high regard by her masters in a Christian home, and managed carefully the task of looking after its daughters. She disciplined them firmly when they needed discipline, strong with a godly firmness, and a reserved wisdom in teaching them. For example, except at those hours when they were most temperately fed at their parents' table, she would not allow them, even when parched with thirst, even to drink water. It was thus she forestalled a bad habit, adding a wise word: 'You are drinking water now because you have no wine, but when you are married and become mistresses of your own cellars and cupboards, you will scorn water, but the drinking-habit will stay with you.' By such teaching and the authority of her command she held in the greediness of younger years, and so shaped the very thirst of the girls towards moderation, that anything improper no longer appealed to them.

Yet, as your handmaid told me her son, there crept upon her a love of wine. For when, as the manner is, a responsible girl was bidden by her parents to draw wine from the cask, with the jug under the open tap, before she poured the wine, she would taste a little with the tip of her lips, her conscience forbidding more. It was not done out of drunken desire, but rather out of the ridiculous and daring indiscipline of youth, commonly kept under control, in those earlier years, by the authority of their elders. So with the daily addition of another 'daily little' (for whoever scorns 'little' falls 'little by little') she fell into the custom of greedily gulping cups almost full of wine. Where then was the wise old woman with her strong prohibition? Is anything strong enough against a hidden malady, Lord, unless we are under the guard of your medicine? Father, mother, guardians were not there. But you were there, the creator who calls us, and sets over us the good folk through whom you work for our soul's salvation. What did you do then, my God? Whence the cure, the healing? Did you not from another person produce a hard sharp rebuke like a healing lancet from your secret store, and with one cut sever that gangrene at the root? A young maid with whom she used to go to the cask, when they were alone as usual together, quarrelling with her small mistress, in a most bitterly insulting manner charged her with being 'a wine-guzzler.' This taunt stung her, she saw her foulness, condemned it immediately and cast it off. As flattering friends corrupt, so quarrelsome enemies sometimes correct, but you repay them not according to what you do through them, but by the measure of their intent. That angry girl tried to upset her little mistress, not to do her good, and that in secret, either because the place and occasion of the altercation so befell them, or because she herself might fall into danger by letting it be known so late. But you, Lord, ruler of all in heaven and on earth, who bend to your own ends the depths of the swift river, and with steady hand the wild tide of the ages, by the anger of one soul cured another. So let no one, observing this, ascribe it to his own power, if another whom he desires to be corrected, should find correction by a word of his.

IX

Monica's Married Life

Brought up thus with modesty and discipline, she was made subject by you to her parents, rather than by her parents to you. When with the passing years she reached marriageable age, and was given to a husband, she served him as a master. She worked hard to win him to you, preaching to him by her character, by which you made her beautiful, submissively lovable and admirable to her husband. She so endured his marital infidelities that she never had a quarrel with her husband on this account, for she still looked for your mercy upon him, that, believing in you, he might become chaste. Generally speaking, he was exceedingly kind but also bad-tempered, but she knew not to oppose an angry man by deed or word. If it happened that he had been too thoughtlessly aroused, she would explain what she had done at the right time, when he had cooled down and was calm. In a word, though many married women, who had better tempered husbands, bore on their faces the marks of shameful blows and gossiped among their friends about the way their men lived, she rebuked their tongues, half seriously, half in jest. She would advise them that, from the time they heard the marriage contract read to them, they should consider them documents which made them servants, and that thus, remembering their condition, they should not set themselves up proudly against their masters. And when they expressed amazement, knowing what an evil-tempered husband she put up with, that nothing had been heard or by any means had been made apparent, that Patricius had beaten his wife, or that they had ever fallen into the strife of domestic disagreement, and confidentially asked why, she taught the rule I have mentioned. Those who took notice of it, after a trial, thanked her. The others, kept down, suffered.

At first her husband's mother was incensed by the whispers of wicked servant girls. However, with Monica persevering in patience and gentleness, she was so won over by her obedience in all ways, that of her own accord she reported to her son the meddling gossip of the household servants, by which domestic peace between herself and her son's wife had been upset, and requested punishment. When he, obeying his mother, and with an eye to household discipline and harmony among its members, had flogged those reported to him, as the one who reported them suggested, she promised like reward for anyone who, currying favour, spoke any ill of her daughter-in-law, and so no one from then on dared do so, and they lived in notable sweet kindliness.

This also, God, my mercy, you gave as a great gift to the servant in whose womb you made me – where she could, between those in disagreement and discord, she bore herself as such a peacemaker, that though she heard mutually the bitterest words from both parties (of the sort which crude and swollen discord regurgitates when to a present friend about an absent enemy a burning heart breathes out the corrosive speech of mingled hate) she betrayed nothing from one to the other save what might avail for their reconciliation. This good gift might seem small to me, unless I had known to my sorrow many groups who, by some horrible sinners' infection, spread widely abroad, betray, not only words said by angry enemies to their equally angry enemies, but add words not said at all. On the contrary, it should be held a small obligation to a civilised man not to stir up the hatreds of men, nor increase them by evil speaking, but rather to give attention to cooling them down by speaking well. Such a one was she, you, her heart's instructor, teaching her in her own breast.

Finally even her own husband, now in the last days of his earthly life, she won to you, and in him as a believer she had no more to complain of those things she endured in him before he believed. She was the servant of your servants, and anyone of them who knew her found much to praise in her while honouring and loving you, seeing that you were at the centre of her holy way of life to which its fruits bore witness. For she had been 'the wife of one man', had paid the debt she owed to her parents, had managed her household religiously, had a reputation for good works, she had brought up her children, as often 'travailing for them' as she saw them swerve from the path. Finally, Lord, for all of us (since, for this gift, you allow your servants to speak, those of our group who, before she fell asleep in you, lived together, after receiving the grace of your baptism) she exercised as much care as if she were the mother of us all, and served us as if we were all her parents.

X

Conversation with Monica

When the day was near for her departure from this life (you knew it though we did not) it happened, I think by your secret guidance, that we two should be standing alone leaning on a window. It was at Ostia-on-Tiber, and the window looked on to a courtyard garden in the house we had. Removed from the bustling crowds after the fatigue of a long journey, we were building up strength for the sea voyage. So we were conversing most pleasantly, 'forgetting the things behind and reaching for those before', and speculating together in the light of present truth (which you are) about what the eternal life of the saints will be, which 'eye has not seen, ear heard, nor has it come into the heart of anyone'. Yet we panted, as though our hearts had lips, for those upper streams of your fountain, the fountain of life which is in your presence, so that sprinkled from it, as we are able to receive, we might set our thoughts on so vast a theme.

We agreed that the greatest imaginable delight of the senses, in the brightest conceivable bodily context, set beside the sweetness of that life, seemed not only unworthy of comparison, but not even of mention. With deeper emotion we tried to lift our thoughts to that Reality itself, covering step by step all things bodily, and heaven itself whence sun, moon and stars shine above the earth. We soared higher, and by the heart's meditation, by speech, by wonder at your work, penetrated to our naked minds and past them to reach the place where plenty never fails, from which store you feed

Israel for ever with truth for food, where life is the wisdom with which all this universe is made in the past and in time yet to be. This wisdom is not created but is as it was and forever will be. Indeed, to have been and to be about to be are irrelevant terms in this wisdom, only eternal being. While we talked and panted after it, with all our heart's outreaching we seemed just to touch it. We sighed and left captured there the firstfruits of our spirits and made our way back to the sound of our voices, where a word has both beginning and end – unlike your Word, our Lord, which endures in itself without ageing yet renewing all.

So we were saying: If for anyone the tempest of the flesh should grow still, the phantasies of the earth, the waters and the air be quietened, along with the axis of the skies, if the very soul should fall silent and transcend itself by forgetting itself with its dreams, imaginary insights, and speech, and all else taking form from the transient (for they all say to him who has ears: We made not ourselves but he who abides eternally made us), if all these, at such words, could fall silent, because they are straining their ear to their creator, and if he should speak alone, not through them, but by himself and audibly, not by human speech nor voice of angels, the sound of thunder nor obscure similitude, so that we should hear only him whom in such matters we love (in such fashion as we were straining and in swift thought touching the eternal wisdom in all things immanent) if this state could go on, leached utterly of all alien conceptions, and if this one rapture could seize, absorb, and so envelop its beholder in more inward joys, so that eternal life should be quite like that moment of understanding to which we aspired, would not this be: 'Enter into the joy of your Lord'? When? When we shall rise again, though 'we shall not all be changed'?

Such was our conversation though not precisely in this sequence and these words. Yet you know, Lord, that on that day, when we were speaking thus and the world grew base to us amid such conversation with its delights, she said: 'Son, as for me, I find nothing in this life which delights me. I do not know what I have left to do here or why I am here, now that my hopes in this world are gone. There was one thing for which I used to desire to stay on a little in this life, to see you a Catholic Christian before I died. God has granted me this more abundantly, in that I see you his servant, all earthly happiness cast aside. What am I doing here?'

XI

Monica's Passing

What reply I made to her I do not well remember, but about five days later, she took to her bed with a fever. One day, in the course of her illness, she lost consciousness and for a brief time was out of touch with what was happening. We hurried to her but she quickly came to herself, saw me and my brother standing by her, and asked with a questioning air: 'Where was I?' Then looking at us distraught with grief, she said: 'Here you bury your mother.' I was silent and controlled my weeping, but my brother said something to her about his hope that she would more happily die at home than in another land. At these words, with a concerned look, as though checking him from entertaining such thoughts, she turned her eyes on me and said: 'Listen to him!' And to both of us she said: 'Put this body anywhere. Let not that concern you. I ask only this that, wherever you may be, you will remember me at the altar of the Lord.' When she had said this in what words she could, she fell silent in the grip of her worsening illness.

For my part, God invisible, considering your gifts, which you put into the hearts of your faithful, and from which fair fruits emerge, I rejoiced in gratitude. I had remembered, what I knew before, the care she had always cherished about her burial. She had purposed and prepared to lie beside her husband's body. Because they had always lived in deep harmony, her desire also was (so little can man's mind grasp things divine) to add this happiness to the other, and to have it generally remembered that it had been granted her, after long pilgrimage across the sea, that the earthly part of both of them should be covered by the same earth. When, in the fullness of your goodness, this triviality had begun to leave her heart, I did not know. I rejoiced in wonder that the fact had been made clear to me. In fact, in the conversation we had at the window, when she said: 'What am I doing here now?' no wish to die in her own land was apparent. I learned later that, while we were at Ostia, she had a conversation one day with some friends. In her motherly confidence she spoke of how lightly she held this life, and what a blessing death was. I was myself not present. They were astounded at the woman's courage – you gave her that gift – and when they asked whether she was not afraid to leave her body so far from her native city, she replied: 'No place is far from God, nor is it to be feared that at the end of the age he will not know whence to raise me up.' So, on the ninth day of her illness, and the fifty-sixth year of her age, and the thirty-third year of mine, that devout and holy soul was released from the body.

XII

Lamentations

I closed her eyes and enormous grief poured into my soul and overflowed in tears. My eyes at the same time, by the mind's fierce command, drew them back to dryness, and it went ill with me in such a struggle. When she breathed her last breath, the boy, Adeodatus, cried out in lamentation until, restrained by all of us, he fell silent. So too, something childish in myself which, in the heart's youthful voice, dissolved into weeping, was restrained and silenced, for we judged it unfitting to solemnize those obsequies with tearful plaints and lamentation which customarily mark the misery or absolute extinction of the dying. She was dying not in misery nor altogether and utterly. This we held by sure reasons, and by the witness of her character and unfeigned faith.

What, therefore, was it which caused me such agony of heart, but a wound newly dealt from a sweet dear custom of association on a sudden torn apart? I rejoiced that in that last and final illness, mingling her endearments with my care for her, she called me dutiful. And she said more than once, with great show of love, that she had never heard tossed from my lips at her a harsh or insulting word. But, God who created us, what comparison is there between the honour I paid to her and the service she rendered me? Because, then, I was bereft of her so great comfort, my soul was wounded and my life lacerated, a life blended of hers and mine together.

With the boy now stilled from his weeping, Euodius took up the psalter and began to sing a psalm. The whole household responded: 'I will sing to you, Lord, of mercy and judgment.' When this was heard, many brethren and Christian women gathered, and when those whose task it was were arranging the funeral, I, in a part of the house where I might properly do so, along with those who thought I should not be left alone, talked about what was fitting at such a time. By such balm of truth I eased the torment which was known to you. They did not know, attentively though they listened to me, thinking I lacked all sense of sorrow. But in your hearing, where none of them could overhear, I blamed the weakness of my feelings, and restrained, in spite of waverings, my tide of grief. But then I would be borne along by its current, not to the point of bursting into tears, or showing it on my face, well though I knew what I was holding down within. And because I was most displeased at the power such human traits had over me, things which in the order of nature and the necessity of our condition must come to pass, I grieved for my own grief with another sort of grieving, and was worn by a double sorrow.

And, see, when the body was carried out, we went, we came back, without tears, for neither in those prayers which we poured out before you, when the sacrifice of our ransom was offered up for her, with the body by the graveside, as the local custom is before burial, nor yet in the associated prayers, did I weep. Yet, through the whole day, was I deeply sad in secret, and with troubled mind I begged of you as I might, that you would heal my grief. You did not, by this one demonstration, I believe, revealing the chain all habit is upon that soul, even the soul which is not fed on deceiving doctrine. It seemed to me good, too, to go and bathe, for I had heard that the Greek for bath, from which the Latin word derives, meant 'that which drives sorrow from the mind'. See, Father of the fatherless, this also I confess to your mercy – after I bathed I was precisely what I was before. The bitterness of sorrow was not sweated from my heart. I slept, I awoke, and found my grief not a little part abated. There alone upon my bed I called to mind true verses of your Ambrose:

> *God of all things Maker,*
> *And Governor of the skies,*
> *Clothing with fair light the day,*
> *The night with slumber's grace,*
> *That rest may bring our slackened limbs*
> *Back to labour's usefulness,*
> *May lift the burden from tired minds,*
> *And relieve those stricken with sorrow.*

Then little by little I brought back to their old shape my knowledge of your handmaid, her holy way of life in you, holy in its gentleness and thoughtfulness towards us, of which I was suddenly bereft, and I was glad to weep before you about her, for her, about myself and for myself. I shed the tears I had contained. They overflowed as they would, and I made them a pillow for my heart. It rested upon them for your ears were there, not the ears of some man who would have arrogantly interpreted my grief which, in writing, I confess to you, Lord. Let him read it who will, and pronounce upon it as he will, and if he finds sin in my weeping for a small part of an hour for a mother dead and gone from my sight, who for years had wept over me, that I might live in your sight, let him not deride me, but if he is a man of lofty love, let him rather weep for my sins before you, Father of all my brethren in Christ.

XIII

Prayers for Monica

With my heart now healed of that wound, in which I afterwards found the emotions of the flesh to reprove, I pour out to you our God, on behalf of that servant of yours, another kind of tears, that which flows from a broken spirit, that ponders the peril of any soul which dies in Adam. Although she, brought to life in Christ, when not yet freed from the flesh, so lived that your name was praised in her faith and character, yet I dare not say that from the moment when you gave her rebirth through baptism, no word issued from her mouth contrary to your commandment. It was said by your son, who is truth: 'If any one call his brother a fool, he shall be in danger of Gehenna's fire.' And woe even to a praiseworthy life if, mercy laid aside, you should take it to pieces. It is because you do not with utter strictness probe our sins, we hope in faith to find a place in you. Whoever reckons up his real merits to you, what reckons he which is not of your giving? If only men could know they are but men, he who glories would glory in the Lord.

And so, my praise and my life, God of my heart, setting aside her true deeds, for which I give thanks gladly to you, I beseech you for my mother's sins. Hear me in the name of our wounds' Remedy, he who hung upon the tree and who, sitting at your right hand, makes intercession for us. I know that she has conducted herself mercifully, and from her heart has forgiven those who have sinned against her. Do you also forgive her sins, such as she may have committed through the many years after the water of salvation. Forgive, Lord, forgive, and enter not into judgment upon her. Let mercy be exalted above judgment, because your words are true and you have promised mercy to the merciful, as you enabled them to be, 'you who will be merciful to whom you will' and 'have mercy on him to whom you have been merciful'.

I believe you have already done what I ask of you, but approve the prayers my lips desire, Lord, for she, as the day of her dissolution drew near, took no thought of having her body luxuriously swathed, or embalmed with spices. She coveted no choice memorial, or sought burial at home. She gave no directions for this, but only desired to have her name remembered at your altar, which she had served without one day's break, the altar from which the holy sacrifice was dispensed by which 'the document against us was erased', through which the enemy was overcome, the enemy who, listing our sins and seeking something to bring against us, found nothing in him in whom we conquer. Who shall give him back his innocent blood, who repay the price with which he bought us, and so take us from his hand? To the sacrament which was our price, your handmaid bound her soul by the bond of faith. Let no one pluck her from your protection. Let neither lion nor serpent break in by force or fraud. For she will not answer that she owes nothing, in case she be refuted and seized by the cunning accuser. She will answer that her sins are forgiven by him to whom none can repay the price he paid for us, he who owed nothing.

So let her rest in peace with the husband before whom and after whom she had no other, whom she served 'bringing forth fruit to you', so that she might also win him to you. And, my Lord and God, inspire your servants, my brothers your sons, my masters whom with heart, voice and pen I serve, that as many as shall read this, may remember at your altar Monica your servant, with Patricius, once her husband, by whose bodies you introduced me to this life, how I know not. Let them with holy love remember my parents in this passing light of day, and my brethren under you our Father in the Catholic Mother, and those who are to be fellow citizens in the eternal Jerusalem, for which your pilgrim people sigh, from their birth to their return – so that what my mother in her last words asked of me may be more richly granted her in the prayers of many more, which my confessions inspire, than through my own.

BOOK TEN

The Fight Flows On

Introduction

And thus the story might have ended. 'Home was the sailor, home from the sea', but the moaning of the bar could still be heard, and the swell of the ocean still thrust into the haven. The ancient reader might have preferred to end the story in the garden at Milan, at Verecundus' villa, or at Ostia, after which 'they lived happily ever after'. Book Ten would have surprised him, for it covers a tract of experience. Conversion was not a triumphant ending but the beginning of a battle.

Some vantage points had been reached and taken, and some foes destroyed. Like some modern physicist faced with the evanescence of matter in his hands and feeling reality elude him, Augustine sought in strange ways for the substance of things, and failed to find it. So modern, in the context of their own forms, were the problems which beset his questing mind. The Platonists had cleared his bewilderment here. He had taken heroic stand against the power of the flesh, 'the lust of the flesh the lust of the eyes and the pride of life', but such enemies lurked along his path. Was it right to delight too keenly in the beauty of Creation, and risk forgetting for a moment the Creator? Could the beauty of the Psalms be lost in the majesty of the music in which Ambrose had enshrined them? He was agonisingly conscious that temptation lurked in every natural corner of the life. Men who walk in the light must take care to walk fast lest darkness overtake them. The allurements of smell do not much bother him, but is he deceived, when God 'is sifting out the soulds of men before his judgment seat'? 'I beseech you, God, to show me my full self'.

It is the world of a sensitive man, a 'tormented saint', unable to rest in the Lord, afraid to be presumptuously sure. Have there not always been a host who, in a cumbered humility, find no good in redeemed man? 'Every virtue we possess, and every victory won ... ' emerge computer fashion from him who touches the keys. To be sure the mingling of faith and grace, the roots of faith itself, free will, all touch problems which the time-bound mind cannot grasp, and which it codifies to its confusion. We leave Augustine with the fight still flowing on.

The marvel of memory fills much of Book Ten for he has once or twice been disturbed by the thought that it had its elements of unreliability, and he clearly had a small brush with conscience after the account of his ecstasy at Ostia in Monica's last days. He analyses memory with acute understanding, and elucidates the processes of recollection and recall, immediate and delayed, with the aptest imagery, and with his usual wordiness. As inevitably he tangles himself in the unreal problem of how one can remember forgetting. The mind of Saint Augustine remained the mind Christ rescued from the cult of Mani, and led step by step through the paths of wisdom to the truth. He was a man from another century but not a man from another world. His path to Christ was that which more than a few academic Christians have followed, and are following today. It was a hard path, long and weary, and it is natural enough that when he at last struggled to its end he should be footsore, and scarce believing that he was in the Saviour's hands with nothing left to fear. It is a pity that, as far as the *Confessions* take us he never attained that rest of heart to which his opening words aspired. *Vale Augustine.*

I

Foreword

May I come to know you, who know me, just as I am known. My soul's Virtue, enter my soul, and shape it to yourself to have and to hold it without spot or wrinkle. This is my hope, and for that reason I speak and rejoice, when there is health in my rejoicing. Other things in this life are the less to be wept over in proportion as we do weep over them, and indeed the more to be wept over in proportion as we fail to do so. For, see, you have loved truth, and he who acts in truth comes to the light. And it is in truth I would act in my heart as I confess before you, and in what I write before many witnesses.

II

God Knows Already

From you, Lord, to whose eyes the depths of man's conscience is bare, what is there in me which is concealed, even if I should be unwilling to confess to you. I should be hiding you from me, not myself from you. But now because my cry of pain reveals that I am displeased with myself, you shine out and please me, yes, you are loved and longed for, so that I am ashamed of myself and renounce myself. I choose you, and please neither you nor myself, save it be in you. That is why, Lord, I am fully known to you, whatever I may be. I have already said with what advantage I make confession to you, confession made not in words and with the body's voice, but with the soul's words and the cry of my thoughts, which your ear understands. For when I am evil, to confess to you is nothing more than to be displeased with myself. When I am good it is simply not to ascribe goodness to myself, because it is you, Lord, who bless the just and first you justify the unjust. Confession, therefore, my God, is made in your sight silently and yet not silently. As for sound, it is silent, in love it cries aloud. I utter nothing which men call right which you have not already heard from me, nor do you hear anything from me which you have not first said to me.

III

The Fruit of Confession

What then have I to do with men that they should hear my confessions, as if they could heal all my infirmities? Men are curious to hear the life of another, tardy to amend their own. Why do they want to hear from me what sort of person I am, those who do not wish to hear from you what sort of persons they themselves are? And how do they know whether I am telling the truth, when they hear about myself from myself, since no man knows what goes on in a man but the spirit of the man which is in him? But if they hear from you about themselves they will not be able to say: 'The Lord is lying.' For what is it to hear from you about themselves but to know themselves? Furthermore, who knows and says: 'It is untrue', unless he lies? But because 'love believes all things' (at any rate, among those whom love makes one by knitting them to itself), I too, Lord, confess to you in such fashion as men may hear, though I am not able to prove to them that what I confess is true. But those whose ears love opens believe me.

But do you, Physician of my heart, make clear to me with what profit I so act, for the confessions of my past sins (which you have forgiven and covered to make me happy in you, changing my soul by faith and your sacrament) when they are read and heard, stir the heart, so that it does not sleep for despair and say: 'I cannot.' Let it be wakeful in the love of your mercy and the sweetness of your grace, by which every weakling is made strong who is made conscious by it of his infirmity. It is pleasant to the good to hear of their past evils, those I mean who are now done with them, and it pleases them not because they are evils, but because they are past and not present. And so, with what advantage, my Lord, to whom my conscience, resting more in the hope of your mercy than in its own innocence, daily confesses, with what advantage, I ask, by this book, in your presence, I also make confession to men about what I am now, and not what I was once. That advantage I have seen and have described. For, see, what I am now at the very time I am making these confessions, is what many want to know, both they who have known me in person, and those who have heard something from me or about me. Yet their ear is not on my heart where I am, whoever I am. So they wish to hear as I confess what I am within, in the place where neither eye nor ear nor understanding can penetrate. They desire it. They are prepared to believe. But will they understand at all? Love, which makes them the good men they are, tells them that I am not confessing what is not true about myself, and the love that is in them believes me.

IV

The Theme Continued

How will such a wish help? Do they want to congratulate me when they have heard how near, by your gift, I am come to you, and to pray for me when they have heard how far, by the burden of myself, I am held back from you? To such folk I shall reveal myself, for it is of no small advantage, my Lord God, that by many praise should be given you on my behalf, and that by many prayer should be made to you. Let a brotherly mind esteem in me what you teach is estimable, and grieve for that in me which you teach is grievous. Let that brotherly mind do this, not a stranger's, nor that of 'the sons of the alien whose lips speak vanity, and whose right hand is the right hand of iniquity', but that brotherly mind, I say, which when it approves, rejoices about me, and is sad for me when it disapproves, and does both out of love. To such folk I will reveal myself. Let them breathe freely at my good deeds, sigh for my bad. My good deeds are set up by you, they are your gifts. My bad deeds are my own sins, and lie under your judgment. Let them breathe freely in the former, sigh for the latter, and let hymn and lamentation go up before your face from brotherly hearts, which are your censers. And you, Lord, who once found delight in the odour of your holy temple, have mercy upon me, according to your great mercy, for your name's sake, and, by no means abandoning what you have begun, bring what is imperfect in me to perfection.

Here lies the advantage of my confessions, not in what I have been, but in what I am – to confess this, not only before you with a hidden rejoicing and with trembling but also with a hidden grief along with hope, but also to confess where believing sons of men can hear, those who share my joy as partners of my mortality, my fellow-citizens, and fellow pilgrims along with me, with those who have gone ahead of us, and those who shall come behind, companions on the road I tread. These are your servants, my brothers, whom you willed to be your sons, my masters whom you have bidden me serve, if I would live with you, and in communion with you. But this your word would be a small thing, if it gave command only in speech and did not go before in deeds. And this I do in deeds and in words, this I do beneath your wings, too perilous an enterprise were not my soul sheltered under your wings, and my weakness known to you. I am but a tiny child, but my father ever lives and he who guides me is sufficient. For he is the very one who begat me and protects me, and you are all the good I have, you the omnipotent one who are with me, before I am with you. To such folk, therefore, I shall reveal myself, those whom you bid me serve, revealing not what I have been, but what I am. I do not judge myself, so let me, on these terms, be heard.

V

Man's knowledge of Himself and God

It is you, Lord, who judge me. No one knows what belongs to a man but the spirit which is in man, but, at the same time, there is something in man which not even the spirit within him knows. Yet you, Lord, who made him, know all about him. So I, though in your sight I may despise myself, and reckon myself earth and dust, yet know something of you, which I do not know about myself. Truly 'we see now, dimly as in a mirror, and not yet face to face.' For that reason, as long as I wander from you, I am nearer to myself than to you. Yet I know that in no way can you be profaned. For my part I do not know what temptations I can resist, and what I cannot. There is hope because you are faithful, you who do not allow us 'to be tempted above what we are able, but will with the temptation make a way of escape so that we shall be able to bear it.' I will therefore confess what I know about myself, and what I do not know about myself, because even what I do not know about myself, I know by your illumination until my darkness becomes as the noon-day before your face.

VI

How God is known

It is not with a doubting but an assured consciousness that I love you, Lord. You smote my heart with your love, and that is why I loved you. But heaven and earth and all that is in them, look, from all sides they bid me love you, nor cease to tell it to all 'so that they should be without excuse.' But more profoundly will you 'have mercy upon whom you will have mercy, and show compassion to those on whom you have had compassion.' Otherwise heaven and earth sound your praises to deaf ears. What is it that I love when I love you? Not the beauty of a body nor the comeliness of time, nor the lustre of the light pleasing to the eyes, nor the sweet melodies of all manner of songs, nor the fragrance of flowers, ointments and spices, not manna and honey, nor limbs welcome to the embrace of the flesh – I do not love these when I love my God. And yet it is a kind of light, a kind of voice, a kind of fragrance, a kind of food, a kind of embrace, when I love my God, who is the light, voice, fragrance, food, embrace of the inner man, where there shines into the soul that which no place can contain, and there sounds forth that which time cannot end, where there is fragrance which no breeze disperses, taste which eating does not make less, and a clinging together which fulfilment does not terminate. It is this that I love when I love my God.

And what is this? I asked the earth and it said: 'I am not it', and all that is in it made the same reply. I asked the sea and the nether deep, and the creeping things with life, and they made answer: 'We are not your God. Seek above us.' I asked the moving breezes, and all the air, and all that inhabits the air, all made reply: 'Anaximenes is mistaken. I am not God.' I asked the sky, the sun, the moon and stars. 'Neither are we the God you are looking for', they say. I said to all those things which besiege the doors of the flesh: 'You speak to me of my God, but you are not he. Tell me something about him.' They cried out with a mighty voice: 'He made us.' My questioning was the action of my mind, their reply was their beauty. I turned to myself and I asked myself: 'Who are you?' I replied: 'A man.' And, look, in my person are body and soul, one without, and the other within. Through which of these two should I have looked for my God, for whom I had, through the body's faculties, made search from earth to heaven as far as my eyes could see? Better is the inner self. For to it all the body's messengers made report, as though to a president and judge, about the replies of heaven, earth and all the rest which they contain, saying: 'We are not God, he made us.' These things did my inner self know by the service of the outer self. I, the inner man, understood these things, I, the soul, through the body's sense. I asked the whole mass of the world about my God, and it replied to me: 'It is not I, he made me.'

Is not this semblance obvious to all who have sound wits? Why then, does it not say the same to everyone? All creatures great and small see it, but cannot question it, because reason does not preside as judge over the senses which make report. But men can question, so that 'the invisible things of God are seen and understood by what is made.' But by love they are made subject to them, and subjects cannot be judges. Nor will the material things themselves answer, unless the interrogators be their judges. Nor do they change what they have to say (their outward semblance, in a word), if one man simply sees, while another sees and asks, so that they appear in one way to the former in another way to the latter, and, though of the same appearance, have no message for one, but speak to the other. Indeed, they have something to say to everyone, but only they understand, who refer the message which comes from without, to the truth which dwells within. For truth says to me: 'Neither heaven nor earth, nor any other body is your God.' Their very nature says this. Obviously there is less bulk in the part of a thing than in the whole of it. To you, my soul, I say that you are the better part, because you animate the mass of your body providing it with life which no body can give to a body, but your God is the life of my life to you.

VII

God is not Found by any Bodily Faculty

What is it then that I love, when I love God? Who is he who is above the summit of my soul? By my soul itself I will climb to him. I will rise beyond that power of mine by which I cling to the body, and fill its whole structure with life. It is not by that power that I find my God, for a horse and a mule, which are without understanding, and who possess the same power by which their bodies live, might so find him. There is another power, that by which I give life, but also by which I give feeling to my flesh, which the Lord constructed for me. He commanded the eye not to hear, the ear not to see, but ordered the eye for me to see by, the ear through which I might hear, and the other senses, each by each, in their own places and functions. They are various. I, the one mind, act through them. I will, I say, rise beyond that power of mine, which I share with horse and mule, who also perceive through their bodies.

VIII

The Power of Memory

So I will rise beyond that natural power, by degrees rising to him who made me. I arrive at the fields and broad mansions of memory, where are laid up the treasures of countless images, brought there by all manner of experience. There is stored away also whatever we think by way of enlarging or lessening, or in any way modifying, what sense has encountered, together with anything else approved and put away, which forgetfulness has not yet devoured and buried. When I am there, I order what I wish to be brought out, and some things appear right away, others require longer search, as if they are produced from remoter storerooms. Some things rush out in a heap, and while something else is sought and looked for, they crowd forward as though to say: 'Perhaps we are what you want.' With the hand of my heart I dismiss these from the face of my remembrance, until there appears at last what I want, coming into view from its hidden storage. Other things are stacked up promptly as required, and in ordered sequence, those in front making way for those behind. As they give place they are packed away, to be forthcoming again on demand. It all takes place at once when I repeat anything from memory.

There all things are systematically stored, each under its

proper head, in accordance with its delivery, each through its proper gate – light, for example, and all colours and corporeal shapes by way of the eyes, through the ears, too, all kinds of sound, and all scents by the nose's ingress, and tastes through that of the mouth, by the sense of touch all things hard or soft, hot or cold, smooth or rough, heavy or light, whether within or without the body. All this that huge storage place of memory, with its unimaginable secret nooks and indescribable corners, receives, to be recollected and brought back at need. They all enter by the appropriate gate, and are there laid up. The things themselves, however, do not go in, but only images of things perceived. There they are at hand for the thought which calls them up. Who tells us how such images have been formed, though it is obvious by which senses they have been seized and packed away inside? Yet even when I am dwelling in darkness and silence, I can draw colours into my memory, if I wish, and distinguish between white and black and any other colours I will. And sounds do not intrude and confuse what I have drawn into consideration by my eyes, though these, too, are there, as though lying stored apart. And if I choose to call for them and they present themselves at once, though my tongue be still, and my throat silent, I sing as much as I will. Those colour images, which notwithstanding are still about, do not get in the way and break in, when another deposit is called for, which poured in by the ears. So with the rest, which through other senses have been imported and stacked. I remember them as I will. I distinguish the scent of lilies from that of violets, while smelling nothing. I prefer honey to sweet wine, smooth to rough though, at the same time, neither tasting nor touching anything, but simply re-membering.

I do this within myself, in the great hall of my memory for there are to my hand heaven, earth and sea, and all I have been able to perceive in them, except what I have forgotten. I meet myself there, too, and recall myself, what, when and where I have done something, and my reaction when I did it. Everything is there which I have personally experienced, or believed and remember. Out of the same store, I continually weave into the past new and newer images of things which I have experienced, or, on the basis of experience, have believed. And from these too I fashion future actions, events and hopes, and reflect on all these things again as if they were there. 'I shall do this and that', I say to myself, in that great receptacle of my mind full of so many and so great images, 'and this or that is what follows.' I say: 'If only this or that could be!' 'May God turn this or that aside!' So I speak with myself, and when I speak there are the images of all I speak about from that great treasure house of memory, nor should I be talking of any of them, were the images not there.

Great is the power of memory, great indeed, God, a vast, a boundless inner room, whose depths none can reach. And this is a power of my mind and is part of my nature, and I myself do not understand all that I am. Therefore is the mind too narrow to contain itself. And where should that be which does not contain itself? Can anything be outside itself and not in itself? How does it not contain itself? Wonder and great amazement burst upon me and lay hold of me at this. Men go to wonder at the heights of mountains, and the huge billows of the sea, the broad sweeps of the rivers, the curve of ocean and the circuits of the stars, and yet pass by themselves, nor wonder that, though I speak of all these things, I have not been seeing them with my eyes. Yet I could not be speaking of them unless, in my memory, I saw, in their immensity before me, the mountains, waves, rivers and stars which I have looked at, and the ocean which I have heard about. But I did not make them part of me by seeing them, when I looked on them with my eyes, nor are the realities themselves with me, but only their images, and I know by what corporeal sense each was stamped upon me.

IX

Remembering Abstract Things

But this is not all which the mighty capacity of my memory carries. Here are all those principles of liberal sciences, which have not yet been forgotten, removed to some remoter place – or no place at all! And I hold not the images, but the principles themselves. For what literature is, what skill in argument may be, or categories of questions, whatever I know of such matters, is not in my memory in such a way that I have taken in the image and left out the reality, to utter its word and pass away like a voice striking the ear, to be recalled by a trace, a voice as it were, but no longer a voice. Or like a passing odour, dispersed upon the wind, leaving its image on the memory which we can recapture in recollection. Or like food which in the stomach has no taste, yet retains a sort of taste in the memory. Or like anything which is apprehended by the body's touching it, which can retain an image in the memory when remote from our body. Those realities, to be sure, are not admitted to the memory. Their images alone, with wondrous speed, are captured, and laid up in some way, in wondrous compartments, and by an act of recall wondrously produced.

X

Memory and Perception

In truth, when I hear that there are three kinds of questions: 'Does a thing exist? What is it? What is it like?', I retain the images of the sounds of which these words are composed, and I know that they passed through the air with a noise, and no longer exist. But the realities which are indicated by those sounds were never reached by any sense of my body, nor in any way discerned save by my mind. In my memory I stored away, not their images, but the things themselves. Whence they entered my person, let them say, if they can. I review the doors of my body, and light on none by which they may have gained entry. My eyes say: 'If they were coloured, we announced them.' My ears say: 'If they made a noise, they were announced by us.' My nostrils say: 'If they had a smell, they passed our way.' My sense of taste says: 'If they had no savour, do not ask me.' Touch says: 'If it was not a solid, I did not handle it, and if I never handled it, I did not take notice of it.' Whence, and by what way did they enter my memory? I do not know. For when I first learned them I gave no credit to another mind, but understood in my own. Approving them as true, I commended them to my mind, storing them away for later reference when I would. They were therefore in my mind before I learned them, but not in my memory. Where were they, or why, when they were put into words, did I acknowledge them and say: 'Yes, this is true', had they not been already in the memory, but so removed and buried, as it were, in deeper hiding-places, that, had they not been extracted by someone, I would not perhaps have been able to think of them.

XI

Memory is the Soul

We therefore discover that, learning those things whose images we do not ingest through the senses, but perceive them, as they are, in ourselves without a medium, is simply to receive by perception things which the memory already contained unclassified and unarranged, and to take knowledge of them and be careful that they should be placed near at hand, in the same memory where before they were scattered, unheeded and hidden, and so should readily come into the mind, now aware of them. How many details of this kind of knowledge does my memory carry, which are already discovered, and, as I put it, placed near at hand, things which we are said to have learned and to know. They are things which, should I chance not to recollect them for some short lapse of time, become so covered up again, or slip back again as if into remoter rooms, that they must once more, as though they were new, be thought up from those same hiding-places, their only retreat, and considered again, in order to be known. It is as if they had to be collected again from some dispersion. Hence the word 'recollect', which is allied to 'collect', after a common fashion with verbs. The mind of man has appropriated this word, so that in familiar parlance it is not anything in general that is gathered together, but only what the mind gathers together that is said to be 'recollected'.

XII

The Mathematician's Memory

Likewise, the memory contains those reasons and laws beyond counting of numbers and measurements, none of which have been imprinted on it by the senses, for they have neither colour, nor sound, nor taste, nor smell, nor feeling. I have heard the sound of words which express these ideas in discussion, but the sounds and what they signify are different one from another. The sounds are different in Greek and Latin but the things they signify are neither Greek nor Latin, nor any other language. I have seen the lines drawn by architects, the finest thin as a spider's web. These, too, are different. They are not the image of those realities which the eye of the flesh makes known to me. He knows them, whoever, without envisaging any body, apprehends them within himself. I have also perceived, with all the senses of the body, the numbers we use when we count. But the numbers we use in counting are different again. They are not the images of things and so truly exist apart. Let him who does not see these things laugh at me for talking about them, and I will pity him who laughs at me.

XIII

Remembering Memory

I hold in memory both these things and how I learned them. I have heard and remember, too, many false objections to what I have said. False though they are, it is not false that I have remembered them. This also I remember that I have distinguished those truths and these falsehoods, alleged in contradiction. I remember this, too, that I find myself now discerning them in another way from that in which I once did frequently in thinking about them. I remember then that I have often understood these things, and what I now discern and understand I store up in memory, so that in the future I may remember that I have understood now. And I remember that I have remembered, just as if, in the future, if I shall call to remembrance that I have now been able to remember these things, assuredly I shall remember by the power of memory.

XIV

Mind and Memory

My memory contains also the emotions of my mind, not in the same manner as the mind does at the time of the experience, but far differently, as the strength of memory is. When I am not happy, I remember that I have been happy, as I remember past sadness when I am not sad. I remember without fear that I have at times been afraid. Without desire, I remember past desire. On the contrary, in gladness I remember my past sorrow, and past gladness while sorrowing. This is not to be wondered at if we speak of the body. The mind is one thing, the body another. So that, if I remember with joy a past pain of the body, it is not a cause for wonder. Memory itself is mind. When we give an order for something to be remembered, we say: 'See that you keep it in mind', and when we forget we say: 'I did not have it in mind', or 'It slipped my mind', we are calling the memory the mind. How then does it come about that, when in gladness I remember a sadness that is passed, and the mind holds gladness and the memory sadness, my mind is glad because joy is in it, but my memory is not sad because it has sadness in it? Can it perhaps be that the memory has nothing to do with the mind? Who would say this? The memory is like the mind's stomach, and joy and sadness are like sweet and bitter food. Committed to the memory, they are like food passed into the stomach. They are stored there, but cannot be tasted. The comparison is ridiculous, but contains an element of truth.

Look, I bring out of my memory the statement that there are four disturbances of the mind, desire, joy, fear and sorrow. Whatever I am able to discuss about them, dividing each into its several parts and defining it, it is in my memory that I find what to say, and from my memory that I produce it, while at the same time I am not disturbed by any of the named disturbances. Calling them to mind, I remember them, and before I recalled them and brought them back, they were there, and that is why by recollection, they could be produced. Perhaps, then, as food can be regurgitated for the cud to be chewed, so are they brought out of the memory by recollection. So why does not the one who discusses these things perceive in the mouth of his thinking, as he remembers, I mean, the sweetness of joy, and the bitterness of sorrow? Is the comparison invalid because it does not apply in all points? Who would willingly speak about such matters, if, at every mention of sorrow or fear, we were compelled to be sad or fearful? Yet we could not speak of them unless we found in our memory, not only the sounds of the names corresponding to the images imprinted on it by the body's senses, but also the ideas of the things themselves which we received by no doorway of the flesh, but which the mind itself, by the experience of its own passions, committed to the memory, or which the memory itself retained without any act of committal.

XV

Remembering Absent Things

Who can easily say whether this is by images or not? For example, I name a stone or the sun, when the realities are not present to my senses. The images of them, however, are present in my memory. I name a bodily pain, but it is not present. Nothing is hurting me. But if the image was not there in my memory, I should not know what to say, nor in discussion distinguish it from pleasure. I mention bodily health, when I am sound of limb. The reality is present with me. And yet, had not the image of health been also in my memory, I could in no way recall what the sound of this name signified. Nor would the sick know, when health had been named, what had been said, unless the same image were held by the power of the memory, although the reality of health was far from the body. I name numbers whereby we number. See, they themselves are in my memory, not their images. I name the image of the sun and that is present in my memory. And I do not call to mind the image of that image, but I call to mind the image itself. It is there itself for my remembering. I name memory, and I recognise what I name. Where does that recognition take place but in the memory itself? Is the image itself at hand for me by means of its image and not by its own reality?

XVI

Remembering Forgetfulness

And what when I name forgetfulness, and in the same way recognise what I name? Whence do I recognise the thing itself, if I do not remember it? I do not speak of the name itself, but of the thing which it signifies. If I had forgotten it, I would not be able to recognise what that sound denoted.

When I remember memory, memory itself is present with me, by itself. But when I remember forgetfulness, then both memory and forgetfulness are present, memory, by which I have remembered, and forgetfulness, which I am remembering. But what is forgetfulness, but a deprivation of memory? In what way, therefore, is it present for me to remember it, when I cannot remember it when it is present? Now, if what we remember we retain in the memory, unless we did remember forgetfulness, we should not in any way be able, on hearing that name, to recognise its meaning. So forgetfulness is retained in the memory. It is present, therefore, so that we may not forget that which we do forget, when it is present. Is it from this to be understood that, when we remember it, forgetfulness is not by itself present, at the time when we remember it, but only by means of its image, because, if forgetfulness were to be present by itself, it would not cause us to remember, but to forget. Who will now unravel that? Who will understand how that can be?

Certainly, as for me, Lord, I toil in this, and I toil within myself. I have proved a heavy soil that needs much sweat. We are not now examining the spaces of the sky, or measuring the distances of the stars, nor seeking the balances of the earth. It is I who remember, I, the mind. It is not so wonderful, if the knowledge of what I am not is so far removed from me. What is nearer to me than I myself? And, see, I am not able to understand the power of my memory, for I identify myself completely with it. What shall I say when I am convinced that I remember forgetfulness? Shall I say that what I remember is in my memory? Shall I say that forgetfulness is in my memory for this very purpose, so that I shall not forget? Both questions are absurd indeed. What comes third? How shall I say that the image of forgetfulness is kept in the memory, and not forgetfulness itself, when I am remembering forgetfulness? How shall I say this, too, seeing that, when the image of anything is imprinted on the memory, it is first necessary for the thing itself to be present from which the image can be impressed. Thus I remember Carthage and all other places where I have been, the faces of people I have seen, and what the other senses have reported. Thus, too, it is with the health and sickness of the body.

When these objects are present, the memory receives images from them, which, being there, I can contemplate, and bring back to mind, as I remember the absent objects. If, therefore, forgetfulness is held in memory not by itself, but by its image, assuredly it was once present itself, for its image to be captured. But when it was present, how did it write its image on the memory, when forgetfulness blots out, by its presence, what it finds already noted? Yet, in whatever way, past comprehension and understanding though that way may be, I am sure I remember forgetfulness itself, that by which what we remember is effaced.

XVII

Remembering God

Great is the power of memory, my God, awesome in a way, a deep and boundless complex. And the memory is the mind and the mind is I myself. What am I, therefore, my God? What am I by nature? A life various, manifold, exceedingly vast. See, in the numberless fields, caves and caverns of my memory, beyond numbering and full of numberless kinds of things, be it by images, like everything corporeal, or by their own presence, as with art, or by undefinable ideas and impressions, as with the activities of the mind, which the memory retains, even when the mind does not experience them, since whatever is in the memory is also in the mind – through all this mass I rush about, and flit this way and that. I penetrate it as far as I can, but there is no bottom. Such is the power of memory, such is the power of life in a being who lives, but yet must die. What then am I to do, my God, who is my true life? I will go past even this power of mine called memory, go past it, I say, to reach you, sweet light. What are you saying to me? I am climbing up by my mind to you, who live above me. I will pass, too, this power of mine which is called memory, in my desire to reach you by the path by which you may be reached, and cling to you at the point at which you may be held. Even beasts and birds have memory, or they could never find their dens and nests again, nor much else to which they are accustomed, nor, indeed could they ever become accustomed to anything save by memory. Therefore I will pass beyond memory, too, to attain to him who set me apart from the animals and birds of the air, and made me wiser than they. I will pass beyond memory, too, to find you ... where, truly good, and sweetness without care – to find you ... where? If I find you apart from my memory, I am not remembering you. And how shall I find you, if I do not remember you?

XVIII

Nature of Remembering

A woman had lost her drachma, and looked for it with a lamp. Unless she had remembered it, she would not have looked for it. When it was found how she could know whether it was the coin she sought, had she not remembered it? I can remember many things I have lost and found again, and I know this, because while I was searching, it would be said to me: 'Perhaps this is it – or that?' And I went on saying: 'No', until what I was looking for was brought to me. Had I not remembered it, whatever it was, I should not have found it, even if it were brought to me, because I should not have recognised it. It is always the same, when we look for anything lost and find it. However, when anything is lost from sight, but not from memory, if it is a visible body, its image is retained within, and sought until it is restored to sight, and when it is found it is recognised by that image which was retained within. Nor do we say that we have found what had been lost, if we do not recognise it. It was lost from the eyes, but not from the memory.

THE CONFESSIONS OF ST. AUGUSTINE

XIX

The Theme Continued

What about when the memory itself loses something, as in cases where we forget and try to recollect it? Where, in the final analysis, do we seek but in the memory? And there, if perhaps one thing is brought forward instead of another, we reject it until that which we are looking for comes up. And when it does we say: 'This is it'. We would not say this unless we recognised it, nor recognise it unless we remembered it. Certainly then we had forgotten it. Or was it that it had not totally escaped us, and the lost part was looked for from what was retained, and the memory, conscious that it was not carrying on in its completeness what it was in the habit of so carrying, and limping because an old habit had been mutilated, demanded that what was missing should be restored? For example, if we see, or think about a man we know, and are trying to recall his name which we have forgotten, anything else which comes into our mind does not link up, because it was not customarily connected with the man in question. It is, therefore, rejected, until the one appears which the memory comfortably accepts from customary acquaintance. And whence does that appear, but out of memory itself? That is where it comes from, even when we recognise it from the prompting of someone else. We do not believe it as something new, but upon recollection approve the truth of what was said. Were the name utterly erased from the mind, we should not remember it even when it is put to our mind. We have not yet forgotten utterly what we remember we have forgotten. It follows that, what we have utterly forgotten, though lost, we shall not be able even to look for.

XX

The Blessed Life

In what way, then, do I seek you, Lord? When I seek you, my God, I seek the blessed life. I shall seek you that my soul may live, for my body lives by my soul, and my soul by you. How, therefore, am I seeking the blessed life, for it is not mine until I say in the proper place: 'Enough, here it is'? How am I seeking it? By remembrance, as if I had forgotten it, and still grasping that I had forgotten it? Or through eagerness to learn a thing unknown, or something I had never known or had so forgotten as not to remember that I had forgotten? Is not the blessed life what all desire, and there is no man at all who does not desire it? Where did they come to know it, since they so desire it? Where did they see it, so to love it? No doubt, in a way, we possess it. And there is a kind of way by which, if one possesses it, he is blessed, and some there are who find their blessedness in hope. These have it on a lower level than those who have it in reality, yet none the less are better off than those who are neither blessed in deed nor hope. Yet even they, unless they had it in some fashion, would not so desire blessedness. That they do so is beyond doubt. Somehow they have come to know it, and thus have some sort of knowledge of it. I am not sure whether that is in the memory or not. If it were, there must be times when we knew blessedness. Whether this was so with us individually, or in that man who first sinned, and in whom we all die, and through whom we are all born in wretchedness, I offer no opinion. But I do ask whether the blessed life is in the memory, for we should not love it, did we not know it. We have heard the name, and we all admit we strive for it. It is not the sound alone in which we take delight, for when a Greek hears the name in Latin, he gains no pleasure, because he does not understand it. But we do, as he would do, if he heard it in Greek. The reality itself is neither in Greek nor in Latin, to attain which both Greeks and Romans eagerly strive, as do men of other tongues. So it is known to everyone, so that if, with one voice, they could be asked whether they wished to be happy, undoubtedly they would reply that they did. This would not come about, unless a reality which goes by this name, were not held in the memory.

XXI

Remembering what we Never Possessed

Is not this just as I remember Carthage which I have seen? No, it is not, for the blessed life is not seen by the eyes because it is not something solid. Is it like remembering numbers? No, for he who holds them in knowledge seeks nothing beyond them. But the blessed life we have in knowledge, and that is why we love it. Yet we still desire to attain it, and know its blessedness. Do we remember it as we remember eloquence? No, although at the mention of this name, some, not yet eloquent themselves, recall the reality, and many desire to be eloquent, whence it appears that eloquence is within their knowledge. Having, by their bodily senses, observed others to be eloquent, and having enjoyed the experience, they desire to be eloquent themselves. However, they would not have enjoyed it, but for some inward knowledge, nor would they wish to be eloquent save for that enjoyment. The blessed life, for all that, we do not experience in others by any bodily sense. Or is it in the same way as we remember joy? Perhaps that is so, for I remember my joy, even when I am sad, just as I remember, in unhappiness, the blessed life. Yet never, by bodily sense, did I ever see, hear, smell, taste or touch my joy. I experienced it in my mind, whenever I was glad, and its knowledge clung to my memory, so that I was able to recall it, at times with disgust, at others with desire, according to the difference between those things in which I remember that I took pleasure. I have been flooded with joy of a sort, even over disgraceful things, the memory of which I now detest and execrate. At other times, I rejoice in good and honourable things, which I call to mind with longing, though they are not perhaps at hand, and for that reason I am sad as I recall my former joy.

Where, then, and when have I experienced the blessed life, so that I should remember, love and long for it? Nor is it I alone, or a few along with me. We all wish to be happy. And unless with a certain knowledge we knew what this meant, we should not with so firm a will desire it. How does it come about, that if two men are asked whether they wish to go to war, one of them would conceivably reply that he was willing, and the other that he was not. But if they were asked whether they wanted to be happy, both would without hesitation say that they did, and for no other reason would one wish to be a soldier and the other not, than to be happy. Is it, perhaps, that one finds joy in this situation and the other in that? So do all agree that they want to be happy, as they would agree if they were asked whether they wished for joy. Joy itself they call the blessed life. Though one pursues his joy in this way and another in that, one end only they strive to attain, that they may be glad. And since no one can say that they have not had the experience, it is recognised because it is found in the memory, when the name of 'the blessed life' is heard.

XXII

It is Simply Joy in God

Far be it, Lord, far be it from your servant's heart, who is making confession to you, that I should consider myself happy whatever joy I feel. There is a joy which is not granted to the ungodly but to those alone who worship you for your own sake, and whose joy you yourself are. This is the blessed life, to rejoice in you, to you, on account of you, this and nothing else. They who think it other than this, pursue another joy, which is not true joy. Yet from some semblance of rejoicing their will is not completely deflected.

XXIII

What and Where the Blessed Life is

It is not therefore certain that everyone wants to be happy because those who do not wish to rejoice in you, which is what the blessed life is, simply do not want the blessed life. Or, on the other hand, is it the case that everyone wants it, but 'the flesh lusts against the spirit, and the spirit against the flesh, so that they do not what they wish.' That is why they fall on what they can do, and are content with that, and because they cannot do it, they do not wish urgently enough to make them able. I ask everyone whether they prefer to rejoice in the truth rather than in falsehood. In the truth, they reply, as confidently as they reply that they want to be happy. Indeed, a happy life is rejoicing because of the truth, and this is rejoicing in you, who are the truth, God, my Light and 'the Health of my countenance'. This blessed life all desire, this life, which is the only blessed life, all, I say, desire, just as all desire to rejoice because of the truth. I have encountered many people who wish to deceive, but no one who wishes to be deceived. Where, then, did they become acquainted with the blessed life, but where they also became acquainted with the truth? This truth they love because they do not wish to be deceived, and when they love the blessed life, which is only rejoicing because of the truth, then also they love the truth, and they would not love it were there not some knowledge of it in their memory. Why, then, do they not find joy in it? Why are they not happy? Because they are more preoccupied with other matters which make them unhappy, rather than what they faintly remember makes them happy. There is still a faint light in men. Let them walk and keep on walking, lest the darkness overtake them.

But why does truth engender hatred, and why does your man become an enemy to those to whom he preaches truth, though the blessed life is loved, which is nothing else but rejoicing because of the truth? Unless it be that truth is so loved, that, whoever loves anything else wants what they love to be the truth, and because they do not wish to be deceived and are unwilling to be convinced that they are deceived. And so, for the sake of that which they love instead of the truth, they hate the truth. They love truth when it enlightens, hate it when it reproves. Because they do not wish to be deceived and want to deceive, they love truth when it reveals itself, and hate it when it reveals them. That is how it will repay them, revealing in their despite those who do not wish to be revealed by it, without revealing itself to them. Thus, thus, does the mind of man, blind, sick, foul and ugly, wish to lie hidden, but does not wish to have anything hidden from it. It falls out on the contrary that it is not hidden from the truth itself, but truth is hidden from it. Yet even so, in its wretchedness, it would rather take joy in truths than in falsehoods. It will therefore be happy if, with nothing hostile coming in between, it will find joy in truth alone, by which all things are true.

XXIV

Memory also holds God

See, Lord, how great a tract of my memory I have traversed in search of you and outside my memory have not discovered you. For I have found nothing about you that I have not held in memory since I first learned about you. From the time when I learned of you, I have not forgotten you. Whenever I found truth, I found my God, truth itself from which I first learned it, and I have not forgotten. So from when I first learned of you, you abide in my memory, and there I find you, whenever I recall you, and take delight in you. These are my holy delights, which in your mercy, and with an eye to my poverty you gave me.

XXV

Where in my Memory

But where do you abide in my memory, where do you abide there? What sort of sanctuary have you built for yourself? You gave this honour to my memory, that you should abide in it, and I am pondering where this may be. I have passed such parts of it as I have in common with the beasts, when I recalled you to mind, for I did not find you there amid the images of corporeal things. I came to those parts where I stored the processes of my mind, and did not find you there. I went on to my mind's very seat, which it possesses in my memory because the mind can remember itself. Nor were you there, for you are not a corporeal image, nor the movement of a living mind as when we are joyful, sympathise, desire, fear, remember, forget, and anything of this kind. Nor are you the mind itself, for you are the Lord God of the mind. All these things change, but you remain unchanged through all. And yet you deigned to dwell in my memory since first I learned of you. Why am I seeking now in what part you dwell, as though the memory had any parts at all? Assuredly you dwell in it, because I remember you since the time I first learned of you, and I find you there when I call you to remembrance.

XXVI

Where, then

Where, then, did I find you that I should learn of you? You were not in my memory before I learned about you. Where, therefore, did I find you in order to learn about you, but in you, above me? There is no place anywhere. We go forward, we go backwards, but there is no place anywhere. Truth, everywhere you give audience to all who consult you, and give simultaneous reply to all who consult you, various though their questions be. Clearly you answer them, though they do not all clearly hear. All seek your counsel on what they will, but do not always hear what they wish. He is your best servant who looks not so much to hear from you what he wishes, but rather to wish that from you which he hears.

XXVII

How God Draws Us

Late I came to know you, Beauty ancient yet new. Late I loved you. But, see, you were within me while I was abroad. There I was seeking you. Deformed though I was, I was rushing upon those beauties of your creation. You were with me, but I was not with you. Those beauties kept me far from you, beauties which would not have existed, were they not in you. You cried and called aloud, and broke my deafness. You flashed, shone and shattered my blindness. You breathed fragrance, I drew in my breath, and I pant for you. I tasted, I hunger and thirst. You touched me, and I burned for your peace.

XXVIII

The Wretchedness of Life

When I shall with my whole being hold fast to you, sorrow and toil will have no more part in me. My life will be alive, wholly full of you. But as it now is, because you lift the one you fill, and because I am not yet full of you, I am a burden to myself. Lamentable joys strive with joyous sorrows, and I do not know on which side victory stands. Alas for me. Lord pity me. My sorrows which are evil, strive with my joys which are good, and I do not know on which side victory stands. Alas for me. Lord pity me. Alas for me. Look, I do not hide my wounds. You are the physician. I am sick. You are merciful. I am wretched. Is not the life of man on earth nothing but temptation? Who wants trials and difficulties? Your command is that they be endured, not loved. No one loves what he endures, though he loves to endure. For although he rejoices that he endures, he would prefer to have nothing to endure. I long for prosperity in adversity. I fear adversity in prosperity. What middle place is there between these two where human life is not all temptation? Woe, again and yet again to the prosperities of the world, for fear of adversity and joy's corruption. Woe, again, twice and three times for the adversities of the age, from longing for prosperity, and because adversity itself is hard, and lest it shatter endurance. Is not the life of man on earth all temptation without respite?

XXIX

Hope is in God Alone

My whole hope is in your mercy. Give what you command and command what you will. You enjoin continency upon us. And when I came to know, says someone, that no one can be continent save by God's enablement, this also was a part of wisdom to know whose gift it was. By continence, in fact, we are gathered and brought into a unity from which we were scattered widely abroad. He loves you too little who loves anything along with you which he does not love because of you. Love, which burns for ever and is never quenched, lovingkindness, my God, set me on fire. You enjoin continency. Give me what you bid, and bid what you will.

XXX

Dreams

Certainly, you command me to contain myself from 'the lust of the flesh, the lust of the eyes, and the self-seeking of the age.' You ordered me to abstain from sexual promiscuity, and as for marriage itself, you counselled me to follow something better than you allowed. Because you gave it, that is what I did before I became a dispenser of your sacrament. And yet there live on in my memory the images of such things as my way of life had fixed there. Of this I have had much to say. They assail me, but without strength, when I am awake. But in dreams they come, not only with delight, but even to command consent, and something very like the act. So strong is the illusion of that image in soul and flesh, that the true visions persuade me to that end in sleep, which the false cannot do when I am awake. Lord, my God, at such a time, am I not myself? Is there so much difference between myself and myself at the moment of passing from waking to sleeping, and sleeping to waking? Where, at that moment, is my reason by which my mind, when it is awake, resists such temptations, and which would remain unshaken if the realities themselves assailed me? Is my reason closed with my eyes? Is it lulled to sleep along with the senses of the body? And whence comes it that, even in sleep, we put up a resistance, and, mindful of what we have set before us and abiding true to it with perfect chastity, we give no assent to such enticements. And yet, so great a difference is there that, when it falls out otherwise, we return on awakening to peace of conscience, and by this space of time realise that we have committed no such deed. Yet we are sorry that it was, in a manner, done to us.

Can it be, God omnipotent, that your hand is not strong enough to heal all the sicknesses of my soul, and with your more abounding grace to quench even the lewd movements of my sleep? You will increase your bounties towards me more and more, so that my soul may follow me to you, freed from the birdlime of lust, so that it may not be a rebel against itself, and not only in dreams not commit those corrupt acts of uncleanness by way of sensual images to the very response of the flesh, but may not even give assent to them. For that such a thing should not give the slightest pleasure, no more than the smallest act of the will could check in the pure emotions of a sleeper, not only in this life but even at this time of life, is a small thing for an omnipotent one, for you, who 'can do more than we ask or think'. What I yet am in this part of my evil, I have confessed to my Lord, rejoicing in trembling in that which you have given me, and grieving in that in which I am still imperfect, hoping you will make your mercies perfect in me to the plenitude of peace, which my inner and outer man will have with you when 'death is swallowed up in victory'.

XXXI

Eating and Drinking

There is another evil of today to which I wish it were 'sufficient'. We repair the daily wear and tear of our body by eating and drinking, until the day arrives when you destroy both food and stomach. Then you will kill this emptiness of mine with a wondrous fullness, and clothe this corruptible thing with everlasting incorruption. But now the need is one which I enjoy, and against that enjoyment I do battle, lest I should be made its captive. I wage daily war in fastings, often bringing my body into subjection, and my pains are routed by pleasure. For hunger and thirst are pains of a kind. They burn and kill like a fever, unless the medicine of food comes to our aid. It is readily at hand, as part of the comfort your gifts provide. Our frailty is served by earth, water and sky and our calamity is called enjoyment.

You have taught me this, so that I have come to take my food as a medicine. But while I am passing from the discomfort of want to the comfort of replenishing, there lies in ambush by the pathway the snare of inordinate desire. To pass that way is pleasure, and there is no other pathway, save that which need dictates. And since health is the reason why we eat and drink, a perilous pleasure links itself to us like a maid in attendance, and often enough tries to show the way so that I may do for its sake what I say and desire to do because of health. Nor has each the same standard, for what is enough for health is not enough for pleasure, and it is often not clear whether it is the necessary care of the body which seeks aid, or the pleasurable deceit of greed, which is offering its services. My unhappy soul takes pleasure in this uncertainty, and finds in it a protection for self-justification, glad that it is not clear what is enough for the ordering of health, and under the pretext of well-being, disguises the business of pleasure. I try every day to fight against these temptations, and call upon your right hand, and to you I refer my troubles, for in this I find no firm counsel.

I hear the voice of my God who bids me: 'Do not let your hearts be loaded with excess and drunkenness.' I am clear enough from drunkenness, and in your mercy, may it not come near me. But greed has often crept up on your servant. In your mercy, let it be put far from me. No man can be self-controlled save by your gift. You give us much that we pray for, and whatever good we receive before we pray for it, we accept from you. We receive it in order to recognise it afterwards. I have never been drunk, but I have known many a drunkard made sober by you. Therefore it was your doing, that they should not be drunkards who never were, and that those who were drunkards should not always be so, and that both should know to whom they owe the benefit. I heard also something else you said: 'Do not pursue your lusts and turn away from your pleasure.' This saying, too, which I have much loved I heard by your favour: 'We lose nothing by not eating, and gain nothing if we eat.' That is to say: 'The one will not land me in plenty, nor the other make me miserable.' And I have also heard: 'I have learned, in all circumstances, to be content. I have learned abundance. I have also learned to endure want.' 'I can do all things in him who makes me strong.' See a soldier of heaven's army, not the dust we are. But remember, Lord, that we are dust, and that out of dust you made man, and that he had been lost and was found.

Nor could he do this of himself, for he was of the same dust, he whom I loved, who, by your inspiration, said: 'I can do all things in him who makes me strong.' Make me strong, so that I may be able. Give what you command and command what you will. He confesses that he has received, and his glorying is in the Lord. I have heard another asking to receive. He says: 'Take away from me the greediness of my appetite.' So, my holy God, it appears, that you are the giver when that is done which you order to be done.

You have taught me, good Father, that 'to the pure all things are pure' but 'it is evil to the man who eats with a guilty conscience', that 'everything you have made is good, and nothing is to be rejected that is received with gratitude', and that 'food does not commend us to God', and that 'no one must judge us in the matter of food or drink', and that 'he who does not eat should not look down on him who does.' These things I have learned, thanks and praises be to you, my God and master, who knock at my ears, and enlighten my heart. Deliver me from all temptation. It is not the uncleanness of the food which I fear, but the uncleanness of greed, for I know that Noah was permitted to eat all manner of food which was good to eat, that Elijah was fed with flesh, and John, though he was endowed with marvellous abstinence, was fed and was not polluted by the living creatures, locusts, which fell to him for food. And I know that Esau was led astray by desire for a dish of lentils, that David blamed himself for a desire for water, and our King was tempted by bread, not flesh. And so, the people in the wilderness earned reproof, not because they longed for flesh, but because, in that desire, they murmured against the Lord.

So, set in the midst of these temptations, I most surely do daily battle against inordinate desire for eating and drinking. It is not of the sort that I can cut off once for all, and decide never to touch it again, as I can with sexual activity. The bridle of the gullet is therefore to be held with a disciplined looseness, and firmness. And who is there, Lord, who is not pulled a little beyond the limits of need? If there is such a man, he is a great man, and let him praise your name for it. I am not that man, for I am a sinner. But I, too, glorify your name, and may he make intercession to you for my sins who overcame the world, he who counts me among the weak members of his body, because his eyes have seen my imperfection, and all shall be written in your book.

XXXII

Smell

I am not much concerned with the allurement of smells. When they are not there, I do not look for them. When they are, I do not reject them, but I am always ready to be without them. So it seems with me, unless I chance to be mistaken, for there is a lamentable darkness, in which what I can do and what I cannot do lies hidden, so that when my mind itself enquires about its own powers it is not certain whether it should believe itself. What is there is concealed for the most part, unless experience reveal it. No one can be secure in this life, which is mostly a trial whether, just as he who is capable of worse can become better, so from being better he can become worse. Our one hope, confidence and certain promise is your mercy.

XXXIII

Hearing

The pleasures of hearing have more firmly bound and subdued me, but you loosened and freed me. Now, I confess, I rest a little in sounds to which your message gives life, when they are sung with a good and well-trained voice, not so as to be gripped by them, but to rise and go when I will. Yet the thoughts by which those sounds live and gain entry to me, seek in my heart a place of no small dignity, almost beyond what I can supply. I seem to myself at times to accord them more honour than is fitting, when I feel my mind to be stirred to a more holy and ardent flame of devotion by those holy words when they are sung, than if they were not sung, and that the varied emotions of our spirit have each their appropriate measures in voice and song by which, according to some hidden association, they are moved to life. But the delight of the flesh, to which the mind must not be surrendered to the point of weakness, often deceives me, the senses not so much accompanying reason as following patiently behind. Having for reason's sake gained admission, it tries to run on ahead and play the leader. Thus I sin unaware in such matters, and realise it afterwards.

At times, guarding too carefully against this very deception, I err by too great severity, so far at times as to wish that all the melodies of sweet music which accompany David's psalter so frequently, were banished from my ears and from the whole Church. What I have been told of Athanasius, bishop of Alexandria, seems safer to me, who instructed the reader of the psalm, to express it with so small a modulation of the voice that it was more like speaking than singing. Yet when I recall the tears I shed at the hymns of the Church, in the first days of my recovered faith, and now, too, when I am moved, not by the singing but by the words which are sung (when they are sung in a clear voice and a truly appropriate tune) I admit again the great usefulness of this institution. Thus I waver between the peril of pleasure, and a wholesomeness of which I approve. I am the more inclined, though my opinion may not be final, to approve the custom of hymns in the service, that by the delight of the ears, less sturdy minds may rise to a feeling of devotion. Yet when it happens that the music of the voice moves me more than the words it sings, I confess myself to have sinned in a way that merits punishment, and then I would rather not hear the singer. Just see my position! Weep with me. Weep for me, those of you who entertain any good within you which can produce action. If you are not one of these, such considerations do not stir you. But you, Lord my God, hear, regard me, look and pity. Heal me, in whose eyes I am now become a problem to myself. That is my infirmity.

XXXIV

'Lust of the Eyes'

There remains the pleasure of these, my body's eyes, about which I make my confessions to you. May the ears of your temple, fraternal and holy, hear them, so that we may end what is to be said of the temptations of the body's desires, which still batter me. I groan over them, and long to be clothed with my heavenly habitation. My eyes love beautiful and varied forms, bright and lovely colours. Let them not take possession of my soul. Let God hold it, who made all these, for he is my good, not these, good though they are. They affect me in my waking hours daily, nor is any rest given me from them, as rest in silence is given at times from the sounds of music. For light, the very queen of colours, bathes everything I see, wherever I am by day. Gliding by me in many ways it charms me, when I am otherwise engaged in paying no attention to it. So strongly it entwines itself, that, if it is suddenly withdrawn, I look for it with longing, and if it is long gone it saddens my mind.

O light, which Tobias saw, when with those closed eyes, he directed his son in the way of life, and went ahead with the feet of love, never losing the path. Or the light which Isaac saw, when, with his earthly sight dimmed and darkened, it was granted him to bless his sons, without recognising them, but to do so as he blessed them. Or the light which Jacob saw when, blind in extreme old age, he shed light, by the heart's illumination, on the predestined tribes of a people yet to be, and laid his hands, mystically crossed, upon his grand-children by Joseph, not as their father, by outward sight, corrected him, but as he, by inward sight, discerned. This is the true light, the one light, and they are all one who see and love it. But the light of the body, of which I was speaking, seasons life for the blind lovers of this world with beguiling and dangerous savour. But they who know how to praise you for it, 'God, of all things creator', take it up in your hymn, and are not, unawares, taken up by it. That is how I would be. I resist the lust of the eyes, lest my feet by which

I tread your way be tangled. I lift up to you the eyes of the spirit, so that you may pluck my feet from the snare. There are times when you do this, for they are in the snare. You go on doing it, for I am often caught in the traps laid everywhere, for 'you who keep Israel will neither slumber nor sleep.'

How beyond number are the things men have added to the allurements of the eyes by different arts and crafts, in clothes, shoes, utensils and such like, in pictures and works of the imagination, far beyond what is necessary, moderate or religiously significant, outwardly following what they are making, inwardly forsaking the one who made them, and spoiling what has been made in them. For my part, my God and my glory, I sing a hymn to you, and make sacrifice of praise to him who makes me holy, for those things of beauty which pass through the souls of men into their clever hands, all derive from that beauty which is above our souls to which, day and night my soul aspires. But those who create and cultivate the beauty of outward things, derive thence a code for judging them, not a way of using them. He is there, though they see him not, so that they may not stray too far, and conserve their strength for you, and not waste it on that which wearies while it gives joy. I see this and speak about it, yet still clutter my feet with such things of beauty. But you will pluck me back, Lord, you will, because your mercy is before my eyes. I am made miserably prisoner, but mercifully you extricate me, sometimes without my being aware of it, when I have been but lightly involved, at other times painfully, because I had been held fast.

XXXV

Intellectual Curiosity

There follows another kind of temptation, dangerous in many more ways. For apart from the desire of the flesh, which is an ingredient in the enjoyment of all the delights of the senses, in the service of which all who depart from you perish, through those same bodily senses, there infiltrates the soul a sort of useless but eager longing, not so much for carnal pleasure itself, as for trying out carnality. It is masked by the name of knowledge and learning, and is called in God's language the 'lust of the eyes', because in the search for knowledge the eyes are the principal agent of sense. To see relates properly to the eyes, but we also use the word in relation to the other senses when we employ them in the search for knowledge. We do not say: 'Listen how red it is', or 'smell how it shines', or 'taste how it glitters', or 'feel how it gleams'. All these things are said to be seen. But we say not only: 'See how it shines', a function of the eyes alone, but also: 'See how it sounds, smells, tastes, how hard it is.' So, as was said before, the lust of the eyes comprises the general experience of the senses, for the function of sight in which the eyes have preeminence, is taken over metaphorically by the other senses, when they explore some sort of knowledge.

Thus it may be more clearly seen, how pleasure, and how curiosity works through the senses. Pleasure follows after things beautiful, melodious, sweet, savoury, soft, but curiosity, for the sake of the experiment involved, seeks the opposite of all these, not for the trouble they bring, but for the urge to experience and understand them. What pleasure is there in seeing a dead and mangled body, which makes you shudder? Yet if one is lying thus, they flock around, to be made sad, and to turn pale. They are afraid to see such a sight in dreams, as if someone had made them go and see it while awake, or some report of beauty had induced them to do so. Illustration could be multiplied from the other senses. From this disease of desire rise some strange sights in the theatre. So they go on to pry into natural phenomena, not beyond our knowledge, but which it is not to our profit to know, and which men simply are curious to understand. Hence, too, when occult arts are used for this same end of perverted knowledge. Hence, even in religion itself, God is tested, when signs and wonders are demanded, not for any salutary end, but merely for experience.

In this vast forest full of traps and perils, see, I have cut off and banished much from my heart, as you, God of my salvation, have granted me to do. Yet when dare I assert, since so many things of this sort buzz round our everyday life, when dare I assert that nothing like this captures my attention, or stirs a fruitless ambition to acquire it? True, the theatres do not now snatch me away, and I am not eager to know the courses of the stars, nor has my soul ever sought answers from the dead. I loathe all unholy compacts Lord, my God, to whom I owe all lowly and unfeigned service; with what strong artifices of prompting has the enemy tempted me to seek a sign from you. I beg of you in the name of our king, and of our true, chaste homeland of Jerusalem that, as any consenting to those thoughts has been far from me, it may ever recede further and yet further. But when I petition you for someone's salvation, the end of what I seek is far different, and since you are doing what you will, you grant, and will grant me to follow willingly.

And yet, who can number in how many trifling and contemptible ways does our curiosity daily tempt and often stumble us? How often do we first almost tolerate people who tell empty stories, in case we hurt the weak, and then gradually listen willingly to them. I do not now go to the races to see a dog chasing a hare. But in the country, should I chance to be passing, the hunt might divert me from some important thought and claim my attention, not so as to compel me to turn my horse's head, but deflect the attention of the mind. And unless you should quickly prompt me, revealing my weakness, or, using the very spectacle, by some train of thought to lift my mind to you, or to treat it with contempt and pass on, I stand like a dolt. And what when, sitting at home, a lizard catching flies, or a spider entangling them as they rush into its web, captures my attention? Is the process different because they are small creatures? I pass on to praise you, the wondrous creator and orderer of all, but that is not how I begin to be interested in them. It is one thing to get up quickly, another not to fall. Of such matters my life is full. My only hope is in your great and wondrous mercy. When our heart becomes the receptacle of such things, and carries piles of this abounding uselessness, our prayers are often interrupted and distracted, and while, before your face, we direct the heart's voice to your ears, such vast concern is cut off by the inrushing of nameless trivial thoughts.

XXXVI

Pride's Sinfulness

Shall we list this also among things to be despised, or will anything restore us to hope but your well-known mercy, since you have begun to change us? And you know to what extent you have done that .You first of all healed me of the lust for proving myself right, so that you could become gracious to all the rest of my iniquities, 'heal all my maladies, redeem my life from destruction, and crown me with pity and mercy, and satisfy my desire with good things.' You curbed my pride with your fear, and tamed my neck to your yoke. I bear it now and it is light to me, because so you promised and so you made it. It was truly so, but I did not know it when I was afraid to submit to it.

But, Lord, you who alone rule without pride, because you are the only true Lord who own no lord, tell me, has this third kind of temptation ceased to trouble me, indeed, can it possibly cease to do so in this life, the wish to be feared and loved by men, for no other reason than our private satisfaction, which is really no satisfaction at all, but a wretched life and disgusting ostentation? Thus it happens that men do not love you most of all, nor purely reverence you. That is why you 'resist the proud and give grace to the humble.' You thunder down upon the ambitions of the world, and 'the hills' foundations tremble.' So, since in some positions in man's society, it is necessary to be loved or feared of men, the enemy of our true blessedness presses hard on us, everywhere spreading his snares: 'Well done, well done!', so that while we greedily collect them, we may be trapped before we know it, cut our gladness off from truth, and deposit it in the deceptiveness of men, liking to be loved and feared, not for your sake, but instead of you. Thus the adversary claims us, making us like himself, not in any oneness of love, but in a partnership of punishment. He has set his throne in the north, that dark and frozen they might serve him, while bent and crookedly he tries to be like you. But we, Lord, look, we are your little flock. Possess us. Stretch over us your wings, and let us escape beneath them. Be our glory. Through your indwelling, let us be loved and feared. Whoever wants to be praised of men, when you are blaming him, is not defended by men when you judge him, nor will he be rescued when you condemn. But 'the sinner is not praised in the desires of his soul, nor is he blessed who works iniquity.' When a man is praised for some gift you have given him, and he is made more glad for the praise he has, than for the gift that wins the praise, he proves to be another who is praised while you condemn him. Better is he who praised than he who receives the praise, for the former took pleasure in the gift of God to man. The latter was better pleased with the gift of man than of God.

XXXVII

Praise and its Opposite

We are tried daily by these temptations, Lord, incessantly we are tempted. Our daily furnace is the tongue of men. In this way, too, you bid us be continent. Grant what you bid, and bid as you will. You know how my heart groans in this matter, and the tears which flood my eyes. I cannot easily discern, how I am cleaner from this pestilence, and I fear much my secret faults, which your eyes know when mine do not. I have some power of examining myself in other spheres of temptation, but not much in this at all. For from the pleasures of the flesh and the superfluous greed for knowledge, I see how much I have won by reining in my mind, when I do without such things, by my will or when I do not have them, for then I ask myself how much more or less it is to me not to have them. For riches, which are coveted for this reason, simply that they may minister to one of these three lusts, to any two, or all of them, if the mind cannot understand whether it despises them when it possesses them, they may be banished, and so it can be tested. To do without praise, and thus try out our strength, must we live a bad life, and live so desperately and evilly, that all who know us may detest us? Can we say or think anything so mad? But if praise commonly is, and must be what goes with a good life and good deeds, we ought as little to forego such company as the good life itself. I do not understand how well or ill I can be without anything, except when I experience the lack.

In this kind of temptation, Lord, what am I to confess to you? What, save that I am delighted with praise, yet with the truth rather than the praise. For were it put to me whether I should prefer to be mad, and astray in everything, and yet be praised by everyone, or firm and confident in the truth, and to be censured by all, I see what I should choose. Yet I should not wish that approbation spoken by someone else should increase my joy for any good I have, though, I confess, that praise does, in fact, increase it, just as censure makes it less. When, however, I am troubled by this unhappiness, there does slip into my mind an excuse – and you know of what sort it is, because it leaves me in doubt. For since you have bidden us not only to be continent, that is telling us from what to withdraw our love, but also righteous, telling us, that is, on what we should bestow it, and further, that you would have us love our neighbour as well as you, I sometimes think I am glad because of the openness and goodwill of someone near to me, when I am made glad by an understanding praise. Likewise I am saddened by evil in him, when I hear him censure what he fails to understand, or what is actually good. I am even saddened by my own praise at times, when either those things are praised in me which I dislike myself, or even smaller, indeed trivial, good things are prized above their worth. But once more, I do not know whether I am moved in this way because I do not know whether I do not want the one who praises me to differ with me about myself, and not because I am moved by concern for his advantage, but rather because those same good things which I find pleasing in myself, are more pleasant in my estimation when they please another too. There is a way in which I am not praised, when my own opinion of myself is not praised, for either those things are praised which do not please me, or those things which please me less are too much praised. Am I not uncertain of myself in this?

See, in you, Truth, I see that I should be moved by my own praises, not on my own account as for the advantage of my neighbour. I do not know whether this is the case with me. In this I know less of myself than I do of you. I beg you, my God, show me myself, so that I may confess to my brothers who will pray for me, that which I shall find damaged in me. Let me question myself with greater care. If, in the matter of my praises, I am concerned with my neighbour's advantage, why am I less put out, if another person is unjustly censured than when I am? Why am I more annoyed by the reproach that is hurled at me than against another, out of the same wickedness, and in my hearing? Do I not know this too? Or is the conclusion that I deceive myself, and express not the truth before you in my heart or on my tongue? Put this madness far from me, Lord, lest my mouth be made the sinner's oil to anoint my head.

XXXVIII

Vainglory

Needy and poor I am, yet better when, in my unseen lamentation, I am displeased with myself, and look for mercy until my lack is made good, and perfected into a peace which the eye of the proud does not know. The words of the lips and the deeds known to men have in them a most perilous temptation, arising from the love of praise. It gathers the solicited votes of men, for some private excellence of its own. It is a temptation, even when shown up by myself and in myself. 'Shown up' is the right word. It often boasts emptily over its very scorn for empty boasting, which thus ceases to be the scorn of which it boasts. The boaster does not in truth despise it, when he boasts about it.

XXXIX

Self-Love

Deep inside us, too, is another evil, in the same category of temptation, in which people who are given to pleasing themselves show their emptiness – though, in fact, they neither please nor displease others, and do not care whether they do so or not. Pleasing themselves, they greatly displease you, not only because they please themselves in evil things, as if they were good things, but in dealing with your good things as if they were their own – or even if they acknowledge them as yours, they act as if they had deserved them, or while acknowledging your free gift, it is with no thought of neighbourly rejoicing, but rather grudging it to others. In all dangers and trials of this sort, you see my heart's trembling, and I feel rather that my wounds are healed by you than inflicted on me.

XL

The Battle

Where have you not walked with me, Truth, teaching me what I should guard against and what I should pursue, when I brought to you the things I have seen on earth, as I could, and sought your counsel? With the senses and to the best of my ability, I scanned the world about me. I gave attention to my body and my senses themselves. Then I went into the caverns of my memory, those many and mighty spaces, wondrously full of numberless stores. I thought about them and stood amazed. I was not able, apart from you, to understand anything, and yet found none of these things actually to be you. Nor was I the discoverer, I who had gone through them all, and tried to distinguish and assess everything according to its worth. I received some things by way of my faltering senses, with questioning, sensing also other matters which were mixed up with myself. I distinguished and enumerated the messengers themselves. I went through other items stored in the vast treasures of memory, putting some back, and pulling others out. When I was doing this, I was not myself, and by 'myself' I mean the strength by which I did it, nor was it you, because you are the unfailing light which I consulted on everything, its existence, nature, worth. But I could hear you teaching and commanding me. This I often do. This delights me, and I retreat to that joy, whenever I can free myself from what I needs must be doing. Nor, in all these things, which I run over under your counsel, do I discover a safe place for my soul except in you, in which my scattered remnants can be gathered together, and nothing be withdrawn from me. There are times when you admit me to an inner love quite extraordinary, a sweetness beyond description, which, could it but be made perfect in me, something beyond this life would be in it. But I fall back to what I am under these grievous loads, and I am sucked back into these things of everyday. I am held fast, weep much and am still firmly held. So mighty is custom's burden. Here I can remain, but do not wish to do so. There I wish to be, but cannot be. I am wretched in both ways.

XLI

The Alternatives

Thus I have considered the maladies of my sins under lust's threefold head, and called on your right hand to help. I have seen your splendour with a wounded heart, and, beaten back, I have said: 'Who can reach it?' I am cast forth from the sight of your eyes. You are truth, which is over all supreme. Through my covetousness I did not wish to lose you, but did wish to possess a lie beside, just as no man is so eager to speak falsely, that he does not know what truth is. So I lost you, because you would not be possessed along with a lie.

XLII

No Angel Mediator

Whom could I find to make my peace with you? Was I to petition the angels? With what plea? With what sacraments? Many, trying to come back to you, and unable to do so of themselves, have, I hear, tried this way, fallen into a longing for strange visions, and been thought deserving of delusions. They have been highminded, sought you in pride of learning, thrusting out their breasts rather than beating them, and were so conditioned in their hearts that they have attracted their fellow-conspirators, the allies of their pride, the 'powers of the air', by whom through the powers of magic, they are deceived, as they sought a mediator through whom they might be purged – and there was none. It was the devil, transforming himself into an angel of light. And it strongly drew proud flesh, because he was spirit himself. For they were mortal sinners, but you, Lord, to whom they wished to be reconciled, are immortal and sinless. A mediator between God and man must have something like God and something like man, lest, being in both like man, he should be far from being like God, and being in both ways like God, he should be too remote from men, and thus not a mediator. So that deceitful mediator, through whom, in your secret judgment, pride deserves to be deluded, has one thing in common with men, namely, sin, and desires to seem, in something else to have a part with God – to wit that, because he does not share the mortality of flesh, he may boast himself to be immortal.

But because 'the wages of sin is death', this he has in common with men, that along with them he should be condemned to death.

XLIII

Christ, the One Mediator

The true mediator, whom in your secret mercy you revealed and sent to men, that by his example they might learn true humility, that 'mediator between God and men, the man Christ Jesus', appeared between mortal sinners and the immortally righteous one, mortal with man, righteous with God, so that, since the wages of righteousness is life and peace, he might, through the righteousness which is linked to God, make void the death of the sinners who had been justified, the death he willed to share with them. This was revealed to holy men of old, so that they, through faith in his suffering yet to be, like us, through faith in his suffering past, should be saved. As a man, he was a mediator, but as the Word, not standing midway between, because he was equal with God, he was God with God, and together one God.

How have you loved us, good Father, who 'spared not your only son', but for us sinners surrendered him. How have you loved us, for whom he 'did not consider equality with God something to be usurped, and was made subject even to the death of the cross', he alone, free among the dead, 'had power to lay down his life and power to take it up again'. For us, in your sight, he was both victor and victim, and victor for the very reason that he was a victim. For us, he was, in your sight, both priest and sacrifice, and priest for the very reason that he was a sacrifice. From slaves he made us your children, born of you, serving you. Well then stands my hope firm in him, because through him you will 'heal all my infirmities', through him 'who sits at your right hand making intercession to you for us'. Otherwise I should despair, for many and great are those infirmities, many and great, but your medicine is greater. We might think that your Word was far from any union with man, and so despair of ourselves, had it not been 'made flesh and dwelt among us'.

Terrified by my sins and the burden of my wretchedness, I turned it over in my heart, and considered flight into the wilderness, but you forbade me and strengthened me, saying: 'Therefore Christ died for all, that they who live should no longer live for themselves, but for him who died for them.' See, Lord, I cast my care upon you that I may live, and I shall consider 'wondrous things out of your law'. You know my inexperience and my weakness. Teach me and heal me. Your only son, 'in whom are hidden all the treasures of wisdom and knowledge', redeemed me by his blood. Let not the proud speak evil of me, because I think about the price of my redemption, eat, drink, give alms. Poor myself, I desire to be satisfied by him, among those who eat and are satisfied. And they shall praise the Lord who seek him.

E. M. Blaiklock:
A Christian Scholar

Trevor Shaw

All those who have appreciated Professor Blaiklock's masterly translations will enjoy this illuminating biography of a great scholar and a fine Christian. For twenty one years he held the Chair of Classics at the University of Auckland, New Zealand, where he became established as a respected teacher and accumulated many academic distinctions.

During his fifty year writing career he produced no less than eighty books as well as writing a popular weekly column for New Zealand's largest daily newspaper. But many will remember Professor Blaiklock particularly for those moving and gently erudite books such as *Kathleen* that reveal the human face of the redoubtable Christian apologist.

Trevor Shaw, journalist and author, has combined careful research with his personal knowledge of Professor Blaiklock to create an inspiring tribute to his life and work.

The Hodder and Stoughton Christian Classics Series

The Hodder and Stoughton Christian Classics are original translations, adaptations or abridgements of the great classics of devotional spirituality. Chosen for their reference to the needs of today's Christians, for their theological and spiritual perception and for the timelessness of their message, each of the titles in the series will enrich the faith of the reader.

The Confessions of St Augustine
New Translation with an Introduction by
E.M.Blaiklock

The Cloud of Unknowing
Edited by Halcyon Backhouse

**The Twelve Steps of Humility and Pride
On Loving God**
Bernard of Clairvaux

The Little Flowers of St Francis
*(incorporating the Acts of
St Francis and his companions)*
Translated by E.M.Blaiklock and A.C.Keyes

The Institutes of Christian Religion
John Calvin

The Practice of the Presence of God
Brother Lawrence

The Greatest Thing in the World
Henry Drummond

The Imitation of Christ
Thomas à Kempis

A Serious Call to a Devout and Holy Life
William Law

At the Feet of the Master
Sadhu Sundar Singh

Revelations of Divine Love
Julian of Norwich